What Would You Like To Know About The Catholic Church?

Answers by
Father Kenneth Ryan and
Monsignor J. D. Conway

CARILLON BOOKS   ST. PAUL, MINNESOTA

**WHAT WOULD YOU LIKE TO KNOW ABOUT THE
CATHOLIC CHURCH?**

A CARILLON BOOK
Published by Pillar Books for Catholic Digest
Carillon Books edition published October 1976

ISBN: 0-89310-004-8

Printed in the United States of America

CARILLON BOOKS is a division of
Catholic Digest
2115 Summit Avenue
St. Paul, Minnesota 55105
U.S.A.

"What did Pope John say on the occasion of the appointment of the new archbishop of Ravenna?" What the Pope said might have been important, striking, and even entertaining, but a critic could not help doubting that the question was ever really asked and whether the editor was not filling space instead of rendering a service to his public. The department in the *Catholic Digest* made it a point never to succumb to such temptations but to keep the department what it was designed to be—a source of interesting and pertinent information about the Catholic Church.

In presenting these questions and answers we feel justified not because we have compiled anything like an encyclopedia on the Catholic faith but because the ordinary inquirer will find here his question and an answer to it. Our trust is that it will be enduringly useful to the cause of religion and understanding.

Contents

5

Introduction

The questions and answers found in this book are from the department, "What Would You Like to Know About the Church?" in the monthly magazine *Catholic Digest*. The purpose of the department was to furnish answers in depth to inquiries about various facets of the Catholic faith. It was at the risk of giving the correspondent more information than he wanted or asked for, but each answer was developed according to the original plan. On the face of them, many questions could be answered with a simple yes or no, and, to go by the phrasing of the writer, in many cases that would have been satisfactory. But in most religious questions there was a clear indication that the writer would not understand the answer unless he were acquainted with the historical, theological or philosophical background of his query. He was seldom the first ever to have asked his question, and in most cases it had been treated many times over in Catholic apologetic writing. The editorial problem was to adjust the content of the answer to the writer's capacity to use and understand. Accordingly the material is not so elementary as to lose the average reader, nor so erudite as to be beyond his interest.

The quality of the answers depended entirely on the quality of the questions. But this was a kind of feedback operation; good answers in turn stimulated more good questions. Departments of this kind were for many years standard features of nearly all Catholic magazines and newspapers, but, frankly, they were not all good. Busy or lazy editors often suffered from a shortage of good questions, and too often would make up their own, such as, "What did Pope John say on the occasion of the appointment of the new archbishop of Ravenna?" What the Pope said might have been important, striking and even entertaining but a critic could not help doubting that the question was ever really asked and whether the editor was not filling space instead of rendering a service to his public. The department in the *Catholic Digest* made it a point never to succumb to such temptations but to keep the department what it was designed to be—a source of interesting and pertinent information about the Catholic Church.

In presenting these questions and answers we feel justified not because we have compiled anything like an encyclopedia on the Catholic faith but because the ordinary inquirer will find here his question and an answer to it. Our trust is that it will be enduringly useful to the cause of religion and understanding.

I

The Newest Questions

Question and answer columns have their trends just like other magazine features. Lately the questions are mostly concerned with changes, proposed changes, and possible changes in church discipline and practices.

1

Why the Changes in Saint's Days?

THE LETTER:

I am in favor of a good many of the changes in the Church that help make our religion more meaningful and alive. However, one change puzzles me. All my life I have celebrated certain saints' feast days on specific dates. Now I find, since Vatican II, the calendar of saints has been revised and many feast days have been changed. I thought that most feast days represent a special day in the life of a particular saint, the day on which he died, or some other significant occurrence. Why this general upheaval?

Lillian A. Amend

THE ANSWER:
By Kenneth Ryan

Why indeed? And the upheaval is bigger than you indicate. Since the time of Roosevelt, Thanksgiving has been jumping back and forth between the last two weeks of November. In many states Washington and Lincoln now share a birthday and Armistice Day has had its name changed to Veterans' Day and its place on the calendar expunged. The suspicion is inescapable, Lillian, that the post-Vatican reformers are bandwagon riders.

It would take some efficient investigative reporting to find out who is responsible for the changes in the Church's calendar. They are made in the name of some committee or other and, of course, the membership of the typical committee changes often enough to cover the trail of individual responsibility. Many persons deprived of their patron saints and name days would like to know the answer to "Who done it?"

Personally, I dislike the changes because I knew the old calendar by heart. I worked for three years with a Catholic wall-calendar company and was charged with getting all feast days down correctly, the date numerals in the proper color, and Sundays and feasts given preference according to their importance. In all the three years, I made only one mistake. What were known as double major feasts—unlike doubles, simples, feasts of the first class, and so on—were, in the fine print in the front of the missal, subdivided into two classes. One of these enabled the double major to take over on Sunday and the other did not. I got one wrong, and the chuckles of our competitors over my ignorance and unreliability still resound in my ears.

Until the recent revision of the calendar, I could go into the sacristy any morning to prepare for Mass and know just from the newspaper's dateline what saint's day or feast it was. I even had a good grasp of movable feasts such as those celebrated on "the Saturday following the First Friday" and never had to look at the *Ordo,* the enigmatically abbreviated, printed Latin guide for Mass celebrants. Now I look at the *Ordo* carefully every day out of a well-founded fear that it may be the day for a feast I never heard of (such as the Fourth of July) or that Christmas is being celebrated in September.

Old-timers are pretty much all alike. I remember my first pastor who wouldn't eat meat on Friday even on Christmas, though the Pope had allowed one and all to do so. My pastor was conscientious in other ways and every three years or so would take the big parish missal down to the local church-goods house to have the new feasts inserted. Invariably, a still newer feast would be promulgated and I well remember his fretting and fuming at the reobsolescence of his missal. I tell you all this to make the point that changes were always with us and were usually resented. Maybe we can avoid resentment over calendar changes if we go over the contents of the old calendar and then try to figure out why specific changes were made.

The earliest liturgical books we know about had Masses only for great feasts like Christmas, Easter, and Pentecost, and for Sundays numbered according to their occurrence after such feasts. (That's a little oversimplified, but you get the idea.) Masses for saints' days came in during the Middle Ages and grew gradually more important, so that they crowded out the Sunday Masses. My first pastor used to hark back nostalgically to the days of his early priesthood (circa 1890) when he never had to check on what Sunday after Pentecost it was, but only on what saint's day it was. So, about 1911, a little liturgical reform was in order, The ancient and lovely old Masses for the Sundays were reinstated as they should have been. The trouble was that thereafter someone or other always wanted an exception here and there. Soon feasts were again being assigned to Sundays, despite criticism and opposition. Occasionally the Church would be accused of politics as when the new Feast of Christ the King was made to coincide with the Reformation Sunday of the Protestants.

When the modern liturgical movement began in the early decades of this century, its promoters were suspect for such things as saying that even the Solemnity of St. Joseph should not displace a Sunday. They began the deemphasis of the "Sanctoral cycle" (saints) which has now resulted in the skipping over of even the ancient Roman saints in reciting the Roman Canon of the Mass. We may properly regret such skipping, but the fact of the matter is that for liturgical purposes the saints needed some thinning out. First of all, there are only 365 days in the year and there are enough reputed or canonized saints to provide dozens for each day. The great majority cannot have days to themselves.

Many saints had fine legends but no historical credentials, so in the present reform we have had the sad disappearance of the non-Saints Christopher and Philomena. In the good old days of nonecumenical controversy, Catholics were often taunted with Veronica and Longinus whose names (translated as True Picture and Long Spear) obviously derived from their roles in the Passion story. By implication they were thus betrayed as fictional characters. In preparation for the new post-Vatican calendar, saints whose physical existence could not be historically established were taken not only from the calendar but from the general list of saints. Even Linus, successor to Peter himself, did not stand up historically, and was removed from the calendar.

A good many accretions in the old calendar had been the result of what we could call the public relations efforts of various religious societies. This is not to say the efforts

were wrong, but what would come up usually on the death
of a founder of a society would be a decision on the part of
the members to have him or her canonized. Once this was
accomplished and his or her feast day placed on the local
calendar, the effort would be expanded to make the day
observable by the universal Church.

None of this activity was reprehensible, of course, but it
did lead to a cluttering of the calendar. Most such saints
have now been taken off the universal calendar, though
wide latitude has been left to societies and local Churches
to venerate their own saints. In the overall, however, the
number of saints' days has been greatly decreased, and the
priest thumbing the *Ordo* before Mass has more and more
occasion to mutter "Ah, another nothing!"

All this removal I can understand and accept, but date
changes I find more darkly mysterious. As you say, the old
feast day of a saint was the day he died, his "birthday in
heaven" as the Martyrology calls it. Inevitably in the old
calendar there was overlapping (the frequent phrase in the
Martyrology about two saints is that they died "the same
day but not the same year").

In the old days, if the newly canonized saint was sufficiently popular or his promoters had enough clout, he
could take over another saint's birthday. It might just be
that this is an explanation of what seems to be random
rearrangements of saints' days. Surely such takeovers gave
rise to objections, and it may be that the calendar reformers were responding to them.

Speculation may be idle, but it is fun trying to figure out
why specific changes were made. In a cursory, once-over
count I made, 140 feasts' and saints' days remained un-
changed, though the upheaval seems greater than that.
More than 200 saints have been taken off the calendar,
many of whom had only secondary positions on it anyway,
in that their feasts were celebrated on the same day as
some greater one. It is just a thought, but it seems likely
that these second-place saints had all been downgraded in
long-past, forgotten revisions, and have now been given the
coup de grâce. Some 80 saints have been kept on the calendar, but have had their dates changed.

Since there are only so many days in the year, it is easy
to see the reasoning behind the doubling up of saints who
previously had private feast days. Joachim and Anna, parents of Our Lady, very reasonably have been given a com-

mon feast. Timothy and Titus, both recipients of Epistles from St. Paul, have been doubled up. But groups of unrelated saints (Bede, Gregory VII, Mary Magdalene de Pazzi) have been assigned to May 25, and June 22 now has Immaculate Heart of Mary, Paulinus, John Fisher, and Thomas More.

Sometimes it looks like the revisers tried their best to keep things the same and, for reasons otherwise inscrutable to us, changed feast dates by only one day. Bonaventure was moved from the 14th to the 15th of July; Alphonsus Liguori from August 1 to August 2; Cosmas and Damian were moved only one day. I haven't done the research, but would guess that such cases were probably instances of restoring to the saint his "birthday in heaven," denied him in the old calendar by an older and equally revered occupant. The older calendar managers had gotten him as close as possible to his birthday in heaven.

Among the more easily solvable mysteries is the change of St. Thomas the Apostle to July 3 from December 21 where he was interfering with the orderly presentation of the glorious "O" antiphons in the Breviary just before Christmas. His proper readings and antiphons caused an unconscionable amount of page fingering in the Divine Office, and were in that sense a real distraction from the spirit of the season. If you ask why the Visitation was changed from July 2 to May 31, I can only conjecture that it was part of a larger shuffling of the feasts of Our Lady, to cut them down in number or at least space them out.

Occasionally we get a glimpse of ecumenism in the changes. The feast of Christ the King no longer conflicts with Reformation Sunday but has been made the last Sunday of the year. I would hesitate to see ecumenism at work in the new and smaller set of feasts of Our Lady, but must recognize that some conservatives have dark suspicions in that regard.

Feasts which celebrated things rather than persons, such as St. Peter's Chains and the Finding of the Holy Cross, have been taken off, though I think technically you could say that the Chains feast celebrated the dedication of a church named for St. Peter and that it was St. Helen who was really honored for the Finding.

Curiously, nearly all of the Doctors of the Church have had their dates changed and many of them have been assigned only "optional" status. I don't know why I keep thinking of such things, but surely it could not be that the revisers wanted to deemphasize doctrine.

In numbers removed, martyrs surpass even the founders of religious societies and orders. It may be that martyrdom is growing less popular; there haven't been many martyrs since Vatican II. But it is more likely that since so many of them lived long, long ago, they have been really forgotten and to keep them on the calendar would not in practice foster devotion.

Even in the face of my old prejudices, I would have to say that clearing the calendar of so many saints was mostly to the good. Yet it is true that most Vatican-II type reformers were intent on upgrading religion whether it needed it or not. They saw relics of paganism, local gods, and spirits in the cult of saints. The mixture of veneration of saints, devils, and old pagan deities still practiced by the more primitive people of, say, Brazil and Haiti, is far from Christian and should have, they thought, no recognizable counterpart in fully civilized worship of God. So, removing saints from the calendar was possibly regarded by the reformers as a step in the right direction.

At this point the whole matter of praying to the saints and praying to God works its way into discussion. Prayers for intercession by the saints is old standard Catholic practice; but the reformers are right in trying to make official worship direct itself to God. It is a psychological fact that when you pray sincerely and immediately to God for some earthly benefit, you usually argue yourself out of wanting it. You succeed in reaching and knowing the joy of submitting to God's will in the matter. Somehow, when you just pray to a saint and ask him to ask for you, you don't reach the higher level of prayer and are secretly relieved to let the whole matter stand as a simple request, uncomplicated by considerations that would bring you to giving up your momentary heart's desire.

So, after all, my answer, Lillian, to your question "Why the upheaval?" is "I don't know." My speculation is that the general effort was to deemphasize the veneration of the saints. Why the saints' days were shifted around has never been revealed, and anything I say about it can be either right or wrong, so that a detailed official account of what was changed and why would make engaging reading.

In a sense, the trimming away of the saints from the calendar is an extension of the cutting away of popular devotions of all kinds. Without going into the question as to whether the popular devotions become unpopular by the will of the people or were made so by activists among the clergy, we can only wait to see whether the new calendar will result in more churchgoing. That must have been its ultimate purpose.

2

How About Women's Hats in Church?

THE LETTER:

I am a man 75 years old and of the old school. With all the changes in the Church taking place, many things puzzle me. I try to accept them, knowing that the Church has to concern itself with the future as well as the present generation. But there is one thing I wish you would clear up for me. What does the Church teach on the passage from I Corinthians, chapter 11, regarding women covering their heads in church? I know that if I dared to go to Mass with my hat on, I would scandalize everyone in church, including the women who have no covering on their heads. Please comment. I have always subscribed to *Catholic Digest* and will continue to do so. So if you use my question, send the subscription to a worthy missionary.

P.Z.

THE ANSWER:
By Kenneth Ryan

You win the ten-year subscription, P.Z., but it was really by lot. Nobody will mind that since you are giving it to a missionary anyway. Your question was chosen because it was asked by more people than any other. Of all the "changes in the Church" this one apparently has grated on the most nerves.

The older a custom, the more people love it, and the

newer a custom, the more people dislike it. Within the
Catholic Church the custom of women covering their heads
at Mass goes way, way back. The *Liber Pontificalis,* a continuing account of the lives of the Popes, which was started
in the 7th century and was continued into the 16th, says
that Linus, the next Pope after Peter, made it a formal law
for women to cover their heads in church.

Of course, Linus was following St. Paul, who said they
should be covered "because of the angels." By "angels"
Paul probably meant the ancient equivalent of ushers, but
we still don't know why they should make any difference.

Paul was a conservative at heart, despite a spectacular
conversion to a revolutionary new faith. As a conservative,
he believed in the observance of what sociologists now call
folkways, and head-covering for women must have been
among those he knew and approved of back in his home
town of Tarsus. The notes in the old Rheims-Douay Bible
say that Paul probably wouldn't write that way about
women were he writing today.

It is intriguing that head-covering should in so many cultures be associated with religious ceremony. I was discon-
certed once as a young priest away from home for the first
time. On a ship going to Europe, I had tipped a steward to
get access to the first-class library where, I had been told, I
could make arrangements to say Mass. On entering, my
first reaction was that a mockery of the Mass was going on
in there. I was so shocked, I backed out to gather my wits.
There was chanting around an altar, lighted candles, and a
group of men wearing what looked to me like Benediction
veils. The mockery seemed to come from their all wearing
Homburg hats. Second thoughts came quickly as I realized
that it must be a sincere religious ceremony.

I suppose head coverings, veils, and long garments for
women are all tied in with the more than natural physical
modesty of the pious followers of the monotheistic religions—Jews, Moslems, and Christians. It must have been
that the Canaanite fertility worship with its obscenities so
offended the Jews of ancient times that they have ever since
required modest dress of all men and women and passed
the custom on to the Moslems and Christians.

And, despite the pressures of religion and respectability,
women's fashions that become nation- and world-wide have
usually had their origin in the more raffish elements of society. In my youth, when there was opposition to women's

bobbed hair and knee-length hosiery, it was on that basis.

You might expect that an archeological sociologist would find that in ancient days respectable women wore head coverings and women whose thought was to attract men did not. But among the odd things you turn up in writing oddball articles like this is that such was not the case. The bas-reliefs of old Assyria show that head veils were worn for lovemaking. Where does that leave our presumption that women always wear head coverings for modesty?

Of course, most people tend to approach even questions dating from antiquity in a modern frame. For instance, in terms of heated churches: it could be that head coverings became prescribed because they were worn for practical reasons (to keep warm or hide a poor hairdo) for so long a period that the practical purpose was forgotten. Monks singing in choir to this day symbolically cover and uncover their heads with their hoods according to the rubrics and type of prayer they are reciting. But there is no doubt that hoods or cowls originally were just ordinary attachments to the medieval monks' garb, and were worn on or off the head, in or out of church, according to how hot or cold it was. Maybe hat-wearing was always for warmth or protection.

Just the other morning, I was sitting alone in church after saying Mass and found it cold there. I unthinkingly put on my old fur cap and continued my meditation after an idle thought about how Pope John had revived the use of a warm, fur, papal headpiece that his predecessors had abandoned. At breakfast a fellow priest, who unbeknownst to me had seen me, archly inquired whether I had converted to the Jewish religion. After a moment's puzzlement, I got the point and later thought how outraged I would have been had I seen a student with his hat on in church. There is undoubtedly some deep psychological connection between head-covering and being in church, but it is hard to pin down the complete symbolism.

The military man, of course, when in uniform and bearing arms never removes his hat or cap. This, I suppose, is because the hat is the modern equivalent of the helmet and to remove it would be a sign of surrender, like throwing down your sword. A man not bound by military protocol still follows this symbolism when he removes his hat in church; it is a sign of submission to the Lord in his sanctuary. Don't ask me whether the same symbolism applies to

women. St. Paul says they were symbolizing subjection (to
men) by *covering* their heads. This military symbolism
would mean they were showing subjection (to the Lord)
by *uncovering* them. It gets complicated.

Actually, of course, women cover or uncover out of style
and do not even think of symbolism. In pre-Vatican II
days, children were routinely taught to make visits to the
Blessed Sacrament and few little girls wore hats on week-
days. Everyone old enough remembers how they would
wear a piece of Kleenex or a handkerchief on their heads
as temporary hats. There was usually a lot of giggling
about it, but the memory of the reverence they wanted to
show is heart-warming. The other side of the picture is that
those who didn't have a hat, handkerchief, or Kleenex
didn't make a visit. Few people realized that they were welcome to the Lord with or without hats so long as no irreverence was intended.

Maybe that is the attitude we should take toward the
women of today who don't wear hats to church. The argument would be that real enforcement of the rule (Canon
1262) would require that they should be turned away. This
enforcement would in turn raise the question of whether it
would be better to keep the rule of hat-wearing or the law
of churchgoing.

Another question that would arise is whether there was
any ancient positive law on hat-wearing or whether female
hat-wearing was just an optional custom. Since 1918 we
have had Canon 1262, but for its source you can't really go
back to Pope Linus, because, as I purposely neglected to
mention before, the *Liber Pontíficalis* is not held in high
regard by scholars as a source of authentic history. And
even if it were, the parts written in the 7th century about
what happened in the 1st century would be open to reasonable doubt. The authors might just be reaching for an explanation of a fact of their own time (head-covering) in
attributing it to a law of Linus.

One of the commonest misunderstandings of the way the
Church enforces its law is thinking that all laws are enforced for all Catholics in all places for all time. It's a beautiful ideal and is true of divine law but not of minor matters
like hat-wearing. The Pope can legislate for everybody but
not for all time. At his death his successor can enforce his
laws or let them go by the board. The whole Code of
Canon Law is now undergoing revision.

Heads of the Pope's congregations, who are something like United States cabinet officers, are charged with enforcement of law within their departments. Bishops can enforce for their own dioceses and until the recent introduction of parish councils, pastors could rather easily enforce law for their parishes. Now, head-covering for women can be enforced at any of these levels. However, we know that neither Linus' legislation nor Canon 1262 is being enforced everywhere, although some bishops and pastors may be attempting local enforcement. So it is very difficult to answer people who frame their questions unspecifically: "Why doesn't the Church enforce the law?"

The only way to get an answer would be to find which bishops and pastors have not made rulings and only then could you go on to inquire (and it would have to be of those individuals, not of the Church) why there was no enforcement. If you go all the way back to the Bible and St. Paul,* you likewise find that enforcement is not automatic. Interpretations differ and there has not been universal agreement that what he wrote was by that fact universal law for the Catholic Church.

On reading the text of Canon 1262,** one finds that head-covering for women is really legislated in the framework of modesty rather than as specific content of divine Biblical revelation. It says that women should have their heads covered and be modestly dressed, above all when they receive Communion. And when you realize this you see that the real issue is the modesty traditionally required of women in church. A woman or girl clothed with normal decency would not offend anyone but the fanatics by appearing in

---

* Canon 1262

1. It is to be hoped that, according to old custom, women in the church building be separated from the men.

2. Men, either in or out of the church building, when assisting at holy rites, are to have their heads uncovered unless established popular customs or special circumstances interfere; women, however, are to have their heads covered and be modestly dressed, above all in approaching the Lord's table.

** From 1st Corinthians 11: 5-15

. . . every woman praying or prophesying with her head uncovered disgraces her head . . . A man indeed ought not to cover his head because he is the image and glory of God. But woman is the glory of man. For man is not from woman, but woman from man. For man was not created for woman, but woman for man. This is why the woman ought to have a sign of authority over her head, because of the angels.

church without a hat. The normal reaction would be to think she forgot it. However she would be technically in violation of the canon.

This consideration leads to another point that at least partly explains the present nonobservance. It is that the opening paragraph of that same Canon 1262 says "it must be hoped" (*optandum* in Latin) that, following ancient custom, women in church should be separated from the men. This hope is fulfilled now, I suppose, only in remote rural districts of Catholic countries. Such separation would be unthinkable in a modern suburban American parish. The canon's nonobservance shows how custom can get so strong that enforcement of the canon would verge on the ridiculous. Custom also has overwhelmed another Canon law (1264) which says that nuns singing in church must stay out of sight (in the old sense, of course). Many of them now lead congregations "in song" and I am sure there are very few twinges of conscience over obedience to Canon 1264.

So, despite St. Paul, Linus, and immemorial custom, head-covering for women is unlikely to be among the new revised Canons of the Church. What we are witnessing is not really a rebellion against law so much as an ignoring of it out of a desire to observe fashion instead. For all we know, the fad may change and, out of no obedience to anything but fashion, female heads may very soon be routinely covered both in and out of church.

So, P.Z., thanks for saying "Please comment" instead of insisting on a cut-and-dried answer. In closing, I would ask that you read *all* of Canon 1262, note what it says about *men,* and keep your hat off in church.

3

Who Can Go to Communion Now?

THE LETTER:

I recently met a young Catholic student (age 20) who told me this touching story. She and a group of non-Catholics attended a weekend retreat. During subsequent months, a close relationship developed in this group which included a desire by non-Catholics to attend Mass.

Several of the non-Catholics asked their Catholic friend if they could receive Communion. The young girl's love for her friends was such, that, after telling them she didn't think it was possible, she became so sad she began to cry and had to leave the service.

My question: Is there any way these beautiful youngsters can receive Communion without formally embracing the Catholic faith? What would Jesus have done if He saw this yearning?

J.M., M.D.

THE ANSWER:
By Kenneth Ryan

Doctor, I dislike any suggestion of repartee in connection with a question that involves the Holy Name, but I think the Lord would have told them to go and take instructions, join the Catholic Church, and make their First Communions according to standard operating procedure.

A good deal of the interest in intercommunion, meaning the reception of the Eucharist in one denomination by members of another, comes, as it seems to me your question comes, from an excess of sentiment, as distinguished from sound Eucharistic devotion. I frankly confess, that I (long ago and far away) in preparing children for First Communion did my best to instill sentimental piety. I still do not think it an entirely misbegotten emotion. If it is instilled before the age of adolescent skepticism, it stays with a person an incredibly long time.

I know this because my wearing of the Roman collar on trains and planes used to attract many apparently lonesome fellow travelers who sometimes boozily, but often just dreamily, would confide that the day of their First Communion had been the happiest of their lives. Often their stories went on into details of rather sordid lives and too often their First Communions were among a total of very few Communions. But to each of them the memory of First Communion came like an incense-bearing breeze from Heaven.

How could it be otherwise? *Communion,* the word itself,

is a synonym for *love,* the most blessed of all emotions. But
love, sentiment, and sentimentality shade into one another
so subtly that the question "Which is which?" arises in the
discussion of nearly every act of devotion toward God, including Holy Communion.

Religious thought, like religious writing, extends from
the aridities of theological footnotes to the sopping-wet sen-
timentalities of the amateur hymn writer. Some of the divisions in the Christian faith have arisen over the question of
which end of this wick should be clipped off. Ronald Knox
quotes an example of the wet end, telling us how among
the members of the Church of the Brethren (1746 A.D.) the
wound in our Lord's heart came to be described as "the
dearest little opening of the sacred, precious, and thousand
times beautiful little side." And I suppose Teilhard de
Chardin could represent the dry end: ". . . in the cosmos
system there would appear to be no structural reason for
localizing and delimiting within the whole sphere of existence and action of each individual center considered on its
own." In solving the difficulties of intercommunion, truth
and reason are found between the extremes of loveless ab-
straction and brainless pietisms.

Of intercommunion, whether motivated by brain power
or love power, I think the official Roman Catholic Church
is unready to approve, though the truth is that under certain very specific conditions she does allow the reception of
Communion by persons who have not gone through the
ceremony of "formally embracing the Catholic faith." This
permission is found not in any formal, clearly infallible
pronouncement addressed to the whole world by the Holy
Father, but only in an "Instruction on who may be permitted to Eucharistic Communion" issued by the Secretariat
Promoting Christian Unity, the members of which, under-
standably, are in favor of stirring up a little action. But
even they insist that the outsider: 1) believe the same
things about the sacrament that the Catholic Church does;
2) be in a state of "urgent necessity"; 3) be unable to have
recourse to his own minister; 4) ask for the sacrament
spontaneously, not at the prompting of a Catholic.

Personally, I can't bring to mind any such combination
of person and circumstances in all my wide experience. It
would seem to me this person would on these terms be on
the brink of converting to the Catholic faith anyway. The
proposed recipient would have to be a baptized person,

well-instructed in the Catholic faith, ready to obey the Catholic bishop, in physical or spiritual danger, cut off from his coreligionists, and in possession of an extraordinary actual grace.

Obviously, Doctor, this concoction of legalisms would not permit your friendly young representatives of a non-Catholic faith to receive Communion at a Catholic Mass. The young Catholic girl of your letter was right in her judgment, if a little sentimental in her reaction.

It would even seem that the commission members were trying to prevent, rather than promote, intercommunion. Of course, other denominations are openly opposed to it. The Church Council of the American Lutheran Church, in a statement in 1871, said that no Lutheran should receive Communion in a Catholic church even if he is invited by the priest in charge. The statement points out the implications of such Communion, including that of submission to the local Catholic bishop and the Pope.

I suppose that a detached atheist would say that the spokesmen in both Churches were probably jealous of their own authority. But if he were logical as well as detached, he would see that both authorities were, paradoxically, promoting unity. The disobedient (those that receive Communion in another denomination with no one's permission) make up a kind of third force and surely there is less unity in a division into three parties than there is into two.

You see, Doctor, the Eucharist has always been a symbol of unity not only in love but also in belief and discipline. I don't mean to parallel the following situation with the one you described, but let me tell you about the worst violation of this principle I can remember.

I was Sunday assistant in a parish that was unhappily to witness the defection of all three co-pastors. Among the outrages they perpetrated before leaving their posts was a Sunday evening Mass with music by a hired all-Baptist combo: trumpet, drums, and piano in the sanctuary.

Good feeling ran high and at Communion time the celebrant went first to the musicians, who were in the midst of a selection. Of course, this celebrant did not expect them to break off their tune to receive the Eucharist. But he was, nevertheless, foiled in his intentions when they pursed their mouths and shook their heads like babies refusing food, with him like an anxious mother trying to force acceptance, even pushing the trumpet from the trumpeter's lips. It might have been that the musicians just felt too busy at he moment, but I like to think that as good Baptists they understood the symbolism of the Eucharist, unity of love, *belief*, and *discipline*, better than the celebrant.

So, Doctor, while I take no exception at all to your feelings in what is really a delicate religious matter, I do think that this conception of the Eucharist as symbol of unity of belief and discipline, as well as of love, is important. When you use the Eucharist to promote unity of belief rather than to symbolize, by restricting participation, a unity already achieved, you are abusing the symbolism. As for unity of discipline, the Lutheran 1971 statement only echoes what the Secretariat Promoting Christian Unity said. Reception of Communion in the Catholic Church means identifying yourself with a group bound to obedience to the Catholic bishop named in the Eucharistic prayer.

The proclamation of this symbolism goes back to the early centuries when the Church was converting the Roman world. The Eucharist was only for the baptized, who had been instructed in its meanings. The catechumens, those under instruction, were allowed to attend only the first part of the Eucharistic assembly. They heard the Liturgy of the word, and were then dismissed. Only the confirmed faithful could stay for the offering of the Sacrifice and reception of the Body and Blood of Christ.

There were, of course, practical as well as symbolic reasons for this exclusion. In the days of the persecutions, each catechumen had to have a sponsor, not only for future guidance in the Faith, as babies now have a sponsor at their Baptisms, but to exclude spies seeking the secrets which underground Christians needed to keep for survival in that hostile society. Only after a trial period were converts admitted to the Eucharistic celebration, the core and substance of the Christian faith and life.

It seems clear that well-intentioned Christians should not offer the Catholic Church their allegiance in the Eucharistic sign of unity and obedience, since they do not believe as we do, nor want to obey the same authorities that we do. The Church is not denying them anything, only insisting on rational behavior.

Doctor, in these popular-level articles, I can really give only the gist of the documents covering this matter of intercommunion. To fill in, one should read the Vatican II *Construction of the Sacred Liturgy* (1964), the *Decree on Ecu-*

menism (1965), and the Papal encyclical, *Mysterium Fidel* (1965). For 1975 material, read page 584 of the Seabury edition of the *Common Catechism,* the work of an international team of about 40 equally represented Protestant and Catholic theologians: ". . . numerous Christians in both Churches regard any form of intercommunion or concelebration as dishonest, while the leadership of both Churches continue up to the present to repudiate every experiment in this direction. . . ."

On the Catholic side the higher powers leave the local bishop with authority only to apply the four points made above. He cannot interpret them, for instance, to see in a golden wedding anniversary or in an interfaith marriage, the "urgent necessity" required by the Instruction for the giving of the Catholic Eucharist to a person who has not "formally embraced" the Catholic faith.

Doctor, after my writing all this, I can see you reading it and, at this point, leaning back, stroking your chin, and protesting. You quite possibly know as much about all this legislation as I do, and look on me as one who has missed your point. You are not overly sentimental, you are simply interested in increasing the love of people for each other and for the Blessed Sacrament, and in a general increase of understanding. Your point, you might reiterate, was to be done with all this petty legislation and get on with the fuller message of the Gospel.

Well, I still cannot go along with you. But I have just had an insight that might bear on the whole question. You are thinking of the Eucharist as the sacrament of love, the one in which God expresses his love for us and we our love for Him. This I agree with, but in the Gospel of John, chapter 6, our Lord has promised the Eucharist, and some of the disciples found the saying hard and walked no more with Him. Jesus did not call them back.

This would seem to mean that though the sacrament was to be one of love, it was not necessarily for everyone. This is the foundation of all the bothersome legislation of the Church upon the Eucharist.

The sacrament of universal invitation for which you seem to be groping is not the Eucharist, but Baptism. That is not only open to all who believe, but can even be administered validly by those who do not believe. Again the legalist puts in his point that the pagan, Mohammedan, Jew, or even atheist who baptizes must intend to do what the

Church intends. But despite this restriction on the minister, Baptism is the most ecumenical of the sacraments and the symbol of God's universal invitation.

People understand this. I remember an apostate priest who appeared on a TV talk program some years ago who had a hearty chuckle about what people were doing to his children. Many of his still-Catholic lay friends of former years would visit him, and in the course of the visit somehow entice the prekindergarten kids into the kitchen, hold their heads under the running faucet, and pronounce the holy words of Baptism. The apostate said so many people did this that the kids got used to it and didn't even try to squirm away. The good lay people were, I suppose, somewhat misguided. The story about them affords only tempered amusement, but it illustrates their belief that God's love and grace should be thrust on people be they unknowing or even unwilling.

I go unhorrified at this bestowal of Baptism, because the people were acting out its symbolism of universal invitation. I remain horrified at the priest who tried to force Communion on the unwilling Baptists because he was not acting out the full symbolism of unity of love, belief, and discipline.

But let me try to get back, Doctor, to the tone of your really tender and sincere letter. To be even argumentative when talking about the love of God is a kind of contradiction. Let me say that as I read your letter, the weeping Margaret of the Hopkins poem came to mind. Little Margaret, as you remember, wept at the sight of the falling leaves and the passing of summer. She is told in the last two lines of the poem:

> *It is a blight man was born for*
> *It is Margaret you mourn for*

In other words, there was some question as to what she was really crying about. Could it be that the girl in your letter wept not only because her dear friends could not receive the Eucharist she herself loved, but also because there was between her and them no perfect union of love and belief?

4

Can We Use Violence to Get Justice?

THE LETTER:

I am a student of Kristu Jyothi College at Bangalore, India. Near the college are several villages, in one of which I do social work. The people are very poor and live in subhuman conditions. All the property in the village is owned by one rich man. The people work for him in a large stone quarry. They have no means of fighting for their rights legally; they are ignorant and dependent on the rich man for everything. Relief workers supply them with food (e.g., American wheat), build them houses with money received from benefactors, and evangelize them.

I disagree with this method of helping them because 1) The cause of oppression is in the village itself, and should be tackled by the people there. 2) For a vast country like India, the charity method cannot reach enough people. 3) I know of places in India where Communists, through violent revolutionary methods, have improved the condition of the masses. I feel tempted to join the people and resort to violence. Will I be acting in the spirit of the Gospel? I don't see a clear answer given by the Church in this matter.

My argument is something like this: The present social structure is more violent than even a bloody revolution. Hence a violent revolution against it is morally justified. What is the Church's method of liberating the masses?

Job P.J.

THE ANSWER:
By Kenneth Ryan

I never start an article by making remarks about a correspondent's name, but in your case I must make an excep-

tion not for the sake of any wisecrack but because, Job,
your name epitomizes your problem. By that I mean that
Job in the Bible faced the same problem of evil that besets
you. And, while he had a lot of patience, that alone by no
means solved his dilemmas.

You bring your difficulty to a sharp point with your last
sentence: "What is the Church's method of liberating the
masses?" The blunt answer to the sharp question is, "She
has none. She was not founded to 'liberate the masses.' "
Taking the term in its present communistic meaning, that
answer would be accurate but unsatisfying and would stop
discussion which is really needed for an understanding of
Catholic teaching.

A further reason for going on is the recent publication of
various "theologies of revolution," which by and large
make the same point as you do about violence being no
worse than oppression. Until these liberating theologians
started writing, there was consensus on just war, rebellion,
and use of violence. Speaking very generally, everything
went back to the economic and moral position of the starving man and whether he could take food by force from
those who had more than enough of it. No problem, either
in reason or moral theology, except that he must use as
little force as possible.

But since taking anything by force was usually forbidden
by civil law, the next touch of reason came in recourse to
the Biblical injunction to obey God rather than man. Thus
papal pronouncements on the subject of law and order, such
as those of Pius XI and Leo XIII, would start with an in-
sistence on the need for law and order and go on to make
the point that rebels could not be blamed when someone in
authority was disregarding law and order. In the rulings of
Vatican II the same pattern is followed; its document states
that such rebels must observe "the limits imposed by natural law and the Gospel."

The orthodox theologians have summed up those limits
in necessarily broad terms: rebellion is lawful only when
1) incumbent political power is guilty of extremely grave
abuses; 2) peaceful means have been exhausted; 3) rebellion is the lesser of two evils; and 4) there is reasonable
hope of rebel success.

The Church had first to face questions like these when it
converted the Roman empire and took over the responsibilities to civil society that went with the take-over. Both Au-

gustine and Ambrose had thoughts on the subject. Ambrose said it was wrong not to defend the innocent (wrong not to get involved, that is), and Augustine saw the necessity of war in just causes. But they, too, had "only if" clauses in their declarations. The early Church had to deal with violent situations, but had no thought of adopting violence to attain its purposes.

I suppose Mohammed's followers were the first to use violence in an outright religious missionary effort. They swept from Arabia across Africa, to the Pyrenees, and to the gates of Vienna, taking physical charge of the territories and forcibly converting their occupants. The Romans used violence to put down nonstate religions, but it would seem their motives were political rather than religious. The Muslims were pretty successful, and it is a disturbing thought that violence and religious feeling mix so well. The religious wars of Europe, like those of Mohammed in the 9th century and North Ireland today, were largely political, but there can be no doubt that the igniting sparks were religious.

The theologians of revolution are well-acquainted with the above considerations and that is why they are trying to baptize violence, to "christen" it, make it a Christian thing. Their ultimate object is not really to spread Christianity but to "liberate the masses." Religion is their tool, their means to an end, rather than their end.

But we mustn't forget your rich man, Job. Any violent attack on him would need the same justification as violence against a ruling government. Such justification is possible. You don't furnish many details but that does not matter so much in matters of principle. Before attacking the rich man, you would have to establish his personal responsibility for the oppression. He certainly could be guilty, but if his responsibility were lessened by governmental, economic, or cultural forces working on him, you would have to take them into account. Such responsibility is sometimes not too difficult to establish. It would be a foolhardy historian, indeed, who would call the American Revolution of 1776 immoral, and there are many places in the world today where the oppression is certainly greater than it was in the American colonies.

The second point is that you would have to exhaust all peaceful means before resorting to violence. Again, your letter is lacking in detail, but—also again—it might be easy to prove your point had you done so. In revolutionary situations the use of violence has often been preempted by authority in power, and peaceful means of solution are thereby exhausted. All this you would have to consider before attacking your rich man.

The third point, on the lesser of two evils, depends on a human estimate of the situation. For instance, it might remove the evil of poverty temporarily to divide up the wealth of the rich man, but would you in doing that destroy the means of producing more wealth? Did the rich man have the only available "know how" in making the quarry profitable? Would the workers' immediate prosperity be at the expense of greater future poverty? Maybe not, but you have to make the judgment if you are to act morally.

A press notice in the United States during the Vietnam war quoted an officer as saying he had to destroy a town in order to save it. You must be careful not to do anything like that.

In revolutionary situations the presumption of the rebels is always that the present evil is the greater, but being a rebel does not make you infallible. Rebels tend to forget, for instance, the inevitable, though incidental, killing of the innocent that may be involved. Even when they think of it, they may regard it as of secondary importance. It may have been just a propaganda story, but it was told of Mussolini, during his rebellious rise to power, that his staff car ran over and killed a little girl. When the driver slowed to stop, the great rebel told him not to waste time. "What is one life in this march of history?" is one version of the future dictator's reaction. In traditional thought, human life is of primary importance.

The fourth point, reasonable hope of success, is best illustrated by reference to the present wave of terrorist activity. Hijacking passenger planes, bombing bars, and occupying apartment buildings are basically futile actions. They are not directed against persons who could help or hurt the terrorists. The terrorists have only a remote, not a reasonable, hope of attaining success in higher political areas through the murder of innocent persons. Arafat, the Palestinian terrorist, realized a success in getting the United Nations Assembly to listen to him, but it is unreasonable to suppose that any solution of the Palestinian problem will be reached through his tactics. His "hope of success" is much closer to black despair than it is to bright reason.

I have heard St. Thomas Aquinas snickered at for seeming cautious rather than righteous in writing that rebellion must have a well-founded hope of success in order to be moral, but terrorists could conceivably be morally acceptable in everything but this circumstance. So, before destroying your rich man, at least think of the fourth point.

Now, Job, to go on to another question in your letter, "Would I be acting in the spirit of the Gospel (in using violence)?" Well, you might be acting in the spirit of moral theology, but certainly not in the spirit of the Gospel.

Apply the four points to our Lord himself. Point 1) He lived under the tyranny of the Romans. Their abuses of authority were grave; they planted their heathen standards in the Temple itself. The Jews had their own terrorists, the *sicarii,* who hid their long daggers in their flowing robes, walked in the crowded market place, stabbed those they thought deserving of such treatment, and escaped rather easily most of the time in the noise and panic they caused. Christ did not join them.

Point 2) He kept to the peaceful-means solution. His "Render unto Caesar the things that are Caesar's and to God the things that are God's" was a kind of standing answer to the crowds who wanted him to be their wonder-working warrior king. He told Peter to put up his sword when the hothead cut off the ear of the high priest's servant, who was in the act of unjustly arresting Christ.

Point 3) Christ apparently did not choose the lesser of two evils in his passion. It seems clear from the Gospels that He went willingly to his death though He had alternatives.

People don't read them much anymore, but in pre-Vatican II manuals of devotion, there was always a meditation on the death of Christ which dealt with the excess of his suffering. One drop of his blood, it would be recounted, would have been enough to redeem thousands of worlds, but He shed it all.

Normal human imagination could not evoke a crueler death than that of the thirst, asphyxiation, and pain which He endured. His body and nervous system were perfect and so the sharpness of his agony was unblunted by failing consciousness. Yet all this was by voluntary choice of the greater, not the lesser, of physical evils. His choice was part of the mystery of Redemption and if you claim the name of

Christian, should be considered in your choice between violence and oppression.

Point 4) Just for a touch of modern black humor, how about the 12 legions of angels Christ referred to in reproving Peter? Had He chosen to rebel and had the other three points already in his favor, He could certainly have gone ahead morally on point four with reasonable hope of success. Let's see. In those days there were up to 6,000 men in a Roman legion and so there were about 72,000 angels, not plain soldiers, with whom Christ could have confronted his captors. If you will pardon the so-called humor, He could have taken them as Grant was later to take Richmond. But He didn't call on his heavenly warriors, even though they would have made his hope of success eminently reasonable.

So, Job, be patient. I can't tell you it is always wrong to rebel violently against oppression, but I can tell you it is not the specifically Christian thing to do. I don't think violence can be baptized.

5

What About Birth Control?

THE LETTER:

I take the *Catholic Digest*. However, I am not a Catholic. I have an aunt by marriage and several friends who are Catholic. I certainly agree with the Catholic Church's stand on abortion, but I do not understand the Catholic Church's stand on birth control, with overpopulation such a problem today; and the people with the most children seem to be those on welfare or in those countries where there is starvation. Would it not be better if these children were not born? Can you explain this to me? This is what I would like to know about the Church.

                                              Mrs. R. Austin, Jr.

THE ANSWER:
By Kenneth Ryan

Anyone who takes the *Catholic Digest,* Mrs. Austin, cannot be all bad. You agree with us on abortion, too, so I welcome the opportunity of trying to explain why Catholics who follow the reasoning of traditional morality still oppose artificial birth control.

They are not really as pigheaded as they seem to many of their contemporaries, but to show that I must begin with background considerations. Just what is the issue? Let me say first that it is not a case of the Catholic Church working for an overpopulated world, devoutly hoping that everyone will have as many children as physically possible. Birth control by moral methods is not only permitted by the Church, but in certain cases could be the obligation of the sincere Catholic. The point, of course, is that there is a difference between natural and artificial birth control, the first being allowable and the second sinful.

Despite the implications of those opposed to her stand, the Church is not really relying on starvation, war, and natural calamities to keep population down and the world habitable. Certainly such factors have operated locally in the past and in view of atomic proliferation may well operate on a world scale in the future, but the Church does not rely on them to solve the population problem. The traditional Church regards irresponsible parenthood on a family or national scale as immoral because she believes that God has provided man with a nonsinful, natural birth-control method. I must add that it requires at least intermittent sexual self-denial for successful operation.

It is at this point that I lose all those people who consider they win the argument by exclaiming, "This is the year 1975!" They say it as though the numerals were oversize and underlined. The society we live in lacks any built-in lessons in self-control. Deliberate self-denial of any attainable pleasure is looked on as idiocy. This effect shows through even within the Catholic Church in the agitation to move away from celibacy of the priesthood and the old monastic vows of poverty and obedience. The basic gripe against the Church is that she requires the foregoing of pleasure as a means of controlling population.

I'm sure that you were not even thinking of things like that, Mrs. Austin, so let's go on quickly to a second consideration directly brought up by the question in your letter, "Would it not be better if these children were not born?"

To be or not to be? If life is only a period of agony followed by a return to nothingness, the unbelieving world has the better of the argument—it would seem better "not to be." If, as the Church believes, God creates each person with the ultimate purpose of that person's eternal happiness, the period of suffering between creation and physical death is literally unimportant. This was the thought in Pope Paul's mind when he reproved those who would limit the number of those admitted to the "Banquet of Life."

A second background consideration is in the realm of fantasy. Suppose that all the world were Catholic and that by a greater miracle, all the people followed the Church's traditional teaching about birth control. The population problem would disappear! People would have only as many children as the planet could support.

The rhythm method, known with such great good humor as Vatican roulette, is fallible in a percentage of single family situations. But if the whole human race practiced natural birth control, population could be certainly controlled; in the total world situation the method would be (dare I use the word?) infallible.

In fact in that world of fantasy there would be easier attainment of control. The current complaint of the birth control societies is that people, despite the effectiveness of modern artificial methods of contraception, are continuing to have as many children *as they want,* not as many or few *as they should have* for the best balance of population with world resources. A world of obedient Catholics would not present this problem. So the Church does not see herself as interfering with the march of human progress.

The fantasy approach to the practical problem only annoys and does not dissuade the nontraditional moralists. But from the viewpoint of the Church, the artificial birth control societies want to abolish the natural law. The Church holds that the natural law cannot be abolished, any more than God can be abolished. Both Hitler and Stalin avoided what were to them population problems by genocide, which was basically wrong because it was against natural law, not just because because their respective countries had statutes against murder or even because of the "Thou shalt not kill" commandment published in the Bible. They could ignore statutes, but could not repeal the natural law. If natural law and a statute coincide in scope, abolishing the statute makes no essential difference in the morality of the action.

So political power cannot do away with natural law. Neither can majority opinion. If Vatican Council III were to convene tomorrow and by a 99.4% majority declare that there was to be no canon law against artificial birth control, the action would not change the natural law. No matter how many confessors, canon lawyers, or episcopal false prophets announce themselves in favor of artificial birth control, nothing changes in the realm of right and wrong.

Majority opinion is not the source of natural law. This natural law we are talking about is nevertheless written in the heart of man. It means that there are some things, at least, that a man with his wits about him can discover to be wrong. I would regard my own murder by another as wrong. If I am mentally healthy, I go on to the consideration that it is also wrong for me to kill other men. This mental attitude is natural in man; it is not natural to the other carnivorous animals. Natural law is not self-enforcing. It is often broken by the free will of man, and its application is subject to further reason as in the case of self-defense. But this sense of a natural law is one of the things, along with self-reflection and free will, that raises man above the animals.

Patience, Mrs. Austin, I realize that since you said you were against abortion, you go along with me on natural law, murder, and self-evident wrongs. All this has to be said first.

Artificial birth control is not so self-evidently wrong, since you said you didn't understand the traditional Catholic position. Again, no one will understand the foreground without knowing the background. It might help to say that the Catholic vision of life is greater than the social security type of outlook.

In the rise of the welfare states, the social philosophers began speaking of government care from cradle to grave or from womb to tomb, their definition of the total life span. A more religious definition would be that new life begins

with the twinkle in the father's eye and continues eternally
into the Beatific Vision.

Such things are beyond government control and of little
interest to its agencies, but the traditional Catholic faith is
that interference at any point by man in the continuum of
human life created by God is against natural law. Just as
abortion is a breaking of the continuum, so is interference
with the life forces used by God to create new eternal life.
And just as it makes no difference morally whether the Supreme Court provides for the killing of the person at three
rather than six months of age, it makes no difference morally whether interference with life comes at the time of its
production, in its later stages through euthanasia, or in the
premarriage intention to control it artificially.

Imagine, just for the moment and for the purpose, that
you are God, planning the production of a particular human life. Where do you begin? Is it at emergence from the
mother's womb, at six or three months of fetal life, at the
moment of conception, at the physical union of the parents,
with the intention of the parents to have children, with the
previous production of the parents themselves? It would
seem that man's interference with your plan at any of these
points would be in opposition to your will.

In Catholic tradition the intention to have and rear children is inherent in the marriage contract, for its alternative,
promiscuity, while satisfying the sex and companionship
drives, would take little thought of the children needed to
continue, not the life of the parents, but the life of the human race, part of God's continuum. So, in a very real sense
you could say that the marriage contract and the intentions
of the parties are, in God's view, the beginning of new life.
If you accept all this reasoning, you must agree that artificial birth control is wrong. It interferes with the continuum
of life.

Opponents of the Church's position are often infuriated
with her seeming inability to appreciate the urgency of the
immediate problem. Old-line Catholic moralists are equally
infuriated with the poohpoohing of her philosophical and
logical arguments. One of them is that no faculty of man
should be abused. The use of the word *abused,* according
to one's viewpoint, makes the principle either self-evident
or hypothetical. But calling it hypothetical is not different
from protesting "But this is 1975!"

In the traditional Catholic moral context, saying that the

sex faculty should not be abused implies that its primary purpose is procreation. When those contrary point out that it has also the purpose of mutual comfort and give this purpose more importance than procreation, they are again proclaiming "1975!" A single look at God's total creation shows that procreation is the primary purpose of the sex faculties. The second purpose does not even exist in the lower, unfree-willed, unself-reflecting animals whose actions are ultimately controlled by body chemistry rather than willingness or unwillingness to observe law. Yet the Church insists that the secondary purpose of marriage be fulfilled as strongly as do the new moralists. For instance, it is not fulfilled by artificial insemination, any more than the first purpose (procreation) is fulfilled by a contraceptive act. The Church is against artificial insemination even when the parties are man and wife because there is no human comfort and no expression of conjugal love in it.

The force and fundamental importance of this abuse-of-a-faculty argument is seen more clearly in its disregard by the new morality than in its presentation by traditional Catholic morality. In the new morality, masturbation (called self-abuse in the older, more genteel, manuals) though obviously the abuse of a faculty, is not reproved. It cannot be reproved, and the new moralists must join the liberated women's magazines in encouraging what used to be called solitary vice, because artificial birth control is, physically, mutual abuse.

Vasectomy and sterilization, both mutilations or destructions of a faculty, are necessarily O.K.'d in the new morality. The chief trouble is that there is nowhere for the new moralists to stop. If these methods of population control fail and their purpose must be achieved, they go on logically to abortion and euthanasia as acceptable methods of population control. The only sins left are things like dumping tailings into Lake Superior or not using electronic smoke controls in your smokestack.

It is not a reassuring simile, but it is a fact that Catholic moral principles, like Catholic dogmas, are related to each other as are the cards built into a house by a child. Pull out one of the bottom ones and the whole edifice tumbles, as it has for the new moralists, and as one of them has admitted in print.

That is why the Pope in his encyclical *Humanae Vitae* didn't care that he so bitterly antagonized the fatuous enthusiasts who expected him to give in to the pressure of majority opinion. He can't give in without wiping out the whole structure of Catholic morality, adherence to the natural law, and belief in the God of Judaeo-Christian tradition.

Mrs. Austin, your letter shows you to be a fair-minded, sincere person, so after that outburst you, and thousands like you, are entitled to ask: "If you're so smart, why haven't you persuaded the errant Catholics and, for that matter, the whole world to give up artificial birth control?" The answer is that the official arguments are abstract and, while logical, are not as persuasive as the artificial birth control societies' arguments.

I said they were not as persuasive; I did not say they were not as good. They are in fact better. But the societies can point to the millions of starving babies, we only to a principle to which logic has brought us. They can point to women in real fear of death if they follow the traditional morality; we can only call for heroism in the pursuit of sanctity.

We suffer from the lack of a coercive argument, one that forces peoples' assent. Of course, even the arguments for the existence of God do not coerce everybody. It comes to a question of value; which is more important in our lives, heaven or earth? The new moralists can't see why we cannot have the best of both worlds, but they have to blind themselves to the whole picture of command and obedience, of sacrifice of the temporal for the sake of the eternal, found in traditional Catholic morality.

The new moralists seem now to be the molders of what has become majority opinion. But ever since Adam joined the majority formed by Eve and the serpent, majority opinion can be looked on as a test of right or wrong only with the closed eyes of the new moralists. If you don't understand how they can see anything with their eyes closed, neither can I.

Majority opinion is all in favor of improving the "quality of life" in living populations at the expense of life itself for future generatons. Sort of reminds you of Jack Benny, God rest him. His most famous joke held up the radio program for ten minutes with studio audience laughter. All he did was hesitate overlong in reply to the bandit demanding his money or his life. The audience, obviously with the right set of values, thought it hilarious that anyone could even consider preferring money to life, but that is not the way the world is now. Present majority opinion chooses for itself a more comfortable future (money, really) while denying any future (life, really) to what would ordinarily be a large percentage of the human race.

II
The Eternal Questions

Even though the department was originally set up to provoke questions about the Catholic Church from persons not belonging to it, a surprising number of questions concerned the basics of all religion.

6

What Do You Mean "Have Faith"?

THE LETTER:

I am not a Catholic, nor am I an atheist. It seems to me that the essence of every religion is "You must have faith," often issued almost as a command by the clergy. But how does one really attain faith? To my mind, faith would automatically remove all fear of the hereafter; the contemplation of death would not be terrifying. Faith is not something one can just turn on and off. A man would be a fool, indeed, if he did not want to have the feeling of comfort, fearlessness, and composure that faith can bring him. Is there really an answer, a formula as to how mortal man on this brief earthly span can attain true faith and its inevitable rewards of peace of mind?

Hugo E. Jung

THE ANSWER
By J.D. Conway

You are certainly correct, Hugo, in your judgment that the essence of religion is faith. Religion can be very complex, but it can be viewed simply: religion is my relation as a person to God as a person. Faith is the means by which I establish personal contact with Him.

Again, you are correct in stating that faith is not something we can turn on and off. Faith comes as a gift from God, though, in a sense, we do turn it on when we accept the gift. We cannot attain faith by our own forces, any more than we can grasp a star by reaching. Faith gives us a direct share in God's own knowledge. Only God can grant that.

God has given us power to acquire human knowledge.

Observation, study and reason can lead us to find God in his universe. We can see his power in the unlimited splendors of the heavens, his wisdom in the submicroscopic marvels of the atom, and his patient planning in the genetic marvels of the chromosomes. But all this is natural knowledge; it is not faith. This human knowledge can be a preparation for faith, but I can never attain by study a direct acquaintance with God as a person, nor an awareness of his plans for my salvation and eternal happiness. I must wait until He gives me faith, makes Himself known to me, and reveals his secrets. God makes Himself known as intimately to the child or peasant as to the scientist or philosopher. Often the child's acceptance of God's gift is the more ready and trusting.

Faith is reasonable. It is the assent of our reason to truth made known to us by God. But it is a free assent, not forced by rational arguments nor by God's grace. We accept the truths of faith because we accept God, who makes these truths known to us. The truths themselves do not convince us. God convinces us. We may do a lot of reasoning about the truths of faith once we know them. But starting without them, we could never reason to them. Real faith is firm and final; we do not really know God if we only half believe Him. Real faith is free; ideas forced upon us would not constitute faith.

In a way there is something strange, almost unnatural about faith. Our reason accepts something without coercive arguments, yet is convinced beyond doubt. We could never accept scientific proofs about the natural world in such manner. But faith is not natural; neither is it unnatural. It is supernatural. The knowledge it gives us belongs to a nature superior to ours.

The truth which God teaches us in his revelation, and which we accept through faith, cannot contradict the truths which we learn from the study of God's world. In the course of centuries seeming contradictions have been feared and fought. Some scientists have called revelation ridiculous. And believers often saw science as heresy. Today men of religion realize that God's revelation gives us no short cuts to natural truths. He told us of creation but told us nothing about biology or astronomy. And the man of science does not expect to find in his laboratory an answer to man's eternal destiny.

There is little worry today that science and faith may

contradict each other. The problem is that religion seems to have little relevance to the scientist. He can find so many satisfying natural causes for matter, life, and intelligence that he sees no reason to worry about a first cause. And he is so intent on finding ways to control nature that he has no concern about its ultimate purposes.

Religion is contact with God. In the Christian religion our contact with God is direct and our relationship intimate. He became one of us, came to us in our own nature. The Father's Son became our brother, and through Jesus Christ the Father adopted us as children. We call God "Our Father." To the Christian, God's revelation comes through the Father's own Son, who lived with us and spoke to us in human language. He gave human example; showed human understanding of men's problems, but was able to solve them with divine as well as human power.

The Incarnation of God's Son, while it adds many mysteries to our faith, makes the act of faith more explicit, its object more tangible. But the nature of faith is not changed. It is still our free, personal acceptance of God as a person revealing Himself to us. The manner of his revelation makes acceptance easier. But it still begins with Him and requires a free act of the will from us, with his grace aiding us to perform this act.

Many have been the scholars without faith who, with great learning in languages and history, have studied the life, words, and actions of Jesus Christ with great detail and accuracy. They have appreciated the wonders of his wisdom, the depth of his love, and the noble generosity of his sacrifice, but have never accepted Him as a divine person, or as their personal Saviour. They did not have faith. It is certain that the gift was offered to them. We can hardly accuse them of willfully rejecting it. And probably like yourself, Hugo, they asked, "How does one really attain faith!"

Once again, my point is that we do not attain faith through human study. It comes to us as a gift from God, who alone has divine knowledge to share with us. And our faith is an acceptance of Him. The words and miracles of Christ, his death, and resurrection make the astounding fact of his divinity credible and reasonable, but they do not give us faith. Knowing all about Christ is not enough; I must know Him, receive Him, and commit myself to Him.

In many cases it is this personal commitment that makes

getting faith most difficult. Many people might find it easy to accept with simple trust and consoling confidence a God of power, goodness, and love who takes fatherly care of us here on earth and assures us of some kind of enduring life and happiness. But the Christian faith demands more than that. It involves an awareness of sin and a need of repentance. It requires that we firmly declare ourselves on God's side in the worldly conflict of good and evil.

Faith requires that we live as we believe. If we accept God we must love Him. If we accept Jesus Christ we must follow Him, giving up things of this world that pull us away from Him. And if we accept heaven as our destiny, we must follow the path that leads to heaven.

Faith is more than trust and lack of fear, Hugo; much more than serenity and comfort. It is the discomfort of faith which makes it so hard. The beginning of our movement toward God can become a tough struggle. Sometimes earthly life would seem much easier, more fun, if faith could only let us enjoy its fleeting pleasures in peace. Some people find intellectual problems impeding faith, but probably more are afraid of the real act of faith because of the personal commitment it demands. And more still, having accepted faith, find the daily life of faith discouraging. They turn off its spigot one little twist at a time until its flow is ineffective in producing hope and love, the virtues which should flow from it.

Faith is an act of the intellect, giving us knowledge of God and his truths. As such it is pure gain; it takes away none of our worldly knowledge, impedes in no way our natural wisdom; but it adds knowledge and wisdom that are literally out of this world.

Faith is an act of the will. It demands not only an acceptance of God and his truths, but a commitment of self to God and his plans. It is only through this giving of self, with all the struggle and denial it demands, that faith can grow strong enough to bring hope and serenity and peace of mind with it. I agree with you heartily, Hugo, "A man would be a fool if he did not want to have the feeling of comfort, fearlessness, and the composure that faith can bring him." But these consoling effects can only be obtained at the cost of self-giving.

Religion is a relationship. God gave Himself to us with love in the Incarnation. And the God-Man gave Himself for us on the cross. The faith by which we accept God in his goodness and love demands that we give ourselves. St. Paul said that if he had faith great enough to move mountains, but had not love, it would profit him nothing. So, too, our faith must lead to love or it will wither away.

When faith accomplishes its full purpose in us, the act of faith becomes easier for those about us. One of the most effective ways of announcing God's word to the world is by showing the truth of it in our own lives. If all Christians really lived their faith, religion would be more relevant in the world. It is because the life of the believer often differs little from that of the unbeliever that faith is often dismissed as unimportant.

7

How Do I Know Anything's a Sin?

THE LETTER:

I have a question I would like you to answer: What is the criterion for knowing if a given action or negligence is sinful or not? I ask because I have heard Catholics discuss among themselves the sinfulness of certain actions. Apparently they did not have any criterion by which to judge. They just "felt" that to do such and such would be sinful. They couldn't give me the reasons why.

Charles Mader

THE ANSWER:
By J.D. Conway

The usual complaint against Catholics is the opposite of yours, Charles. We are accused of having all sin classified, so that we can consult a chart to learn which actions are sinful, and which are mortal or venial.

Catholics who merely feel that a particular action is sinful would seem to be going on instinct. For a truly moral life we must have a higher level of understanding and moti-

vation. We cannot know the meaning of right and wrong
unless we know the meaning of human nature: that we are
creatures dependent on God, our Creator. And as Christians we must know our goal in life is union with God in
love. Christian morality is based on the fact that God has
loved us since the moment He created us in his own likeness. The Father sent his Son to show us the reality and the
depth of divine love, and to invite our love in return. And
the Son, Jesus Christ, made it clear by word and deed that
we cannot truly love God unless we love our neighbor also.

A proper understanding of our human nature will direct
our moral life. It will remove the childish concept that
any man is the center of the world: that parents, relatives,
and neighbors live for his welfare and pleasure. If our as-
tronauts got the idea that the earth was turning around
them, they would make fatal errors. For us the beginning
of moral living is to understand our orbit around God.

For Christians, Jesus summed up the norm of morality:
"Thou shalt love the Lord thy God with thy whole heart,
and with thy whole soul, and with thy whole mind. . . .
thou shalt love thy neighbor as thyself." This is our basic
criterion of right and wrong, Charles. Any thought, word,
or action which is an authentic expression of our love for
God and our neighbor is good. Anything which violates or
lessens this love is evil.

However, the love which inspires us to moral action
must be more than sentiment. We must be sure that our
deeds express true love. Instincts are not enough; feelings
are not reliable. We must have positive guidelines, which
the average Catholic gets from his religious education. The
source of the guidelines is the eternal law of God: the un-
changing divine plan for man's happiness, growth, and
sanctity. We can know this divine law through revelation
and reason. God revealed his law to us in two great stages:
the Ten Commandments which He gave to Moses on Mt.
Sinai, and the teaching and example of our Lord Jesus
Christ.

The rules of morality found in the Bible are called the
divine positive law: divine because it comes directly from
God, and positive because it is laid down in explicit terms.
The divine positive law never changes; it is not arbitrary
legislation, but God's own expression of his eternal plan
and of his own immutable goodness. However, his revelation can be increasingly clear and explicit in subsequent

stages. The teachings of Christ are on a higher moral level than the law given to Moses.

Our second way of learning about God's eternal law is by using the common sense God gave us. We can learn only those portions of the eternal law that have been made perceptible in creation. But even if the divine positive law had not been given us, we could learn most of its precepts by using our reason to understand what we are, why we are here, where we are going, and the nature of our relationship to God and to our neighbor. Without revelation we would have gained our insights more slowly, less surely, and often through sad experience.

The natural law is said to be immutable, and yet our knowledge of it grows and deepens as we grow in wisdom and in goodness. Through such moral growth we have gradually come to see the evil of slavery; the viciousness of religious persecution; the equality of all men; the extent of human rights; the immorality of racial discrimination; and the demands of social justice. God's law does not change, but our understanding of it must change, always in the direction of deeper comprehension and wider perception.

Besides the law of God, we have human positive laws: human because they are made by men, and positive because they are spelled out, and are sometimes arbitrary. The men who make laws must have valid authority, either religious or civil. Jesus Christ gave St. Peter and the other Apostles the authority they needed to be shepherds of his flock; and the successors of the Apostles have always used this authority to guide the faithful on the way to sanctity. As a result we have Church laws like those of fasting and abstaining, assisting at Mass on Sunday, and receiving Communion during the Easter time.

In civil society, proper order requires laws that are clear and positive. Some of them may reinforce God's laws, as those which forbid murder, rape, and theft. Others can be quite arbitrary and yet oblige us in conscience. For instance, the laws in the United States require that you drive your car on the right side of the road. If you drive in England, you must keep to the left. Could anything be more arbitrary? There is nothing inherently wrong in driving on either side of the road. Yet you would be guilty of sin if you maliciously drove on the right side of the road in England and thereby endangered lives and property.

I mention this example, Charles, to emphasize by contrast that there is nothing arbitrary about God's law. Murder is not wrong merely because God forbade it in the Ten Commandments. It is wrong by its very nature. It is contrary to our love for God, violates our love for our neighbor, and is unjust.

Opposed to this idea of a natural law are the theories that hold moral good and evil to be relative and changing. Popular today is a theory of situation ethics, by which a person makes his own moral judgments in a given situation. It holds that laws do not have universal validity; that our actions are not inherently good or evil by their nature. Changing situations may alter the morality of our deeds. It is up to us: we must be well-informed, judge with care, take all angles into account, and make an honest decision as to what we should do here and now.

Let us use an example to illustrate the difference between natural-law morality, and the ethics of the situation. We all agree that murder is wrong, and that life is one of our highest values. Now suppose that I am caring for a poor fellow who is dying of cancer, suffering agonies, and begging me to put him out of his misery. As a natural-law man, if I am faithful to my principles, I will know immediately that I have no right to play God. I cannot do evil that good may result from it. I will try to console the man and ease his pain by every reasonable means. I will do nothing extraordinary to prolong his life; but I will not snuff it out.

If I believe in situation morality, my reasoning might be different: The life of this pitiful person is no longer a positive value. Mercy is my motivation; love, I would say, impels me to end his hopeless misery. I decide to kill him.

The judgment I make as a "situationist," Charles, is like that of your friends who simply feel that a certain action is right or wrong. I am influenced by the emotions induced by the situation. Neither feelings nor subjective judgments are acceptable moral norms for a Catholic.

The Church looks to the natural law for reliable principles for moral action. However, like all good things, it can be abused. There are those who confuse the natural moral laws with the laws of nature, and claim that we do wrong when we prevent nature from taking its course. If these people were logical, they would have to label most applied sciences as sinful, especially medicine.

There are those who think that the natural law is merely an intricate exercise in logic. If you start with the right

principles, they say, and are careful in forming your prem-
ises and making your deductions, your conclusions must
conform with moral reality in every case. They would use
the natural law as they would use a computer, but they run
the risk of feeding false or inadequate principles to the ma-
chine. If you put garbage in, you get garbage out. May the
Lord save us from computerized morality!

A third group insist that the natural law is absolute,
rigid, and unchangeable. Possibly they are thinking of
God's eternal law. For all practical purposes, there is no
natural law until we understand it. It is there, but the human intellect has to find it. And it is not something to be
grasped at a glance. We must observe, study, and learn by
the age-old experience of mankind.

The human intellect is marvelous but fallible, and it
tends to learn profound truths slowly. The natural law has
meaning only in the measure that we grasp and understand
its truths. Man's comprehension of the natural law has
grown with his cultural and religious growth, and with
God's help it will continue to grow, always in the direction
of clearer concepts of God's will and greater love for his
goodness.

We make a great mistake, Charles, if we concentrate all
our attention on external laws when we consider morality.
Our acts may be criminal, but unless our personal conscience sees their evil and wills it, we are not guilty of sin.
And our deed may be good, but if our conscience sees it as
sinful, we are guilty of sin.

For a Christian, true morality is not imposed by law
from outside, not even by the law of God; it is rather a
response to an invitation to love, God's invitation. Our human liberty reacts to God's love for us and to our concept
of His infinite goodness. To this morality laws are not binding chains, they are merely useful guidelines to the happy
course of true love. They let us know, not just feel, the
authentic expression of our love.

8

Fit Original Sin into Evolution For Me

THE LETTER:

I have a hard time accepting the Catholic doctrine of original sin. If man has evolved from animals, the first man, Adam, must have been a very primitive man, indeed, much more so than the cave man. I just can't see the doctrine that teaches that this first primitive man was tested and sinned and that this is the reason Christ came to the world, to redeem mankind from original sin.

Could you elucidate? How do we know this happened many millions of years ago? If you could help me to understand this teaching of original sin in conformity with scientific teachings on the age of mankind, I would appreciate it.

Paul Kingseed

THE ANSWER:
By J.D. Conway

You have a difficult problem for me, Paul. I shall try to throw some light on it, but I cannot offer any final solution to all the questions involved. Neither science nor theology has spoken the final word about man's origin, and it is possible that neither ever will.

Science is handicapped by lack of clear evidence; it must deal with indications that are circumstantial, even though strongly convincing. Theologians face the difficulty of translating the truths of revelation out of the primitive world views of the authors of Sacred Scripture into the modern concepts of the evolutionary scientist.

Our revealed knowledge of man's origin and his sin comes to us in the language of men who saw the world as a flat disk protected by a taut blue canopy, with the sun, moon, and stars stuck in it. And while the sacred writers were not being literal in their description of God the sculptor, molding Adam from clay and blowing the breath of life into his nostrils, they certainly had no intimations of the theory of evolution.

In the time of Galileo (died 1642), theologians had problems in adapting the revealed truths they knew in terms of a flat-disk world to the concept of an orbiting planet, insignificant in relation to the galaxies. In the past century our theological problems were even more difficult! Revelation was given us in terms of directly created phyla and species, but we must express it in a manner meaningful to those who view the world as an evolution.

When biological evolution was first accepted as scientific theory, theologians tended to rebel against it. There were rumblings of conflict between science and religion. But they eventually separated the eternal revealed truths from the primitive cosmology used to illustrate them. After this distinction was made, the evolutionary development of the world and its plant and animal life were not in conflict with the Genesis creation story. Slowly theologians saw the possibility of the evolutionary development of man's body. They now find no serious problem in this theory, and they accept the evidence presented by scientists that man has amazing similarities to the animals. While noting that the evolution of man is a hypothesis, they admit that no biologist of today is able to think in other terms.

But theologians are quick to note that the evolutionary process does not apply to man's spiritual, rational, immortal soul. As Pope Pius XII wrote in his encylical *Humani Generis,* "Catholic faith obliges us to hold that souls are immediately created by God." And this is true for your soul and mine, Paul, just as it was for the souls of Adam and Eve.

Up to now we have not been able to translate the doctrine of original sin into terms that anthropologists find entirely meaningful. While there is no conclusive proof of their theory, anthropologists tend to think in terms of the polygenic origin of man. Their scientific studies do not incline them to think of just one man and one woman evolving from animal status, but rather of groups of men and women resulting from genetic explosions or mutations. This theory would not be difficult to reconcile with the Biblical stories of the creation of Adam and Eve, but it seems incompatible with the doctrine of original sin as taught by St. Paul and explained in Christian tradition.

Consequently Pope Pius XII wrote that the faithful cannot believe there were ever true men who did not take their origin from Adam, nor that Adam represents a certain number of first parents. He pointed out the Church's doctrine of original sin: ". . . which proceeds from sin actually committed by an individual Adam and which through generations is passed on to all and is in everyone as his own."

The majority of Protestants believe in original sin, and Lutherans stress more than Catholics the devastating effects of Adam's sin on human nature. However, many liberal Protestants seek a more natural explanation of original sin and its effects on us. Their explanation is that the story of Adam's sin in Eden means simply that sin entered the world from the beginning of man's life on earth; that all men are sinners and share a common state of sin. We are born into a situation of sin. Adam's disobedience set off a chain reaction of sin. Adam turned sin loose in the world, and we all follow the example he set for us.

St. Paul's explanation of original sin seems quite different. I suggest that you read it in his Epistle to the Romans, 5:12–19. For him all mankind had a definite solidarity with Adam, just as we all do with Jesus Christ. In Adam we all sinned and lost life; in Jesus we are all redeemed and receive life. "For just as by the disobedience of the one man the many were constituted sinners, so also by the obedience of the one the many will be constituted just."

Adam's evil deed put all men in the wrong; Christ's good deed puts all men right again. This teaching of St. Paul has been the constant tradition of Christianity, and the Council of Trent defined it formally: Adam's sin hurt not only himself but his descendants; he lost his God-given sanctity and justice not only for himself but for us also; and he passed on his sin to us, so that our souls are dead to grace.

The story of our first parents' sin is told with beautiful and symbolic detail in the 3rd chapter of Genesis. After God had created man and woman, He put them into the Garden of Eden, symbolic of friendliness with the Lord. In the garden they had many special favors, free gifts of God to which they had no natural right. Chief among these gifts was freedom from death, and the tree of life was in the midst of the garden to assure their immortality.

However, God would not force his favors on the man and woman He had created in his own image; they were free to accept or reject them. God put them on probation; the tree of the knowledge of good and evil was in the garden as a symbol of their freedom to disobey God and reject his gifts. They ate from the tree; they refused to obey. They were led into sin by forces of evil outside themselves, as represented by the serpent. We do not know exactly what their sin was, but pride was at the root of their defection, and disobedience destroyed their personal love for God.

As a result of their sin Adam and Eve lost Eden and the special favors that were a part of Eden. They had acquired the knowledge of good and evil by experience, and mankind would never recover from the upsetting effects of that experience. And they had lost immortality; the tree of life was forbidden to them. Now they must suffer and die.

When we read the account of the fall of our first parents, we may enjoy the symbols used in telling it, but we must not be deceived into taking the whole story as myth. It is factual. Our first parents actually committed personal sin, and their sin was not merely symbolic of the subsequent sins of the rest of us, not merely the first fission in a chain reaction. It was a revolt of the human race. At that time they were the whole human race, and when they sinned, all mankind rebelled and broke its bond of union with the Father in heaven.

It seems to me, Paul, that the only answer to your problem is to face frankly the Christian teaching that the first man, whatever his genetic origin or cranial capacity, was raised by God to supernatural status. So he was not merely a primitive man, but a primitive man given extraordinary help from God. It is possible that some of the Fathers of the Church, and some great theologians of past centuries, had exaggerated notions of the gifts God gave to Adam. They believed he was more perfect and beautiful than men are now; he was intelligent, wise, strong, and healthy; in control of his passions, free, and rightly disposed in his will. Sin wrecked him.

These special perfections of Adam resulted from God's free gifts to him, not from his genetic origin. And whether these gifts were few or multiple, whether our first parent was a paragon or primitive, he did have one gift which was essential to the supernatural purpose for which he was created; sanctifying grace. It was symbolized by the close intimacy between God and man in the Garden of Eden. Whatever man's natural origin, he has a supernatural goal: life in loving union with God for eternity. God has great plans for the man and woman He created in His own image and likeness. He wanted them to know Him personally, love Him intimately, and live with Him constantly. But such destiny was far beyond the powers of man, who was only one step removed from the animals.

By his mere natural ability man could never know God, and not knowing God he could never love Him or be happy with Him. So God gave man the gift of sanctifying grace, which let him share a bit in the life of God and equipped him to know God. It is a second and higher form of life engrafted on natural life: supernatural life. This sanctifying grace, and other gifts which Adam may have received with it, were not personal gifts to our first parent as an individual; they were gifts to the whole human race, a sort of family heritage for Adam and all his descendants. The full significance of the fall of Adam lies in the fact that these gifts were lost before they could be given to any of his children. As heirs we can only inherit those gifts which our parents possessed at the time of their death. If they dissipated their wealth, it is lost to us, their descendants. By his sin Adam rejected the gifts of God and thus dispossessed himself of the spiritual wealth which might have been our inheritance.

But all was not lost forever. Many of God's gifts to Adam may never be recovered; man will suffer and die, and his fallen nature will never quite be cured from the shock of sin. But God will not abandon him. "For if by the offense of the one the many died, much more has the grace of God, and the gift in the grace of the one man Jesus Christ, abounded unto the many." God was generous to our first parents because He loved them, but He is more generous to us because He loves us as brothers of his own Son.

9

I Don't Feel Any "Natural Law"

THE LETTER:

In certain parts of some cultures, abortion and abandonment of infants are common practices. The Catholic Church believes in a universal "natural law." How is it that it seems to have no force among the pagans? Until you account for this, I don't see how you can appeal to the natural law in matters of birth control.

Mrs. Roy Von Briel

THE ANSWER:
By J.D. Conway

I would have to say first, Mrs. Von Briel, that Catholics believe in a universal law, but do not claim that all people rightly understand its every precept. We do not even claim that our Catholic ancestors always understood the natural law adequately, or that we right now in the present state of our moral development fully grasp it.

Modern notions of the natural law are often distorted. A classical source of Catholic thinking on this subject is St. Thomas Aquinas. For him the natural law is the participation of rational man in the eternal law of God. This supposes that God has a definite plan for all creation, and that man has a precise purpose in life. It also supposes that man is able to learn God's purpose, and his own goal in life, by using his intellect. God rules the inanimate things of his creation by the laws of nature, which we discover in physics and chemistry. Birds and animals are governed by their instincts, which are laws of action and reaction God has implanted in them. But man can participate in God's eternal law; with his intellect he can learn the law and by his own will freely adhere to it. Therefore, he alone of all creatures on earth is subject to the natural moral laws.

St. Thomas tells us that the basic principle of the natural law is self-evident: good is to be sought and evil avoided. However, when we get down to the detailed problems of life we are likely to encounter uncertainties. Our principles remain right, but our practical judgment may be wrong. In the words of St. Thomas, "the more we get down to particulars, the more defects we encounter." In all these intricate studies, however, we are using our intellect and are guided by the basic principle that good must be done and evil avoided. Once we reach firm conclusions, we may say that we have discovered precepts of the natural law. It is not by pure deduction but by careful study of all the data that we perceive the evil of dropping an atom bomb on innocent children in time of war.

St. Paul wrote about the Gentiles: "They show the work of the Law written in their hearts. Their conscience bears witness to them . . . ." In dealing with this concept of the natural law, we must keep clearly in mind that the natural law is never subjective. It demands a constant, honest study of reality, and a willingness to admit shortcomings and even errors in past thinking and in traditional formulations. The fallible human mind must seek constantly for more penetrating insights.

Among men, the insights of conscience are communicated from one person to another. Gradually they are stated in fixed formulas and made into rules of conduct which are generally valid. In time these formulas are applied to minute details of moral conduct; and in this manner formalism develops. Rules designed to fit every situation may often become quite divorced from the realities of many situations.

Because of its tendency to make rules to fit all occasions, natural-law morality is often accused of fostering infantile attitudes, devoid of adult responsibility and self-reliance. It is said to remove moral emphasis from the person and to place that emphasis on rules and abstractions.

Because it has, in this way, so many rules, the natural law is said to distract the moral and religious person from the unitive love and the I-Thou dialogue with God and with his fellow man, which are means and goals of his goodness. And because of the static nature of its formulas, it is accused of inhibiting the moral evolution of man, depriving him of higher insights and more authentic goals.

Our understanding of the natural law is a developing thing. A good example is the way we understand racial equality. American society had developed some conscience-easing formulas, like "separate but equal." Then as a result of sociological studies, a Supreme Court decision, and many demonstrations, we attained clearer insights into the many realities of segregation, the meaning of human rights, and the implications of equality. Our understanding of the natural law grew rapidly.

There is another sense in which the natural law develops. In a very true sense it is a law of becoming rather than of being. Man attains human perfection by becoming all that God intends a man to be; something better than he is. Man does not become fully himself in isolation: his nature is meaningful only in relation to God and to his fellow man. So the natural law of man's growth requires that man perfect his love for God and his love for his neighbor, not in the abstract, but in daily living. And it is toward this goal of human development that the natural law guides him.

Yet there is one sense in which the natural law is definitely static. It is the enduring norm by which we judge new notions of morality. Man's true development is in the direction of life and love, of justice and rights, and of responsible freedom. So moral concepts which detect immorality in capital punishment or war may well be authentic since they favor life; but a trend to sexual promiscuity is evidently evil since it prevents the development of true, unselfish, enduring love.

The primary competitor of the natural law in modern morality is situation ethics. Both systems have the same purpose: to help us determine which of our human actions are good and which are evil. But natural law is in open conflict with situation ethics, commonly known as the "new morality." Natural law is said to be absolute; it is based on the essence of things as God created them, and it finds some things essentially bad and others essentially good. They are bad or good by their very nature.

The new morality is frankly relativist: willful murder is certainly bad in most circumstances, but you may find yourself in a particular situation in which it is a good and advisable action. The same is true of lying or stealing. Natural law presumes the validity of abstract thought, of generalizations, of valid laws to fit all cases. The new morality holds all moral laws ambiguous. They are said to be generalizations which are not preceisely applicable to any concrete situation. Abstract laws are inventions of the mind; at best they can serve as guidelines or maxims. But each situation is unique, and the moral problems it presents must be judged on the spot, taking into account all the circumstances of here and now.

A Christian disciple of the new morality does not reject the Ten Commandments or Christ's law of love and virtue; he holds in reverence the traditional conventions of society, and the laws of his church and state. All these guidelines help the individual to decide the morality of this particular act here and now, and in these qualifying circumstances. But the primary concern of the new moralist is with the situation itself, and with the unique demands it makes on him.

He is prepared to let the common rules guide him in average situations, but he is ready to ignore the rules, or to violate any given principle, when he is convinced that greater good will be accomplished by so doing. He leaves himself free to decide for himself what is best here and now. For him the highest good is human welfare and happiness. He is concerned only for the good of people. He professes to love persons, not principles. The good of the person comes before any natural law, any law of Scripture, any theory, or any general principles.

In the new morality things are not intrinsically right or wrong. Their goodness or evil depends on the circumstances, the situation, and indeed, on the many complicated, overlapping situations which confront a person at any one instant.

Natural law does not exclude a careful and thorough weighing of all the values involved in a situation. But it does insist that some things are always wrong—murder and adultery, for instance—and that there is no situation that will make them right.

And now, Mrs. Von Briel, having tried to explain to you what the natural law is, I shall not attempt to use its principles and precepts to convince you that birth control is immoral. The arguments usually advanced to prove this point are mainly biological, whereas the natural law is concerned with man's growth and perfection in relation to God and his fellow man. Right now many of our best authorities on marriage and family problems, on world population, sociology, psychology, and theology are studying problems related to birth control in an effort to amass all the data pertinent to a decision on what is wrong, so that it may be avoided; and what is good, so that it may be sought after and done.

10

Tell Me About the Babies in Limbo

THE LETTER:

I am a Lutheran and have read many articles in the *Catholic Digest*. I would like an explanation of the place called Limbo. If unbaptized babies or little children who die without Baptism cannot go to heaven, how do we interpret Christ's saying: "Let the little ones come unto Me, and forbid them not, for of such is the kingdom of heaven"?

Mrs. John B. Sullivan

THE ANSWER:
By J.D. Conway

The word *limbo* comes from the Latin word *limbus,* which means a border, hem, or fringe. Neither the word nor the notion of limbo (as we now understand it) occurs in the Scriptures or in the writings of the early Fathers of the Church. The word and the notion of limbo, as a special place of natural happiness for babies who die without Baptism, seems to be found first in the writings of St. Albert the Great in the 13th century.

In the minds of early Christians you were either in the kingdom of God or outside it. If you didn't go to heaven

you went to hell. Even of the Lord Jesus we say in the
Apostles Creed, "He descended into hell."

The Christians inherited from the Jews, and from other
ancient peoples of the Near East, the notion of a three-
story world. Up above were the heavens, with the sun,
moon, and stars. In between was the earth, floating on water. And down below the waters were the nether regions,
which the Jews called Sheol, a word which the New Testament translated into Greek as Hades. This word is well-
known in Greek classicial literature, first as the name of
the god of the lower world, and then as the place itself, the
house of Hades. In Latin these lower regions were called
infernal. We call them hell.

Until shortly before the time of Christianity, it was considered that everyone died and went to Sheol. But gradually the Jewish people developed the concept of a state or
place of peace for the dead who had led virtuous lives.
They were said to rest on Abraham's bosom. Jesus, in
his story of Lazarus and the rich man, said, "Now the
poor man died and was carried away by the angels to the
bosom of Abraham. The rich man also died and was buried. In his torment in Hades he looked up and saw Abraham a long way off and Lazarus in his bosom."

It would seem that Abraham and Lazarus were in the
lower regions also, but in a much higher, cooler, happier
section. In later centuries the bosom of Abraham came to
be called the limbo of the Fathers, that part of the lower
regions where the virtuous men of Old Testament times
awaited the coming of the Saviour. Seemingly it was evacu-
ated after the visit of Jesus. But it did not become the
limbo of the children.

When the geography of Hades received detailed description, about the 14th century, there were three levels. Down
in the lowest pit sinners were tortured by perpetual fire. On
the second level was the limbo of the children; by this time
most theologians believed that they were comfortable and
happy, but some still held that they were being scorched a
bit by the flames below. On the top floor was the limbo of
the Fathers, but there was no agreement as to who were
the tenants of this once abandoned area. Albert the Great
wrote before the map of hell was so complete, but he explained that *limbus* meant the fringe of a garment, and
limbo was the fringe of hell. Since his time popular imagination has transferred it to the fringe of heaven, which had

long before been moved from the lower regions to beyond
the sky.

We might never have worried greatly about what happened to babies who died without Baptism except for the
Pelagian heresy of the 5th century. It has always been perfectly clear in orthodox Christianity that no one can get
into the kingdom of God or enjoy the Beatific Vision except through the redemptive merits of Jesus Christ. And
from the beginning Christians insisted on Baptism as the
means of being joined to Christ in his redemptive death
and resurrection. But the Pelagian heretics taught that men
could get into heaven by the force of their own free will
and their human merits. But Christian teachers reacted too
strongly. In effect, they bound the hands of God, and limited the effectiveness of his salvific will.

It is true that in the 4th century there was a bit of calm
speculation about what happened to babies who died without Baptism. St. Gregory of Nazianzus, one of the greatest
Greek Fathers of his day, thought that maybe the just
Judge would give them neither the glory of heaven nor any
punishment. But his good friend Gregory of Nyssa had a
more ingenious theory. He thought that these little babies
would start by enjoying God in a natural way; and then as
they matured in the use of their freedom, they would become capable of knowing God more and more until they
came to participate quite fully in the joys of heaven. Later
theologians were quite horrified at the way Gregory of
Nyssa confused the natural and supernatural; but in his
own day, at the 1st Council of Constantinople, Gregory
was named a norm of orthodoxy.

St. Augustine at first thought there might be some me-
dian stage between reward and punishment for unbaptized
babies. But when the Pelagians started putting these unre-
deemed babies right into heaven, Augustine decided that
there was no place for them but hell. It rather bothered
him to see God torturing these innocent waifs; so he had
trouble making up his mind how severe their sufferings
were. His sense of justice required that he make some distinction between the punishment inflicted on hardened sinners and the pangs of these pitiful tots. He finally decided
that their pains were very slight, but they still hurt.

The Pelagians had trouble getting around the words of
Jesus to Nicodemus: "I tell you most solemnly, unless a
man is born through water and the Spirit, he cannot enter

the kingdom of God." But then they remembered that Jesus had also said, "There are many rooms in my Father's house." Surely in one of these rooms there was a place for babies who had died without Baptism.

A council held at Carthage in 418, and later approved by the Pope, condemned this ingenious interpretation of the words of the Lord: "If anyone says that there is, either in the kingdom of heaven or anywhere else, an intermediate place where babies who have departed this life without Baptism may enter the kingdom of heaven, which is eternal life, let him be anathema." Those strong words inhibited the development of any notion of limbo for several centuries. Abelard, the great but notorious theologian of the 12th century, was the first to decide that the very slight punishment decreed by Augustine was nothing more than darkness, the absence of the light of the Beatific Vision.

St. Thomas brought this notion of negative punishment to its perfection. His teacher, Albert the Great, had provided him with the notion of limbo, which Aquinas defined as a state or place in which infants who died without Baptism could live forever in a state of natural happiness. They would never see God in his glory, but they would be joined to Him in sharing his created joys. This benign doctrine of Thomas met opposition from traditionalists in his own day, and even in later centuries there have been theologians who insisted that there must be genuine positive punishment for original sin. Many Thomists reply that the punishment is real, but the infants don't feel it, since they can't know the supernatural joy they are missing.

Bishop Bossuet was an outstanding traditionalist of the 18th century. He insisted that even though the babies didn't get badly burned, they had to suffer some pain perpetually. And a contemporary, Cardinal Norris, figured with exquisite precision just how warm the flames were that caused the infants discomfort without really burning them. A later theologian commented: "I do not know what kind of thermometer he used to determine with such accuracy the degree of heat."

For many centuries theologians who were intensely aware of God's goodness, love and mercy, have tried to free Him from the shackles imposed on Him by the traditional, but otherwise dubious, interpretation of a single text of Scripture. St. Bonaventure was one of the first and greatest, and his most ardent followers deny that he meant what he said. But he did hint that God might grant a special privilege to babies who couldn't receive Baptism, so that they might be sanctified in some other way.

Cardinal Cajetan received his first degree in theology the same year that Columbus discovered America, and he went on to become one of history's greatest Thomists as well as master general of the Dominican Order. But even Homer could nod. Cajetan proposed that the pious prayers of a child's parents might be the means of his sanctification when he could not be baptized. He even recommended that a child in danger of death in its mother's womb should be given a blessing in the name of the holy Trinity in the hope that God in his mercy might grant it grace. For this he came near to getting himself condemned by the Council of Trent, and Pope Pius V ordered that these words be deleted from his books.

John Gerson was a brilliant theologian of an earlier age, but he lived in the difficult times of the Great Schism of the West, and was frequently held as suspect by traditionalists. Along with other theologians of his time he expressed hope in the power of parents' prayer. "Who knows if God will not hear these prayers, and should one not hope that He will be attentive to the humble supplications of those who put all their trust in Him?" The traditional answer is a loud No.

It has been argued that God's tying of his own hands so that He cannot save babies even though He wants to gives little tribute to his wisdom. But there is a traditional refutation of this that has always been found most conclusive. It has been argued that God is unjust to call babies into being without giving them any possibility of salvation, but destining them instead to eternal damnation. The answer: They are not being condemned to hell; they will be naturally happy forever.

Our faith teaches us that God truly desires the salvation of all human persons, and that Jesus Christ died on the cross that all men might have the grace of eternal life. Why then are millions of persons deprived of any chance of salvation by conditions over which only God can have control, conditions which are beyond the range of human fault? The answer: Adam sinned, and in him we are all guilty.

We are told that abortion is murder because the child in the womb is a human person, but that the God of all goodness and love gives that human person no chance or choice. In my own sentimentality I am moved by the arguments given me by the mother of a stillborn child. When she appealed to her pastor, he told her that he didn't think the theologians were working on the problem of limbo at the present time since there did not seem to be a need. Her retort: "Maybe theologians will not consider the problem too seriously until they themselves have fathered stillborn children."

11

Is the Bible Fact or Fiction?

THE LETTER:

I am a 16-year-old junior, attending a Catholic high school. In grammar school, I was taught to believe that the Bible and all its stories were recorded fact and were to be believed. However, in the past three years I have been told by my theology teachers (two of them Sisters) that the Bible is not fact, merely stories that deliver a moral. Although these teachers did explain that Christ's life on earth was recorded history, they said the way events are presented in the New Testament are exaggerations of the truth. Are they?

Kathy S.

THE ANSWER:
By Kenneth Ryan

No. But I think, Kathy, that I will have to restate your question and I hope I get it right. You are asking not only "Why did some teachers tell me one thing and others another?" but also "Which teachers are right?"

On the basis of exact quotes from your letter I would have to say that both sets of teachers are wrong and thus mess up the whole discussion a little more. Taking you at your written word, one set of teachers taught you "the Bible and all its stories were recorded fact" and the other set of teachers taught you "the Bible was not fact." Now unless all of these teachers were very high up in the tree, they did not come out as flatly as that. At least I don't think so. The first set must have known that there are poems and parables in the Bible, and the second set must have known that there are historical books in the Bible well-supported by secular documents and archeological studies. But, Kathy, you did very intelligently catch the gist of two sides of a great continuing discussion and you made simple—at least in the asking—the question "Is the Bible true or false?" It is letters like yours that win the ten-year subscription to the *Catholic Digest*.

Some people insist the Bible is false because it says a fish swallowed Jonah when no fish in the Mediterranean Sea has a gullet larger than six inches. Literal interpreters of the Bible will say there was at least one fish that big because it says so in the Bible. From this type of argument we have to back away immediately. It is the kind of ignorant clashing by night that the Church has always tried to avoid. We at *Catholic Digest* once had a letter from a lady Jehovah Witness denouncing us for something we said in favor of Christmas trees. She pointed out the passage in Jeremiah (10:3,4) "decked it [a tree] with silver and gold"; applied it to the modern Christmas tree (it referred to making wooden idols); and accused us of false religion.

You see, Kathy, when you sit there with a large Bible in your lap it is not an easy thing to get the truth of it. Its parts were written in ancient times, in cultures differing from ours as Brooklyn differs from Babylonia. It was written in various languages, none of them the modern English you and I most easily understand. Even if you trust the translator and he is not trying to shade the meanings to support his own convictions, no translator can do more than paraphrase a poem. Shades of irony and sarcasm may escape him. He cannot possibly catch and transmit the meaning of references to persons, events, political and religious circumstances, mentioned nowhere else in all the world's literature. Sometimes the part of the Bible you are reading has been translated through several languages before coming to you in English and each translator has made his guesses and perhaps had his eye wiped by the next interpreter.

Within a single language the text has often been copied and copies made from copies. Sometimes what the scribe meant for an explanation gets copied into the texts. Sometimes by mistake, he leaves something out. Now, none of this destroys the validity of the Bible, but you will have to admit that trying to read it with *full* comprehension would be as difficult as getting the full force of Shakespearian tragedy in a German translation. Everyone concerned in the translation has done his best, but you just do not have the original. The point of my saying all this is to show the perils of literal interpetations—and offhand decisions that the Bible is false.

It is very easy to come across a text or phrase in the Bible which reassuringly confirms some belief you already have and to take the phrase as proof of the belief. From the time I was a small child, I lisped the Hail Mary with its praise, "full of grace." As a priest for many years on the Feast of the Assumption I started from "full of grace" and explained in my sermons to the people that if she were *full* of grace, there was, so to speak, no room for sin in the Blessed Mother; that no sin meant no corruption of the body (one of the penalties of original sin), and hence the assumption of her body into heaven upon her death.

All that I said was true, and faithful Catholics, among whom I want to be numbered, believed it then and still believe it. But now we believe it even though there is a new translation of the Bible in which Mary is declared by the angel not to be "full of grace" but only "singularly favored." The new translation does not destroy the doctrine of the Assumption, but it does eliminate what I thought was a good argument from Scripture for it. Of course, I had the customary dark suspicions of translators inserting their prejudices into the Scriptures. But as a matter of fact my personal knowledge of the language in which the angel spoke is limited, and I cannot confute the new translation. So my reminiscence should be a warning to you, Kathy, against reading your own convictions into the text of Scripture.

So, if you are still sitting there with a big Bible in your lap, Kathy, you can be sure that almost any meaning you discover there for yourself may be subject to correction by people who know more about the text than you do, and that you should be cautious in jumping to conclusions. But a bigger problem, and I think here we are getting closer to what you had in mind in your question, is that even if by some miracle of scholarship we could be sure we had the exact text as it was first penned by the original human author, we would still have the task of determining what the author *meant*. Sounds silly, but it's true.

You see, the way you express things depends upon what you are expressing. When you are chatting with your friends, you are likely to use the latest slang. Giving the valedictory address at your high school, you skip the slang and keep your demeanor solemn. In written matters there would be similar differences between a letter to a chum and an application for a job. The authors of the various books and parts of the Bible didn't have so free a choice of styles and forms in which to write. In Old Testament days, the languages were not as full of abstract words as our modern tongues. Generally, even when the authors were trying to communicate abstract truths, they used the story form for which the words came easily. Also, generally, they were very good story tellers.

Noah and the Flood, Jonah and the Whale, Judith and Holofernes are such good stories that the question as to whether they were written to record things that in fact happened or written to preserve entertaining folk tales becomes secondary. They fit very neatly into the times and places of their origins and in so doing show they have *meanings* beyond the bare story. Thus the Noah story means that God punishes sin and rewards obedience; the full Jonah story means that the Jews should share their religious truth with the Gentiles; the Judith story means that the weak Jewish people should not give up hope of final victory over their powerful oppressors.

Considering that the day of the paperback had not yet arrived and that there was no financial or other advantage in publishing either fiction or fact it becomes most probable the stories were written to teach lessons. Taken as plain history, they have obviously mistaken details. Noah's ark could not have been big enough to hold a pair each of all the animal species on earth. Nineveh could not have been all that big, either. (In the story it took Jonah three days to walk across it.) Nabuchodonosor, Holofernes's monarch, was never king of Assyria as the story says he was. But, of course, if the stories were told only to teach religious lessons, the problem of their scientific or historical accuracy vanishes. This kind of explanation is not too hard to follow

and should be rather easy to accept as long as we are talking about certain Old Testament books. It is when we come
to the life and works of Christ that we have to dig just a
little deeper into what authors *meant*.

One of the most disturbing terms the average casual Bible student runs into is the word *myth*. Only 50 years ago
its meaning was confined to pagan and ancient tales which
wondrously accounted for the world as the ancients knew
it. Thunder was the voice of Jove and so on. Everybody
knows that isn't so. Then, in the wave of new archeological
and linguistic knowledge, the word *myth* was increasingly
applied to the Jewish and Christian stories in the Bible.
Scholars became able to translate ancient inscriptions that
had been indecipherable. This ability gave them better understanding of equivalent passages in the Bible. It became
apparent, for instance, that the story of the Flood was not
unique to the Hebrew Scriptures but was found in several
other and earlier cultures. *Myth* was the reasonable term to
use when you had to write about this whole class of stories.
It was not intended in the use of the word *myth* to imply
that the Jewish and Christian stories were untrue. But that
certainly is what it sounds like to the average casual Bible
student.

Kathy, if this second set of teachers you had, really said
what you said they said, it was words like *myth* that made
them say it. They must have kept on thinking of a myth as
a false tale, rather than as a class of literature as the competent Bible scholars did. Such a mistake can be destructive
of Christian faith if you are going to call the Bible passages
about the miracles of Christ *myths* without having the
scholars' classification in mind. Pagan literature is full of
stories about dying gods and their return to life. The stories
are poetic personalizations of the dying, dormant, renew-
ing, and flourishing seasons of the year. The question is
whether that is all the story of Christ's death and resurrection means.

At this point we should remember, Kathy, that the chief
difficulty in understanding the Bible is finding out what the
author meant. To stay only on the subject of death and
resurrection: Did the authors of the Gospel mean to per-
sonalize the passing seasons with the story of Jesus Christ?
Did the authors of the pagan tales mean that such characters as Tammuz historically lived, died, and lived again?

It is all right to identify some of the stories of the Bible as being forms of literature contrived to teach abstract religious truths, but there is no need to say that all stories in the Bible have that purpose. Some certainly could have the simpler purpose of recording historical facts for posterity. All we have to ask is "What did the authors mean?"

Millions of faithful Christians have believed that the Gospel authors meant to say that the Son of God came down from heaven, died for our sins, and rose from the dead in proof of his claims. Other millions of people have not believed, never heard the story, or, having heard it, did not want to be bothered with it.

But the question of faith was independent of written Gospel in the first years of Christianity. There wasn't any New Testament yet. Now, as then, people may find the means of salvation without being experts in Biblical literary forms, without having the original or perfectly corrected texts. Our faith is contained in the Bible and practically, I suppose, the Church without it would have had a much more difficult time preserving the original faith. But we need not shiver and shake in the fear that scholars will prove parts or all of the Bible false. They can prove at most that we may have misread the meaning of the authors, but not that we have misread the meaning of the Author. The ultimate fear—that the enemies of the Bible may disprove its historical validity—can never be ours. It is part of our faith that that can never be done.

So after all, Kathy, I may have answered your question in my first two paragraphs. There are various forms of literature in the Bible: parables, poems, and myths, but there is no reason to exclude honest history. In the Catholic view, the more knowledge we acquire about the myths, the surer we can be of the history. In God's ancient providence, the myths were written to uphold the history.

12

What Does "Father, Son and Holy Ghost" Mean?

THE LETTER:

Although I am not a Catholic, I have now been reading the *Catholic Digest* for a year or more. My question is this: I would like to know the Catholic interpretation of the Holy Trinity: God the Father; Son, Jesus Christ; and Holy Ghost, or Spirit.

Through most of the New Testament and in Catholic doctrine it seems as if the first two members of the Holy Trinity are separate, distinct Persons although other literature that I have read seems to say that God the Father and Jesus Christ are one and the same. This is where I am confused. Also, it says in the 17th chapter of John that Jesus prayed to his Father that his disciples might be one, even as He and his Father were one. What is the Catholic teaching on the Trinity?

Pfc. Thomas R. Murphy

THE ANSWER:
By J.D. Conway

When you propose difficult questions, Thomas, you must expect intricate answers. The Trinity is a great mystery, and it is the source of all other mysteries in the Christian religion. Maybe we should preface our answer with a discussion of religious mysteries.

Usually what we call a mystery is something we know but cannot fully understand. There are, for instance, the mysteries of life, thought, and freedom. But these are only natural mysteries, and someday, as we learn more about them, they may cease to be mysteries. In theology a mystery is a truth we cannot know about except by God telling

76

us. There is nothing like it in ordinary human experience.

Religious mysteries like the Trinity involve the activites between God and man: God's redeeming us, and our response in faith and love and worship. That's why we speak of the "Mysteries" of Jesus Christ in his life on earth, his Last Supper, his death and resurrection. And in our response we celebrate sacred mysteries in the Mass and the sacraments.

The mysteries of our religion are the personal dialogue between God and man. The doctrine of the Trinity shows the personal nature of our religion. We are not mere created subjects of a vast and provident power. We can have no real love for a cosmic force, and even less for an omnipotent power above the cosmos. We are persons, and only relations that we establish with other persons, relations of mutual knowledge and love, mean anything to us.

We do establish relations with the forces and beauties of nature. We adapt ourselves to heat and cold, learn to avoid the storm, and are thrilled by the mountains and the sunset. We love, or hate, or fear them, enjoy their beauty, and detest their rigor. But they baffle us by their impersonal response to our love and our hate. The wind and the lightning pay no heed to our curses. The moon and stars kiss us with cold, loveless rays.

With other persons we can discuss and disagree, argue and understand, love and receive love, hate and be grievously hurt. Only in personal relations can persons be truly happy or brokenhearted. The hardships of nature may make us weep with pain. But only a person can make us miserable.

God is a Person, and our relationship with Him is truly personal. That is the basic concept of Christianity. We inherited this concept from the Jewish religion. Jesus Christ made the concept clearer. In Him, as man, God showed He was a Person in a manner easy for men to grasp. However, in revealing his personality to us through Jesus Christ, God found it necessary to open for us the secrets of the Trinity. God is not one lonely Person. He is three happy, intimate Persons who know and love each other completely in the undivided unity of their one divine nature.

Until the angel Gabriel announced to Mary at Nazareth that she was to become the Mother of a Son to be named Jesus, the Trinity had no meaning for mankind. Then the angel said, "He will be great and will be called the Son of the Most High." When Mary wondered how this might be done, the angel replied that the Holy Spirit would come upon her, the power of the Most High would overshadow her and her Child would be called holy, the Son of God.

The doctrine of the Trinity lets us understand who Jesus is, and whose Son He is. Without it, we would never be able to make sense of his words to Mary and Joseph when they found Him, as a Boy of 12, in the Temple of Jerusalem. His Mother complained that she and his father had been looking for Him and were anxious. But He wondered why they should have looked for Him: didn't they know that He must be in his Father's house? How, without the Trinity, explain the words which came from heaven at the time of the Baptism of Jesus in the Jordan, "You are my Son, my beloeved, my chosen One." Or the words of the expelled demons, crying out, "You are the Son of God!"

The mystery of the Trinity is implied in many words of Jesus: that He and the Father are one, that He must return to the Father who sent Him, that the Father is greater than He, that when He returns to the Father He will send the Holy Spirit; and in the prayer of Jesus to which you referred, Thomas: "Let them all be one, as Thou, Father art in Me, and I in Thee, so that they may be in Us, that the world know that Thou hast sent Me." Then there is his anguished cry on the cross: "My God, my God, why hast Thou forsaken Me?" Then a few moments later He exclaims with the calm confidence of a Son, "Father, into thy hands I commend my spirit." And after our Lord's resurrection St. Thomas gave expression to the faith of the Apostles when he exclaimed to Jesus, "My Lord, and my God!"

You and I, Thomas, are persons related to the three Persons of the Trinity. It is in the depths of this mystery that we find the truly personal nature of our religion. In modern terms, God's relationship with us is the I-Thou of a dialogue. He begins with words like these: "I speak to thee, my child, made in my own image; I come to thee and give Myself to thee; and I invite thee to accept Me, to love Me as I have first loved thee, and to return with Me to my home."

However, this is an oversimplified version of God's actual dialogue with us. He is not one Person, but three; and each Person speaks to us and receives our response; each Person intervenes in our sanctification; and each one we love separately as a Person, without trying to separate the three from each other, or from the unity of their nature. Theologians caution us that the relationship of the three Persons of the Trinity is strictly internal, within the divine nature; and that any act of God outside Himself, as in the creation of the human race, is performed by the three Persons as though they were one.

We are told that the Son, the second Person of the Trinity, was able to live on earth and to speak to us as a separate Person because He had a human nature; and his separate personal acts and words came from Him as man. We carefully heed the warning of theologians; otherwise we might end up with a notion of three gods, harmonious, closely united and cooperative, but separate. And that would be contrary to revelation. But still we insist that our relationship with God is personal. I am one person and He is three. The Father is truly my Father, because I am brother to his own Son; and the Holy Spirit, the Person of love, is active in establishing and maintaining this relationship.

Because the Trinity is such a great mystery, we tend to shy from it as too profound for our grasp. We give it an act of faith and then forget it, half wondering why the good Lord ever revealed it to us. But we should immerse ourselves in it, because it has vital, personal meaning to us. We must admit, right from the start, that we never hope to understand it fully; and then proceed to learn all we can.

It is within the Trinity that we find the reason for God's coming to us and giving Himself to us. Giving is the keynote of the Trinity The Father gives Himself to the Son, and gives the Son personality in the process. And the two of them love each other so completely, in their mutual perfection, that the result is the Holy Spirit. The Son is generated by the Father's perfect knowledge of his own infinite Goodness; and the Holy Spirit proceeds from the perfect love of the Father and Son for each other, and is totally encompassed in that love. We are not capable of sharing the love of the Father and the Son as the Holy Spirit shares it. But we share it sufficiently that the Holy Spirit can live in us, not apart from the Father and the Son, but yet in a sanctifying personal relationship.

It may help, Thomas, to state these concepts in various terms. Start this way: God created us in his image: intelligent and free. And from the moment of our creation the

Father loved us, as it is his nature to love, and sought to adopt us as his children. But since we are free, we must accept the adoption freely, or not at all. It will not be forced on us. Because man (Adam) at first refused and rejected God's overtures of love, the three divine Persons worked out a plan of persuasion in which They would all cooperate. The Father sent the Son to become a man. The Son, as man on earth, loved the Father in heaven, and accepted the Father's adoption in the name of all men, sealing the agreement in his own blood.

The Father's sending and the Son's coming were done in the Holy Spirit, the Person of their love, through whom They extended their love, to all men. When the Son, as man, gave worship to the Father, it was done in the Holy Spirit; and when He extends his sonship to us, this, too, is done in the Holy Spirit. And when the three of Them come to live in our souls to sanctify us, we attribute their indwelling to the Holy Spirit, since it is a union and a work of love.

So the Son, sent by the Father, reveals the mysteries of God to us in the Holy Spirit. The Father sent the Son to redeem us, in the Holy Spirit. Through the Son the Father adopts us, in the Holy Spirit. And the three of Them live in your soul and mine to sanctify us. In this union of sanctifying grace, we are joined to God as He is, and He is three Persons. We encounter these Persons in the process of our sanctification, and establish with each one a real relationship. When we join the Son in saying, "Our Father, in heaven," we are speaking to a real, distinct Person: his Father and ours.

The Father's part in the dialogue is to adopt us through his Son in the Holy Spirit. Then our response is through the Son to the Father in the Holy Spirit. We begin this response of faith, which is our acceptance of God and of his gestures of love toward us, and we follow it up in trusting love. Our expression of this faith and love takes many forms: in our feelings, convictions and works, in our ready compliance with God's will, in our love for the brethren whom He loves, and in our prayer and sacrifice. But whatever the manner of our expression, its proper course is to the Father, through the Son, in the Holy Spirit.

We see this most clearly in the Sacrifice of the Mass, in which we unite ourselves to the Son, to offer his own oblation through Him and with Him and in Him, to the Father, in union with the Holy Spirit. And in the prayers of Mass we address the Father, asking that He grant us favors through Jesus Christ, his Son, in union with the Holy Spirit.

13

What Does "The Holy Spirit Proceeds" Mean?

THE LETTER:

My question to "What would you like to know about the Church?" is, "What does the Church mean when it says that the Holy Spirit 'proceeds' from the Father and the Son?"

Arthur Martinez

THE ANSWER:
By Kenneth Ryan

I wish I could treat that question, Arthur, as the Greek Fathers did before the time of St. Augustine. They said it was too mysterious to handle. But since their time there has been so very much written, preached, and propounded on the subject that I could not get by with such a rejoinder.

Proceeds is, of course, a technical theological term with only slight similarity in meaning to the word as we use it in everyday conversation. In the doctrine of the Blessed Trinity, it occurs with other terms, which also must be specially understood: God the Father *is:* God the Son is *begotten;* God the Holy Spirit *proceeds* from the Father and the Son This is the language of mystery, but we can still use our human reason, within its limitations.

So we can begin with the consideration that the doctrine says the Spirit proceeds from the Father *and* the Son, the point being that He does not proceed from the Son alone.

The phrasing suggests, so to speak and pardon me, a triangular God and an equality among the Persons.

There were heretics in the early days of the Church who thought of the Trinity as a composition of persons in which the Son was above the Holy Spirit and the Father above the Son. There was no equality. To condemn any such heresy the Athanasian Creed was made to read that the Holy Spirit was "not created nor begotten, but proceeding."

To get at the meaning of *proceeding,* perhaps we could say first that it is part of a formula, and that no human formula can express anything approaching the full meaning of a mystery. In a sense, *proceeding* has no specific and distinct meaning, since within the Trinity all actions and relations of the Persons are equal. (I warned you this would be mysterious.) But, using human reason as far as it can, the Catholic doctrine on the Trinity runs that the Father generates the Son and that the Spirit proceeds from the Father and the Son. A human analogy to this generation would be a man thinking a thought and expressing it with a word. This is the analogy St. John had in mind when he wrote of Christ as the Word of God. Christ is the perfect and full expression of the Father.

In a similar analogy, the Holy Spirit is the expression, not of the thought, but of the Will of the Father and the Son. As They look on each other, each realizing the perfection of the Other, They have in common the divine Will to love the Other. The Holy Spirit is that proceeding Love; He proceeds from the Father and the Son. An analogy like that leaves us still in the realm of mystery as far as the full meaning of *proceeding* goes, but we need not discard the doctrine as being against the use of reason.

The liberal Protestant theologians of the last century argued that the whole doctrine of the Trinity was a 4th century result of the Church's conflict with Arius, the bishop who denied the equality of Christ with the Father and took nearly two thirds of Christendom with him into heresy. Arius could not accept mystery. I suppose he didn't realize that mystery is beyond reason rather than a contradiction of it. Had the Church defined that one God was three Gods or that one Person was three Persons, it could justly be called unreasonable. But it only says that there are three Persons in one God, which is mysterious, but not at all unreasonable.

It seems to me, too, that the liberal theologians should have given more consideration to Christ's parting words about baptizing in the Name (singular) of the Father and of the Son and of the Holy Spirit (the *ands* make the Persons equal). Even though those theologians didn't believe that Christ was God, at least his words should have shown them that the doctrine of the Trinity goes back to the time of Christ and was not invented in the 4th century. Of course, really up-to-date theologasters (a pilaster is a half-formed pillar, a theologaster is a half-baked theologian) would say that the Church Fathers inserted the doctrine not only into the Creed but into the Gospels, where it was not present before. It goes, I hope without saying, that that insertion is yet to be proved.

At first glimpse, Arthur, your question did not seem like one likely to win the ten-year *Catholic Digest* subscription. Most modern Catholics would dismiss it as irrelevant. This dismissal would be grammatically without meaning unless they went on to say it was not relevant to their immediate personal needs and concerns. But it should be.

Your question takes us back to the early ages of Christianity when men wrestled with the timeless puzzles about the nature of God, the meaning of man's existence, the meaning of history, hopes for the future—the great abstract thoughts without which no philosophical, much less religious, outlook on life could begin. Slaves and emperors took sides on whether the Holy Spirit proceeded from the Father *alone* or from the Father *and* the Son. Those who readily call your question irrelevant are those who consider the brand of pants they are wearing or the kind of grapes they are eating to be of prime relevance. Their theological counterparts are wondering whether a little abortion might not be a good thing and race suicide pleasing in the sight of God.

A further point about your question, Arthur, is that it was chosen even though it didn't fulfill the request to "tell us something about yourself." One of the pleasures of conducting a department of this kind is imagining the appearance and personality of the person who wrote in and trying to figure out what circumstances prompted his particular question.

It can never be more than a guess, but I would say you have some interest in the Pentecostal movement to ask so specific a question about the Holy Spirit. In my view, the

Pentecostals are among the strongest forces now at work in turning men again toward God. Their enthusiasm and joy cancel out a measure of the dullness and sadness that have become a mark of modern religious thinking; their face-to-face approach to God helps the rest of us endure the contentious glaring of modern men at each other. If, by some miracle of grace, men could become chiefly concerned with questions like the one you asked, this earth would be a lot more like heaven than it is now.

14

Is "Doomsday" the Real End of the World?

THE LETTER:

Would you please tell me as clearly as possible about doomsday according to the Catholic Church? I have heard from a Catholic friend that on doomsday Jesus will come, sitting in the clouds, and will judge people. Before this happens, there will come a false Christ, whom they call the antichrist. Of course, I never hear about it in my religion. My Catholic friend cannot give much explanation on it. I am a Moslem.

Soepramono

THE ANSWER:
By J.D. Conway

Doomsday is an ancient popular name for the day of the general judgment. In its original meaning, doom meant decision, with the pronouncement of the sentence. That sentence might be good or bad, but it represented a person's doom. Now we tend to attach the word *doom* only to a condemnatory judgment. We never think of a man being doomed to heaven.

Doomsday is one feature of the several religious events

that we designate as the Last Things. The Greek word for the last things is *eschata*. And from this word we derive the title of a vast, complicated, and important phase of our study of Scripture and theology: eschatology. In most of its outlook the Christian religion is eschatological. It looks forward to coming events, leading to ultimate happiness.

The coming of Jesus Christ into the world, his death, his resurrection, and ascension were eschatological. They were the ways He established his kingdom on earth, his means of preparing man for future judgment and for eternal happiness in heaven. The life and activities of the Church in the world are eschatological. The Church is Christ's present kingdom on earth, which is here to prepare the way for his future kingdom in heaven. The members of Christ's Church are here joined to their Saviour in bonds of faith and love, so that they may share in the glories of his kingdom when the Last Things have been accomplished.

It may help our thinking if we consider what we mean by the Last Things. The ultimate achievement is called the Second Coming, rather generally known by its Greek name of *parousia*. Much is set down about this in the New Testament, both in the words of our Lord and in the writing of the Apostles. It formed one of the most inspiring and pervading beliefs of early Christians. They lived in a life of brotherly love, accepting Jesus as their Redeemer, and joining together in eating the banquet of his love while longing for his Second Coming.

The early Christians acquired the idea, apparently shared by many of the Apostles, especially St. Paul, that the *parousia* or Second Coming would not be long delayed. They were confident that many of them would still be on earth to welcome our Lord back for the final establishment of his kingdom. And they worried a bit about those who died. Would they be able to come back and share in the glories of the Kingdom? On this point, St. Paul gives them assurance.

In a very true sense the existence of Christ's Church in the world is one of the Last Things, one in a series of events beginning with the incarnation of the Son of God, his preaching and miracles, his death and resurrection, his establishment of the Church, and his ascension into heaven. These things were done by our Saviour that the events long foretold and awaited might be fulfilled. The coming of the

Holy Spirit and his activity in the Church and in the souls of men are other steps toward the Last Things.

The ultimate goal of Christ's activity in the world is the establishment of his eternal kingdom, and He makes use of his Church, which is his temporary kingdom. By his death on the cross Jesus liberated us from the kingdom of Satan, so that we could become members of his kingdom on earth. However, Satan has not relinquished his claims on us, and much of the activity of the kingdom of Christ is dedicated to contest against the powers of evil. One feature of Christ's kingdom on earth is that it makes us all members of the same Body seeking sanctification together. In the present plan of God we must have help from others to obtain our own salvation, and we must give help to others for the same purpose. This is preparation for the unity of our life and love in the final kingdom of heaven.

The *parousia,* with the glory of the Second Coming and the general judgment is only a part of the Last Things which await us. Even though our salvation is worked out in the midst of the kingdom achieved through a closely knit body of which we are all members, nevertheless there are Last Things for each one of us individually. The first of these Last Things is our death. In a limited and personal sense death is the *parousia* for each of us. The Lord comes as a "thief in the night." This is true for each of us just as it is for the great final manifestation.

The most consoling feature of Christian belief is that death is not an end, but a transition. It marks a new beginning. In establishing that new beginning there is a particular judgment. And following this individual judgment there will be heaven, hell, or purgatory for the soul immediately. Without delay each soul will begin to live the type of life it had knowingly prepared for itself by its virtues and activities on earth.

For the Christian the meaning of death can be learned only from the death of Christ. Jesus died to prepare us for our death. His death was a sacrifice to the Father, the greatest possible act of love and worship. For all the sons of Adam, prior to Jesus Christ, death was a result of sin, and it seemed to be a victory for Satan, who reaped the fruit of the sin he had sown in the world. With Christ our death became a victory over sin, later shown clearly in his resurrection. It is the role of a Christian to die with Christ and thus to join in the perfect sacrifice offered to the Father.

The Christian has sacraments which are particularly aimed at death. The first is Baptism. It is first of all a symbol of the death and resurrection of Christ, as St. Paul explains to us: "Do you not know that all we, who are baptized in Jesus Christ, are baptized in his death? For we are buried together with Him by Baptism into death. For if we have been planted together in the likeness of his death, we shall be also in the likeness of his resurrection." The Baptism which joins us to Christ in all things joins us particularly to Him in our death.

The Holy Eucharist, the sacrament of our union with Jesus Christ, nourishes us to life everlasting and gives us the pledge that our death is but a prelude to the resurrection. Our Lord has said, "He who eats my Flesh and drinks my Blood has life everlasting and I will raise him up on the last day. He that eats this Bread shall live forever."

We also have a special sacrament of preparation for death, called the Anointing of the Sick. Every Catholic hopes to receive this sacrament, together with the prayers of the Church, before his death.

There is a popular opinion that the particular judgment will be largely a matter of self-judgment. The soul separated from its body will immediately see in proper perspective its entire life of good and evil and will know at once what its lot must be. It is quite possible that this personal judgment does take place, but it is only preliminary. It is truly the Lord who judges in all justice and mercy and love.

One of the doctrines of the Church that offers greatest difficulty to many modern men is that of hell as a place of eternal punishment. Certainly the nature of the punishments of hell exceed our human understanding. Scripture tells us in various places that the souls in hell live in darkness, with weeping and gnashing of teeth; that the smoke of their torments ascends up forever and ever; that they shall be tormented day and night. And Jesus sums it up, saying of the condemned man, "It were better for him if that man had never been born."

Even though it may be difficult for us to accept the idea of hell, we certainly cannot eliminate it from Revelation, which speaks of an "eternal punishment," of going down body and soul into hell fire, of a furnace of fire. St. Paul added a definite note to these punishments when he said that sinners are the ones "who shall suffer eternal punishment in destruction, from the glory of his power." Whatever may be the incidental torments of hell, its essential nature consists in a total and lasting separation from the goodness and love of almighty God.

Purgatory is an intermediate state between the particular judgment and the final happiness of heaven. We know very little about it. Earlier writers used to stress the aspects of punishment in purgatory. Some recent writers have written of its joys. Both attitudes may be true. Purgatory is not primarily a place where the friends of God are tortured, but rather where they are purified from the remnants of their sins to prepare them to enjoy the presence and the love of God in heaven. Probably the essential pain of purgatory is in being separated from the joys of heaven, but even this pain should be lessened by the assurance that these joys will be ours in time. One thing we must remember about the souls in purgatory is that we are able to help them by our prayers, our sacrifices, and especially through the holy Sacrifice of the Mass.

Heaven is the goal of all Christians. It is God's eternal kingdom, prepared for those who love Him. And possibly the best description we have of it was given by St. Paul: "Eye has not seen nor ear heard, nor has it entered into the heart of man, what things God has prepared for those who love Him." Scripture tells us many things about heaven, but when we add them all up, possibly the best idea we can get is of a place of great joy and happiness where God in all his greatness and glory and love and beauty is revealed to us and where we ourselves are advanced to the highest state of perfection possible to our nature.

The New Testament tells us much more about the public events connected with doomsday than about the individual Last Things we have been describing. A great problem, however, is to understand the precise meaning of many of these eschatological pronouncements. They are often obscure, filled with imagery which demands figurative application. Our Lord Jesus Christ spoke in more frightening terms of the destruction of Jerusalem. He possibly intended some of it to refer to the final destruction of the world. Our tendency in reading his words is to apply it all directly to the final judgment. It would seem to me that the early Christians must have understood Him better, because they seemed to look forward with hope and longing for the *parousia,* the Second Coming, and the establishment of the kingdom. They lived for it and hoped for it daily.

In our day we are rather frightened of the whole thing. It has become a day of wrath—doomsday with all its sorrowful indications. Part of our difficulty comes from failure to understand many of the figurative descriptions of that last day. It seems to me that the guiding one should be that of our Lord Himself [separating all mankind to the right and left of Him], as quoted by St. Matthew (25:31–46). The description used by our Lord is humbly fitted to the understanding of men, but there will certainly be some vast, worldwide triumph of his goodness and grace and of those who have shared with Him in faith and love.

One of the favorite occupations of a certain type of Christian through the centuries has been that of figuring out the time of the Second Coming. Since there are dozens of texts in Sacred Scripture that may seem to indicate a time, and since most of them are open to a wide variety of interpretations, even subjective ones, the result has been a series of threatening monitions. Our Lord Himself foretold that there would rise up false prophets trying to mislead the people, telling them that here is the Christ, or there He is, or such will be the time of his coming. Actually our Lord's only reliable prediction was that He would come "as a thief in the night." And these are undoubtedly his own exact words, since none of his disciples would have dared call Him a thief. So for our own individual deaths and for the end of the world the same monition applies. The coming of the Lord will be like that of a "thief in the night." We know not the day nor the hour

Predictions of the Second Coming often make reference to an antichrist. He is some mysterious person or power, and efforts to identify him have been quite contradictory and fruitless. Most of us incline to identify him with our enemies. St. Paul calls him "the man of sin, the son of perdition, who opposeth and is lifted up above all that is called God, so that he sitteth in the temple of God, showing himself as if he were God." St. John said that he was already in the world, that there had been many antichrists. Even more difficult to identify is some force which keeps the antichrist from taking control of the world. St. Paul wrote the Thessalonians that they knew what this withholding power was. In this they were wiser than we. It will be much better for us if we lose our concern about the antichrist and prepare ourselves for the day when our Lord will come.

On that great day Jesus will appear suddenly to the entire world as the lightning strikes to the East, even to the West, and on that day the bodies of the dead shall rise and all will come before Him for judgment. Jesus will be the judge, and He has indicated to us that the basis of his judgment will be love, our love for Him and our love for our neighbors, even our enemies.

The resurrection of the dead causes much trouble, especially to those who have a tendency to materialistic concepts. It certainly cannot be explained in terms of atoms and molecules. It is rather explained by total identity. We will be the same person in heaven that we are on earth. And it is not for us to worry about the physiological or the spiritualizing processes that might produce this identity.

The Last Things are the goal of God's plan for our salvation. The whole history of our redemption and sanctification are directed to them. The Second Coming will be the day of the Lord's great triumph, when his glory and justice will be manifested to the entire world. On that day his eternal kingdom will be inaugurated with all its members gathered together in his own land and in his own home, embraced by his father love. The "end of the world" will probably not be a destruction but a transformation, and achievement of the perfection for which the world was created.

15

Can Anyone Still Believe There is a Devil?

THE LETTER:

I belong to no organized church. Recently I have subscribed to the *Catholic Digest* and have enjoyed its contents very much, especially the December issue in which J.D. Conway explains the mystery of the Trinity.

He says: "In theology a mystery is a truth which we cannot know about except by God telling us. God is a Person, and our relation with Him is truly personal. This is the basic concept of Christianity."

This impels me to ask, "What is the church's concept of the devil? Is the devil also a person, and what is his true relationship to an all-powerful, all-knowing, all-good God?"

I believe that explanations of such mysteries, even involving wide differences of opinions, will help in the synthesis of science and religion, and hasten the fulfillment of the late Pope John's desire "to open the windows of the Church . . . bringing it into step with modern times."

Roscoe Spencer, M.D.

THE ANSWER:
By J.D. Conway

The Church's concept of the devil and his demons, of their fall and their fate, and of their multiple activities in the world of men is also a mystery, Dr. Spencer. We might, by observing the work of demons, see that there are spiritual forces in the world doing evil things and stirring up trouble about us. However, the attitude of the modern enlightened world toward Satan and his satellites is evidence that neither casual nor scientific study would tell us much about diabolical activities, and would give far less hint of the nature and history of the masters of hell.

Today is it hardly fashionable to believe in the devil as a real live person. No one denies that the world is full of evil, suffering, and sin, and a poet may well personify them. But it is thought naive, medieval, and superstitious to admit a host of demons. Nevertheless, in his revelation, God has told us that Satan and his minions are indeed real living persons. They are, indeed, angels, with all the superior intelligence, agility, and power that the Sacred Scripture ascribe to the various choirs of angels. As persons they resemble only faintly the Father, Son, and Holy Spirit. And they probably resemble you and me even less. We know very little about angelic personality. When angels appear in the Scriptures they either act with something like divine power, or they assume human form and speak the words of men.

About the only traits common to the three divine Persons, the angels, and ourselves is that we all have intelligence and free will. But even these faculties we possess in vastly different forms and degrees. The divine Persons know everything, and can love without limit. With the devils we share a lesser ability to know. We have less ability than they at thinking, but our thought is surely less perverted. With the three divine Persons we share the ability to love, and with Satan we share the ability to hate. But the devils have lost the great ability to love.

So the devils are *angels,* sinful angels, being punished for their sins. But they remain angelic persons, if we use that adjective in its literal sense. Their sin did not change their nature or personality any more than Adam's sin changed his human nature or personality. The sin of the angels caused them to lose heaven, even as Adam's caused him to lose Eden. Their sin made them bitter, hateful, full of vengeance, even as Adam's made him and his sons concupiscent, hateful, and prone to murder and deceit. But Satan remained an angel, and Adam remained a man.

The modern sophisticated attitude toward the devil has three bad results for us:

1) We cease to be wary, and so give the devil greater freedom to influence us.

2) We drive a big wedge into our awareness of the supernatural. Our wedge does away with the devil, and it seems good to be rid of him, even in our thoughts. However, if we eliminate bad angels, may we not soon come to ignore the good ones, also? Out of mind are the cherubim and seraphim, along with our guardian angel. May the next step not be unawareness, even doubt, about the Holy Spirit active in our souls by grace?

3) We tear the Sacred Scriptures to shreds. In them we read about the devil under one name or another from early in Genesis to late in the Apocalypse (Revelation). In man's earliest day Satan took the form of a serpent to tempt Eve in paradise; and St. John sees him as a dragon seized by an angel, bound fast for a thousand years, tossed into the pit, and sealed there.

There is a great advantage in our remembering that the devil is an angel. We know that angels are creatures of God, even as you and I. They are more brilliant, intelligent, and powerful than we are; spirits without bodies, able to flit here and there in less than a moment. But in spite of all that, we have no reason to fear the devil, because he remains entirely under God's power. We may rather scorn him, provided that we keep close to God while we are doing it.

The Satan of Judaism and Christianity differs greatly from the prince of darkness of Manichaeism or the archdemon of Mazdaism. These, and other religions of dualism, hold Satan to be an evil god, independent of the good God, an adversary fighting on fairly even terms. Some dualistic religions would even make man a descendant of Satan, or at least hold that man's material body was created by the evil god. Our own Satan has no power against God.

The proper name of the chief of all the devils is Satan: the Adversary. He is a dedicated adversary of God and of all that is good; and he is a vengeful adversary of men, especially when they try to do good and serve God. At one time he was among the most glorious of all the angels; so bright that he was called Lucifer (the light bearer) and was compared in brilliance to the morning star. We know even less about Lucifer's first sin than about that of Adam. It is possible that both of them, each in his own way, strove to make themselves like God. God wanted both of them to share his nature in grace and glory, but they were not content with that; they had their own rebellious plans.

When Lucifer sinned and became Satan, he took with him a host of lesser angels, all similarly rebellious; and they went together into their punishment. And once they had sinned, Satan and his angels—all similarly stubborn—were either unable to repent or were so filled with hate that they wouldn't. Fighting futilely against God is their dedicated purpose, and since they are unable to hurt God Himself, they pick on men. Their vengeful frenzy seems less futile when they can foster evil on earth, separate men from God, and drag them down to hell to share their own miserable futility.

In paging quickly through the New Testament I found nearly 40 references to the devil, and I must have missed many others. St. John in his Gospel and St. Paul in his Epistles pay relatively little attention to Satan, but Matthew, Mark, and Luke, and the Apocalypse abound in references to him.

Jesus Himself was tempted by the devil, but having vanquished him, He went about Galilee casting out devils from those possessed, as St. Mark tells us. When He sent out his

Apostles to preach the Good News of the kingdom He told them they should "heal the sick, raise the dead, cleanse the lepers, cast out devils." Even the 70 disciples were given similar powers for their mission, and they came back boasting: "Lord, even the evil spirits obey us when we use your name." It was on this occasion that Jesus told them He had seen Satan fall from heaven like a flash of lightning. St. Peter in his 2nd Letter tells us that God did not spare the angels who sinned against Him, but cast them into the dark prison of hell until judgment day.

Many of the things we know about the devil come from the words of Jesus. For instance, He told the Pharisees that their father was the devil, that he was a murderer from the beginning, a liar, and the father of lies. In similar, but more friendly fashion, Jesus once called Peter "Satan," because he was trying to tempt Him. On another occasion He told the Apostles that Satan had asked to have them to sift as wheat, but He had prayed for Peter that he wouldn't lose his faith, and after turning back to Christ would strengthen his brethren.

Jesus accepts the popular name of Beelzebub for the prince of devils. He is the father of lies, and Jesus denies any alliance with him in casting out devils. The first three Gospels tell many stories of exorcism. It seems strange to us that so many people were possessed by the devil in those days, whereas so very few seem possessed today. Besides, Doctor, I am sure you would be able to give tentative diagnoses of the diseases of many of those who were possessed. Many apparently had physical or psychic ailments, like the boy, dumb and apparently an epileptic, told about by Mark. An epileptic boy, probably the same one, is frankly called a lunatic by Matthew. Others were deaf, blind, deformed.

However, in writing of these cures the authors of the Gospels do not simply speak of healing; they explicitly say that Jesus drove out the devil, often after conversation with him. And on the strangest occasion of all He drove a legion of devils from a lunatic into a herd of pigs, who promptly jumped into the lake and drowned. For the explanation of these Gospel stories, Dr. Spencer, I am going to refer you to exegetes of the Sacred Writings, and among them you will find differing explanations. However, I am going to make one suggestion based on I John, 8: Jesus came to earth for the express purpose of wiping out the works of the devil. His final accomplishment of that purpose was in

His death and resurrection, but along the way He paused to give Satan a good idea of what was coming.

Satan is allied with death, both spiritual and physical. By His glorious victory over death Jesus gave pledge of final victory over all the forces allied with death: evil, sin, suffering, and the devils. But we must keep close to Jesus if we are to share in his victory. The Trinity is a mystery, Doctor, as you quoted from my earlier article. Satan, too, is a mystery. But one of the greatest of all mysteries is that of our sanctification and salvation: the mystery by which Jesus unites us so closely to Himself in grace that we share with Him his victory over the forces of evil.

Satan can do us no harm while the Holy Spirit lives in us. He may try, because he has a twisted personality, which seems to seek frustration. And he seems filled with envy of man, who shares the divine nature in grace. He sought and failed to be like God; and no divine person ever became an angel. Why should man be so privileged?

16

What Do You Mean by "Soul"?

THE LETTER:

Will you please explain what you understand by the term *soul*. May I also ask why your Church rejects the doctrine of transmigration of souls? It would be of great interest to many of us over here in Ceylon.

Maureen Fernando

THE ANSWER:
By J.D. Conway.

Your question looks simple, Maureen, but the answer is not easy. From the early Fathers of the Church, like Origen and Tertullian, down to the present, writers without number have attempted to give the answer. One reason for the many treatises is that the Sacred Scriptures, while they refer to it often, never try to define the soul. The Old Testament uses three different Hebrew words for it, which translate as breath, breeze, and wind. Holy Scripture uses expressions to mean life, the vital breath of life, or the spirit.

Most of the treatises borrowed the ideas of Greek philosophers but none could improve on the sacred writer of the first book of the Bible. He described God's creation of Adam in figurative language. "Then the Lord God formed man out of the dust of the ground and breathed into his nostrils the breath of life, and man became a living being." This breath of life somehow made man into the image of God. Whatever the soul is, it comes directly from almighty God, like his own breath, and it is the source of life in man.

This figure of speech has its faults. It might give us the idea that the soul is something that is not a part of man, but breathed into him from the outside. However, the sacred author should be studied more carefully: God's "man" is only a figure of clay until the soul is breathed into it. The "breath" makes it a living being. So even from this figure we must conclude that the soul is an integral part of man.

I mention this because there have been some Christians who have held that the soul is like a captive spirit in the body of man, something trapped and straining to be free. Quite the contrary is true. The soul is made to fit the body; and the two of them together are man. In death, the soul and body will be separated, and then neither will be complete or entirely satisfied. They belong together. The body will become dust of the ground again, and the soul will live on. But the soul's life, even in heaven, will be incomplete; it awaits the resurrection of the body, so that they can unite and be man again, as God created them to be.

Christians often speak of saving their souls, but seldom think of saving their bodies. We are saved and sanctified by Jesus Christ, but He did not become man merely to save our souls, but to save us, as men, both body and soul. To accomplish that He became a man, with both body and soul; and He redeemed us with his body as well as his soul.

This point is important because we tend to blame our bodies for all the evil and credit our souls for all the good in us. But it just isn't so. We wouldn't have any carnal passions if it were not for the soul. The guilt of sin is in a decision of the will, and the will is a faculty of the soul. The angels were true spirits (all soul, you might say) but some of them committed sins greater than man is capable of.

The soul is a spirit, and in this fact man finds his greatest resemblance to God, who is all spirit, perfect and unlimited. So it is well for us to consider what a spirit is. It is a being, which means that it is real. But it has no size, shape, color, or weight. We cannot touch, taste, see, or hear it. It occupies no space; it has no parts. Yet it is a being able to know and love. It is powerful. And it always remains itself; since it has no parts it can never dissolve, like the body. Unless God annihilates a created spirit, it will live forever.

The soul is a peculiar kind of spirit, since it is created to be the life-giving principle of man. Other spirits, the angels, were created to remain simple spirits forever. Man's soul requires a special act of God when it is made and breathed into each embryo. The soul requires a special act of God to separate from the body (at death) and to begin life apart from the body. But the greatest intervention of God will come on the last day, when each soul is again united with its body, so that we can live as complete men for all eternity. Jesus gave us an example of this great work of God when his own body rose from the dead on Easter Sunday, and He lived again as man. And as complete man He now awaits us in heaven.

When we die God does something to our souls which permits them to live without our bodies. If we die loving God, our souls go to heaven to enjoy the vision of God while awaiting the resurrection of our bodies. If we die loving evil, our souls will go to hell to await in misery their reunion with our bodies. But neither joy nor suffering will be quite complete until we are complete human beings again. The soul is not in a state of sleep while awaiting the resurrection of the body; it remains conscious and retains its identity. The body separated from the soul disintegrates, and it is only through the living soul, aware of itself, that human personality remains and can be completely restored at the resurrection.

It is because we have souls that we have spiritual powers of thought and freedom; that we are conscious of ourselves and of the world, and can make our own decisions. Our souls make it possible for us to love God, or to hate and disobey Him. Our souls make it possible for us to love our fellow men; yet we never love them as souls; we love them as men.

To take up the second point in your letter, Maureen, we Christians have never believed in the transmigration of souls. What we understand to be a soul could not go from one body to another and survive there. My soul is an integral part of me; and my body has distinctive shape, coloring, and identity. But neither one alone is me. I am a person made up of this body and this soul. God knows and loves each one of us as a person. Jesus Christ loved and redeemed each one of us as a person. We retain our individual personalities in our sanctification, salvation, and eternal life.

The notion of transmigration has been quite unknown in the Jewish-Christian tradition. One early theologian, Origen, did believe that souls were all created long before the bodies were ready for them, and waited in heaven until they were needed on earth. But Origen was very humble in his opinions about the soul; he knew he was merely speculating. If he had lived a bit later he would probably have agreed with other Christian theologians that each soul is created individually for each body at the very moment the body needs it.

Transmigration of souls would contradict Christian ideas of personal responsibility, reward and punishment, sanctity and salvation. Our spiritual souls have two great powers, intellect and free will, and both of them are involved in every phase of our salvation. By the intellect we know God the Father and Jesus Christ, his Son whom He sent to redeem us; by the will we accept the love of the Father as shown to us by his Son. And both the knowing and accepting are achieved through the active help of the Holy Spirit, working through these faculties of our souls.

Without the intellect and will there could be no faith in God, no sanctifying love for God. And while faith and love are the result of God's work in our souls, they are also our own. Each one of us is saved by his own faith, in which his personal soul plays a vital, active part. And each one is saved by his own practical love for God and his fellow man, which is again a personal act of his own soul.

So each one of us is sanctified and saved individually and personally through faculties of our own proper souls, or we reject sanctity and choose evil through the same faculties. Consequently God in his justice and love takes the sanctified soul into heaven on the basis of its own faith and love; or sends it for punishment as it well deserves.

Let me repeat that these sanctifying acts of faith and love are acts of the whole man; and the condemning acts of sin are works of the whole man, composed of body and soul. But it is the soul that receives the reward or punishment first. In heaven or hell it retains the memory of its love or guilt, its sense of identity, so that when the body rises it can with the soul reform the same person, who lived rightly or badly here on earth.

Now, I cannot be rightly rewarded if my identity is lost. I cannot be justly punished unless I remain in hell the same person who sinned here on earth. I do not see God in heaven because of the faith of another person; I am not happy with Him because of another's love. Neither do I suffer in hell for another's sins, but only for my own.

If souls should transmigrate, that is, belong to a variety of persons in succession, there would be no ME hereafter—and the doctrine of eternal personal life is the basis of all Christ's teaching.

III

Questions From and About Other Churches

The Vatican Ecumenical Council stimulated a great many ecumenical questions concerning what the Catholic Church thought about other religions—pagan, Jewish and Christian.

17

The Baha'i World Faith

THE LETTER:

How does the Baha'i World Faith compare with the Catholic religion? It seems to me that it has a wider view of revelation since it takes into account those made through Krishna, Moses, Buddha, and Zoroaster, as well as Jesus Christ, and continues with revelations made to the Bab and Baha'u'llah in the 19th century.

THE ANSWER:
By J.D. Conway

Some of the promotion literature I have seen presents Baha'i as the "one universal faith." It claims to fulfill the Jewish expectation of the Messiah, the Christian hope for the Second Coming, the Muslim prophecy of the "Great Announcement," the Buddhist prophecy about the coming of the Fifth Buddha, the ancient Hindu longing for the return of Krishna, and the Zoroastrians' waiting for the Shah Bahram. According to this literature all religions of the world find fulfillment in Baha'u'llah, who lived about a century ago.

Well, there is an old saying that he who tries to please everyone may actually please no one. To reduce religions to a common denominator is to drain each religion of its peculiar character and doctrines. I don't think religions can be reconciled in this way. Baha'u'llah was a man of considerable religious experience and perceptivity, but he certainly has little in common with the Messiah of the Jews, and less with Christ of the Gospels. A Muslim might understand him as a kind of Muslim heretic; but for the Buddhist and the Hindu he would be completely strange and foreign. The Zoroastrian would not have much in common with him except being Persian.

Perhaps I can show what I mean by tracing the origins of the Baha'i religion and comparing them with the origins of Christianity.

The background of Baha'i is Muslim, in the Shiite tradition of Islam as it prevailed in Persia. According to the Shiite view Muhammad appointed his cousin, Ali ibn Abi Talib, to succeed him. Ali was married to Muhammad's daughter Fatima. Ali's children were direct descendants of the Prophet. The ruling sons and descendants of this family were given the title of Imam (leader). The Imam held temporal power, and the faithful were absolutely dependent on his guidance in spiritual matters. But the Imams led dangerous lives; they were persecuted, poisoned, and variously assassinated by the kalifs of the opposing Sunnite branch of Islam.

There were 13 Imams. The last came to power in the year 260 on the Muslim calendar. For 69 years the last Imam remained in hiding for safety, and communicated with his followers through intermediaries called Babs. Then he disappeared, leaving no successor. The story was that he never died, but lived in a mysterious city, Jabulqa, with a group of faithful disciples, and that at the end of time he would issue forth to fill the whole world with justice.

Just 1000 years after the accession of the 12th Imam, a young Persian named Mirza Ali Muhammad manifested himself as the Bab, spokesman for the Imam. This was in 1844 on our calendar. The religion he established, called Ba'bi', spread rapidly through Persia. Its doctrines were more sublime than those of contemporary Islam, and it soon acquired an extensive literature. However, the Bab and his followers were severely persecuted. The Bab lived only six years after his Manifestation, and he spent most of that time in captivity. But he was able to write to his followers and even to receive them. In due time he dropped the title of Bab, giving it to one of his disciples; and he became Qa'im (the Imam whose return was expected at the end of the world). His followers regarded him as divine.

Before his death he nominated as his successor a young lad of 20, Mirza Yahya, who was given the title Subh-i-Ezel (the Dawn of Eternity). For brevity we will call him Ezel. Most of the followers of the Bab recognized him as their leader. However, he was young and liked seclusion;

so he turned the practical management of affairs over to his half brother, who came to be known as Baha'u'llah. He was 13 years older than Ezel, several years older than the Bab himself. We shall call him Baha for brevity.

In 1852, after a massacre at Teheran in which many Babi leaders were killed, Baha and Ezel took refuge in Baghdad, which was then Turkish, and for the next 11 years Baghdad was headquarters of the Babi, who continued to recognize Ezel as their leader. Meanwhile, Baha had spent some time in the highlands of Turkish Kurdistan—a period of purification and religious preparation. In 1864 the Turks expelled the Babis from Baghdad and took them to Constantinople, where they remained four months, and then were sent farther west, to Adrianople. It was here that Baha publicly announced that he was "he whom God shall manifest," as foretold by the Bab. His followers claimed that the Bab's appointment of Ezel had been only a blind, to prepare the way for Baha's Manifestation.

The Manifestation shook the Babi community into open and intense conflict, during which the half brothers took turns accusing each other of attempted fratricide, mostly by poisoning. Finally the Turks divided them. They sent Ezel and his followers to Famagusta, on the east coast of Cyprus, but with them they sent four Baha'i and their families, seemingly as spies or hostages. The Baha'i were sent to Akka (which is now Israel). Four Ezelis were sent along with them, but all four were killed.

A great schism followed, with Akka and Famagusta glaring at each other across a couple of hundred miles of the blue Mediterranean. The Ezelis had the better claim in law, but their followers were few and their influence dwindled. The Baha'i deprived the Bab of his messianic role, and made him the precursor for Baha'u'llah—a sort of John the Baptist for the real Messiah. They quit calling themselves Babi and became a new religion. Baha'i was their name.

The spirit and thought of the two groups came to differ greatly. The Ezelis tended to mysticism. The Baha'i were more practical and ethical, and they tried to make their religion appealing to the whole world.

But after the death of Baha there was again a bitter schism, with opposing factions led by his two sons, Abbas Effendi and Marzci Muhammad Ali. In due time Abbas Effendi won out, but not before the conflict was carried to the United States. The first Baha'i missionary came here in

1892. He was Ibrahim Kharyru'llah, and he was a follower
of Muhammad Ali. Ten years later, in 1902, other missionaries were sent here by the followers of Abbas Effendi; and
claimed that they sought to kill him.

Baha'i is truly a serious faith, claiming millions of members and worthy to be associated with the more ancient and
widespread religions of mankind, but it can hardly hope to
supplant any of them. Its doctrine rates high in intelligence
and morality, and Christians claim that some of it was borrowed from them.

I can find little in the origins of Baha'i which is comparable with the beginnings of Christianity. There was a certain messianic preparation during the 1000-year Occulta-
tion of the 12th Imam, and there was a precursor in the
person of the Bab. But I see no evidence of an infinite Father who loved the human children of his creation so much
that He sent his own eternal Son, in the personal love of
the Holy Spirit, to become a man, to redeem men from
their sins, to give them a share in his own divine life, to
become a real human brother to them, so that they in turn
might be true children of the Father and share his home
forever.

In the liberal, rational, and humanistic teachings which
modern Baha'i attribute to Baha'u'llah I miss both the personal and supernatural elements of Christianity. There is
no angel announcing to Mary the good news of Christ's
coming, no trusting response of the chosen spouse of the
Holy Spirit, no humble St. Joseph to protect the Mother
and Child, no hidden life in the Holy Family. I do not find
a public ministry of kindness, love, and mercy, filled with
inspiring teachings and frequent miracles, with readiness to
forgive sin combined with severity toward hypocrites.
Above all I miss the personal love and unity of Christ's last
meal with his Apostles, the patient courage and generosity
of his passion and death, and the glorious triumph of the
resurrection, pledge of our own triumph and glory.

Baha'u'llah's meditations in Kurdistan may remind us of
Christ's fasting and temptations in the desert; but his supplanting of his brother, and his alleged attempts at fratricide show how divergent he is from the gentle forgiving
Master of Palestine.

Other things that I miss in looking over the teachings of
Baha'i as set forth in their promotion leaflet are prayer and
a hopeful vision of life after death.

I am edified by the list of teachings they ascribe to Baha'u'llah: the oneness of mankind, free investigation of the truth, all religions on one foundation, religion as the cause of unity and in accord with science and reason, equality between men and women, the elimination of prejudice, universal peace and education, spiritual solution of the economic problem, a universal language, and an international tribunal. But they do not add up to religion as the Catholic knows it: an elevation of man to the supernatural plane, whence he speaks to God as Father, enjoys his personal friendship, and looks forward to a happy union of love forever with Him.

18

Why Do They Say the Jews Killed Christ?

THE LETTER:

I read the *Catholic Digest* for the first time while I was recuperating in a Catholic hospital. The dedication to service of this hospital and the *Catholic Digest* favorably impressed me. I am a Jewess.

But a disturbing thought kept coming to mind. Why are Catholic children taught early in their religious education that the Jews killed Christ? Jews have never accepted this accusation. Our children are taught that evil people of that time killed Christ, and are taught that only when they are in their teens, and are advanced in religious training.

Our children from the time they began to have friends had Catholic friends. They had a wonderful relationship until the Catholic children were taught that the Jews killed Christ. These were children six and seven years old. In keeping with their ability to understand, they tormented our children with taunts. "I can't play with you. You are a Jew. You killed Christ."

It took much effort on our part to explain the fallacy of this to our children and to see that they still remained friends. This was 25 years ago.

Recently my seven-year-old granddaughter came home
from school in tears because some children accused her of
killing Christ. If this has to be taught as part of religion,
then why can't it wait until they are older and can better
understand that every Jew they meet is not guilty of killing
Christ?

Why hasn't this been eradicated from Catholic teaching
long before this? Why is it taking so long now, even as it is
being considered?

Bluma Tepper

THE ANSWER:
By J.D. Conway

I do not know, Mrs. Tepper, how common it is today for
Catholic children to be taught that the Jews killed Christ.
Such teaching has no part in modern education, especially
in these days of the ecumenical spirit. The experience of
your seven-year-old granddaughter is shocking. At least I
can join you in hoping that such teaching will quickly disappear. It is contrary to truth, justice, and charity; it breeds
prejudice, and it contributes to antagonisms in society.

It violates truth. The Gospels inform us that some of the
"chief priests and Pharisees," some "scribes and elders,"
and, indeed, "a whole mob" were active in demanding and
obtaining the crucifixion of Jesus. But certainly this mob
did not include all the Jews in Jerusalem on that day. The
crowds which had acclaimed Him as king a few days earlier had surely not deserted Him so quickly and thoroughly. St. Luke tells us that as He carried his cross "there
was a great crowd of the people, and of women, who were
bewailing and lamenting Him." Can these be charged with
his death?

The vast majority of the Jews of Palestine, among them
his own relatives and friends in Galilee, had no idea of
what was happening in Jersulem on those days. And what
of the Jews in the diaspora, scattered widely in many
lands? Probably the majority of them had never heard of
Jesus of Nazareth. Who can hold them all guilty of what a
mob did? Besides, the sins of the fathers are not to be
charged against the children. The Jews of today share no

guilt in the action of people who lived nearly 20 centuries ago.

Some Christians may claim that even though you can't justifiably blame modern Jews for killing Christ, at least God has repudiated and cursed them for rejecting the Messiah. But St. Paul says the opposite. He was very sad that the majority of the Jews in his day had missed the spiritual opportunities offered them, but he wrote: "I ask, then, has God rejected his people? By no means! I myself am an Israelite, a descendant of Abraham, a member of the tribe of Benjamin. God has not rejected his people whom He foreknew." They have stumbled, but this has not led to their absolute ruin. "Through their false step salvation has gone to the heathen." Their false step has enriched the world. And even from the Jews themselves there was "a remnant, chosen by grace."

St. Paul had great sorrow and unceasing anguish in his heart that his own people had followed their leaders, rather than joining the "remnant," but still proclaimed the enduring glories of Israel. "For I could wish that I myself were accursed and cut off from Christ for the sake of my brethren, my kinsmen by race. They are Israelites, and to them belong the sonship, the glory, the covenants, the giving of the law, the worship, and the promises; to them belong the patriarchs, and of their race, according to the Christ, who is over all things, God blessed forever. Amen."

Our Christian attitude toward the Jews should be one of deep gratitude for the legacy they have given us. From the patriarchs to Christ Himself we owe them our spiritual heritage, including the foundations of the Church and the sacred books of the Old Testament, inspired by the Holy Spirit. They are, St. Paul says, the root which supports us, the branches, the olive tree onto which we as wild shoots have been grafted that we may share its richness.

It is then a sad perversion of the truth for us to teach little children that the Jews killed Christ. Some Jews did. Some soldiers did. Pilate did. We might well use your own words, Mrs. Tepper: "The evil people of that time killed Christ." But the real truth is that all of us who have been guilty of sin had a part in the crucifixion, because the purpose of Jesus' death was to make reparation for our sins. However, He readily forgives us our part in the crucifixion, if we will accept part with Him in his resurrection: his glorious new life of love and grace.

The teaching that the Jews killed Christ is contrary to justice and love. It has been one of the causes of centuries of persecution, and it helps destroy in us the sanctifying effects of the death and resurrection of Jesus. Even while He was hanging with anguish on the cross, Jesus loved those who had crucified Him, and He prayed his Father to forgive them, "for they know not what they do." And He has told us: "This is my commandment, that you love one another as I have loved you." We are not fostering love in the hearts of little children when we tell them the Jews killed Christ. We are giving them scandal by planting in their innocent souls the seeds of hate.

The sad history of anti-Semitism in the Christian world is mostly the result of prejudice, which disguises itself as reason and leads its victims to the point of violence. Prejudice is called the child of ignorance, but the child is much further from truth than its parent, because it stubbornly clings to untruth. Heresies and schisms have often led Christians to violate the law of love, and some of them have endured for centuries. The Saracens were long the prime object of Christian hatred. But our most persistent form of prejudice, from Apostolic times until now, has been anti-Semitism. The Jew has been the occasion to the Christian of more un-Christian acts than any other "enemy."

In their earliest conflicts with the Jews, Christians were largely on the defensive. Peter was thrown into prison. James was put to death, Stephen was stoned, and Paul was often persecuted. Many of the Fathers of the Church wrote treatises against the Jews in this defensive spirit.

However, from the time of Constantine in the 4th century the tables were turned. Earlier pagan emperors had sometimes persecuted Jews along with Christians; now the Christian emperors imposed various civil restraints on Jewish life and activities. For example, Constans decreed a death penalty for marriage between a Christian and a Jew; and Theodosius II forbade the building of synagogues. The rigor of the various emperors was uneven, but their restrictions gradually stamped out organized Jewish political and intellectual life. When the barbarians took over the West there was a brief respite, but it was not long until Jews were being forced to choose between Baptism and banishment in some areas. In the Frankish kingdom they were forbidden to appear on the street at Easter time. It is a reflection on Christians that Mohammedanism offered a measure of relief to the Jews. They were by no means free from persecution in the expanding realms of Islam, but often they took refuge there from Christian severities. In later centuries Turkey became a favorite asylum from the cruelties of Spain and Central Europe.

The Crusades brought times of intense suffering for the Jews. The Crusaders, before leaving for the Holy Land, or along their way, vented their fired-up spirit against the Jews, wiping out whole colonies of them in many cities. Between the various Crusades came periods of peace and prosperity, but each renewal of crusading fervor brought on new anti-Semitic violence. Sometimes the atrocities were sponsored by kings, but more often they were spontaneous outburst of "Christian" hatred.

Ridiculous charges against the Jews were rampant in the Middle Ages: They were accused of using the blood of Christian children in their Passover, of eating the divided heart of a murdered boy, of desecrating the sacred Host, and of poisoning wells and rivers. When a murder took place they were the first suspects, and they often suffered penalties without formal trial.

Frequently anti-Semitic hatred fomented mob violence, which often had a measure of approval from civil authorities. Massacres were frequent; torture was common. Jews were banished from one city to another, and sometimes from entire kingdoms; their goods were confiscated, or they were simply robbed. Some were forced to receive Baptism, after which they were likely to be taken before the Inquisition and charged with insincere conversion.

The 4th Lateran council, besides excluding Jews from public office, decreed that they must wear some kind of identifying dress or badge. Some Popes tried to calm the excesses of their subjects, but others imposed laws which encouraged severity. In the 16th century Pope Paul IV, a man of great severity, put his Roman Jews in a ghetto and forbade them to practice medicine, to own real estate, or to engage in any but petty commerce. They had to wear a badge. A few years later Pope Pius IV expelled all Jews from the Papal States, except for Ancona and Rome. Sixtus V recalled them, but Clement VIII banished most of them again.

In reading the story of Jewish persecutions through the

centuries it is often hard to imagine how any of them remained alive. But their enduring spirit of work and sacrifice enabled them to overcome persecutions, maintain their learning, and acquire wealth and influence.

The Protestant Reformation did not help the Jews. Luther, especially in his later years, was one of their bitter opponents. The French Revolution began their emancipation, but modern concepts of freedom and equality have often been denied them since. The fall of Napoleon brought a setback to their liberties in Europe, marked especially by bloody riots in Germany. But all the hatred and violence of the centuries seemed to culminate in Nazi Germany, in our own times, when a mad Hitler inspired his frenzied followers to seek "the ultimate solution" of the Jewish problem by systematic extermination. He almost succeeded in the lands under his control. In all history the world has never known atrocities so cynical and effective.

I have sketched this horrible history, Mrs. Tepper, to illustrate the evil effects of prejudice, which may well have its origin in our teaching little children that the Jews killed Christ. The inhuman viciousness of nazi crimes should have purged us all of anti-Semitism, but we must admit in all honesty that the Jew suffers from many discriminations in our American society today. He enjoys a full measure of civil rights, but his Christian brethren impose many social restrictions on him.

That controversial play *The Deputy* sadly distorts the character of Pope Pius XII, but it should make us all pause for an examination of conscience. If we retain in our hearts any remnants of anti-Semitism, then we share in a measure in the crimes of the centuries against the Jewish race. We share the same spirit which inspired those crimes. And it is contrary to the spirit of love which was taught by Christ. Lingering anti-Semitism has been greatly discouraged by recent Popes, who have removed its vestiges from our liturgical prayer. For instance, we used to pray on Good Friday, for the "perfidious," i.e., unbelieving, Jews, and we did not kneel in our prayer for them, as we did for Protestants and pagans. Now the offensive adjective is omitted and we do kneel during the prayer.

We can hardly hope for love and fellowship among ourselves when we exclude from the embrace of our love the race that gave us Jesus Christ. The Mother of Jesus was a

Jewish maiden; all of the Apostles were Jews. Nearly all of the early Christians were of the same race. Indeed, St. Peter needed a vision from heaven to prompt him to receive any of the rest of us into the Church.

19

Can or Should a Protestant Rear Catholic Children?

THE LETTER:

Would it be an unforgivable sin for a Protestant couple to raise three orphan Catholic children in a different faith?

My sister-in-law and her husband were killed in a car accident. They were Catholics, and we want to do the right thing about the children. We are farmers, and work and live in an old-fashioned way. I have tried to love and feed them. We were taking them to our little country church along with our own five children, but a lot of gossip among the neighbors makes us wonder if it is right. No one else wants them. They have no money or other place to go. The two boys, 11 and 13, want to stay. The little three-year-old girl is a little darling and everyone loves her.

V.E. Smith

THE ANSWER:
By J.D. Conway

The answer to your question is easy, Mr. Smith. It is evident that you and your wife are good Christians, full of charity and anxious to do what is right. You need have no fear that you will be guilty of an unforgivable sin. I am sure you will follow your honest conscience; and when we do that we are not guilty of sin at all, even though the thing we do may be wrong in itself.

Your basic problem, however, is much more difficult. It would be easy for me to give you a standard answer: That those are Catholic children, and if you keep them in your home you have an obligation to see that they are raised Catholics. Their Baptism entitles them to that, and their parents would surely want it. However, seeking to be honest, I ask myself: What advice would I give if the circumstances were reversed? If you were Catholic people and the children were orphans of Protestant parents, would I say that you were obliged to raise them as good Protestants?

Frankly, we Catholics have a hard time being consistent, in a practical way, about a question of this kind. We are deeply convinced that the Catholic Church is the only true Church of Jesus Christ; that He established it and lives in it and works through it; that our membership in it brings us into personal sanctifying contact with Him; and that our salvation is obtained through it. Consequently our love for our fellow men moves us to desire that they all share the benefits of the Church directly and fully; and we are moved to sadness when we see anyone deprived of the great sacramental benefits of membership in it.

You have probably heard our attitude stated so bluntly that it seems arrogant: "Outside the Catholic Church there is no salvation." This statement needs to be explained lest it be harsh and confusing. It really means that historically Jesus established only one Church, that He lives his continuing earthly life in only one Church, and that He performs his sanctifying mysteries through only one Church. It does not mean that this one Church is surrounded by walls which keep all but full-fledged members from getting any of its graces.

While Jesus lives in and acts through the one Church He founded, He encounters many millions who seem to Catholics far removed from that Church. For other Christians his most effective encounter is in their Baptism and in the faith and love which they have for Him. In fact, many more people belong in effective manner to the Church of Christ than are listed on its membership rolls. No doubt such effective membership belongs to you and your wife and children, Mr. Smith. You were baptized into union with Christ, and you have kept the faith as you understand it, never rejecting it in guilty manner, and you have tried to serve God faithfully as your consciences direct you.

If I may say it without offense, you are in your hearts far more members of the Catholic Church than you are non-members. And those three children who have come under your care might also retain enough membership in the Church to lead them to salvation, even though you were to raise them as Protestants. This would be particularly true of that darling little girl who is only three years old. Her Catholic heritage has not made a deep impression on her conscience. There must remain some question, of course, about the children who are 11 and 13. Can they give up their Catholic faith without awareness of guilt?

Even though salvation may still be practically possible for these children in your church, we Catholics are still convinced that it would be much easier and surer if they had that immediate contact with Jesus of which our Church is an effective sign, that contact which the Mass and the sacraments are divinely designed to accomplish. In plain words, we are deeply convinced that in a practical way a person has a much better opportunity for salvation as a full-fledged member of the Catholic Church.

I am speaking frankly, Mr. Smith, that you may appreciate my problem in adivising you on your problem. A practical solution can be reached only on the basis of personal consciences. First, your own conscience and that of your wife must be considered. But we must not forget the active, tender consciences of those two older children. Neither may we forget the welfare of the little girl nor that of your own five children.

It is a fundamental truth of Christianity that each person has a right and duty to follow his own sincere and certain conscience. This means that he has a right to moral and religious liberty. It does not mean that morality is for each man what he thinks it is, or that all religions are equal. It does not mean that a man may simply believe whatever he wishes without concern for truth. We all have definite obligations toward God: We must investigate the truths He has taught, accept them firmly when we find them, and live by them when we hold them.

Freedom of conscience does not mean that we are liberated from all obligation concerning religion. It means rather that these obligations are inside of us, between ourselves and God. Our beliefs must not be forced on us from outside. Force is unjust, and destroys true faith. We cannot have faith unless we act freely in accepting it. We may be moved to that acceptance by the evidence of truth, and we are surely aided by God's grace, but it remains our own free and personal act. It is so much the nature of faith to be free that when assent to it is forced it ceases to be faith.

Freedom of conscience does not mean that we are free from conscience, free to do as we please, with no obligation on us. It means that no outside force may rightly compel our conscience. St. Thomas once wrote that even though we were to act in accord with objective truth (e.g., accept the true faith), but in doing so act contrary to our consciences, we would be guilty of sin.

I am setting the background for a direct question to you, Mr. Smith. What of your own conscience? You evidently hold your religion important, and have raised your children to believe in its truths as you know them. Can you, without violating your conscience, raise your foster children in the Catholic religion, or at least permit them to grow up in it without your hindering them in any way? The same question must be answered by your wife. No one should try to impose on either of you an obligation that would do violence to your conscientious convictions.

However, and this is very important, yours are not the only consciences to be considered. Most directly concerned are the consciences of those two older children, 11 and 13. They have been taught the truths of the Catholic faith, and their Baptism has given them a right to that faith. They have made their Confessions and received Holy Communion. They both have been taught and have practiced regular attendance at Sunday Mass. Probably they have been Confirmed.

What do their consciences tell them? What do they say when you take them to your church? Do they believe it is perfectly all right for them to forsake their Catholic practices? Because their consciences are tender and timid, they deserve special consideration. With only a little subtle force they can, no doubt, be swayed. But we should have as much respect for young and delicate consciences as for old and hardened ones. It is not fair for us to take advantage of youth and insecurity. We are accustomed to mold young minds in the process of education, but in doing so we must respect their rights as persons. We may help to form but must never violate their consciences. I do believe that I would give the same advice to Catholic parents who had Protestant children come under their care in similar circumstances. It would not be right to try to push these children into Catholic beliefs and practices, or to deny them the practice of the faith which they hold in their own convictions.

With all three of your foster children there is a further point to be considered: the wishes of their parents. True, the parents are deceased, and their wishes are no longer actual on earth. But the children are theirs. While they lived they had the right and duty of educating them, and were responsible for their spiritual welfare. Reverence for their memory admonishes us to treat their children as they would want them treated, as long as we can reconcile their wishes with our consciences. If their accident had given them time to arrange for the religious education of their children what would they have done?

It is to avoid problems like yours that most adoption agencies follow the practice of placing a child in a home where religious practices are the same as those of its natural parents. Your problem cannot be solved, however, by this general practice. The children are in your home and are happy there. You wish to keep them and no one else wants them. It would be a further emotional shock for the children if they were to be torn from their new home.

Your efforts to raise these children Catholics will raise problems of a practical nature. How are you going to get them to Mass every Sunday and to catechism classes? You cannot be expected to teach them their religion. How are they going to learn it? I cannot answer these questions for you. Maybe some of your Catholic neighbors could help.

The natural, easy way is for you to take them to your own church as you are doing. But is it the right way? This is the question you have been asking yourself, and have now asked me. I have shown you my process of reasoning, in the hope that it may be helpful to you.

Another point I have not forgotten: the welfare of your own children. They may be confused in their own religious convictions by a divided family of this sort. Frictions may be created in the home. But with charity and understanding it may be possible for you to develop a truly ecumenical home.

I have tried to ask myself honestly whether I would give the same advice to a Catholic couple who had acquired three Protestant children under similar circumstances. I feel sure I would as regards the two older ones. The things I have said about their freedom of conscience certainly apply both ways. But I must admit that I hesitate about the little three-year old. Here my convictions that the Catholic Church is the one true Church come strongly into play.

There is another factor which cannot be eliminated. It is example. Your three foster children live in a good Protestant home. Even if you see that they are given a Catholic education and are sent regularly to Mass and the sacraments, your home environment will have an influence on them more forceful, perhaps, than their once-a-week Catholic teaching and practice. They may grow up confused about religion. They will see in your home the beauties of Christian life, and may eventually become Protestants themselves. If such be the case you will have no cause to worry about sin. You respected their consciences, and tried to raise them as their parents would want you to. You used no unfair pressures to bring them into your religion. The force of good example is entirely fair.

If I were counseling my hypothetical Catholic couple I would have this factor of example much in mind. I would tell them: Respect the consciences of those Protestant children, try to give them the opportunities their parents would want, and avoid subtle force or influence. But spare them not the persuasion of your good example in true Christian living.

20

Why Do Catholics Restrict Communion?

THE LETTER:

I would like to know why the Catholic Church has a closed Communion. It seems to me that there are several passages in the Bible that tell us all to take, eat, and drink, for it is His Body. He came to save sinners, and the Bible tells us of the adulteress and several more that He forgave, and that when God forgives we are indeed forgiven. Since God does not hold past sins against us how can the Church?

I thank you for the chance to ask this question. My eldest daughter and her two children are Catholics. They give their *Catholic Digest* to me.

Mrs. Earl Enyart

THE ANSWER:
By J.D. Conway

Catholics do not often use the expression "closed Communion," Mrs. Enyart, but we do have it. Only Catholics may take part in our Holy Communion, and it is closed to persons in serious sin. For us it is a sign of faith, unity, and love. "Opening" Communion to persons who do not believe, or do not wish to live in union, or who are in sin (the opposite of love) would not make sense from the Catholic viewpoint.

Our Church has other signs of faith, unity, and love: the other six sacraments. We usually say that a sacrament is an external sign that produces grace in the soul, but that sounds rather mechanical. The sacraments are really very live and personal things. The story of the sacraments begins with the love of God for the human persons He had created. He wanted to bring them to know and love Him, and to have a personal relationship with them.

The problem was that man had no way of meeting God personally. God did find ways of revealing Himself to man in Old Testament times; and man found ways of communicating with God in sacrifice and prayer. But close as God was to his "chosen people" there was still no person-to-person encounter. In due time, God, to make personal encounter with men possible, became a man Himself. The Father sent his own Son to live among men to teach them and do good for them. Finally He died for them and arose from the dead. Those who came into personal contact with Jesus in faith and love were sanctified by Him. There was probably no need for the Apostles to be baptized; they were sanctified by personal encounter with Jesus in the flesh. But St. Paul was baptized because he had not had the privilege of knowing Jesus personally.

Forty days after his Resurrection Jesus ascended into heaven. Was his personal encounter with man only a temporary, local event? Can we, 20 centuries later, have personal contact with Him? The Catholic answer is Yes, in his mystical Body, the Church. The human Jesus now lives in heaven, his Body glorified. But He also remains present and active on earth. He shares his own divine life with the members of his Church, preparing them to live again in heaven.

This mystery of the personal presence of Jesus with his people in the Church is our basic sacrament, a continuing sign. But He has given us seven particular signs to be used on special occasions as a means of personal encounter with Him. These are our seven sacraments. Communion, or the Holy Eucharist, is one of them. In each of them Jesus comes to meet us with spiritual gifts; and in each we respond with faith and love and acceptance of his gifts.

But there is something very special about the sacrament of the Holy Eucharist. You recall the scene of its institution: At the Last Supper Jesus "took bread, and giving thanks, broke, and said, 'This is my Body which shall be given up for you; do this in remembrance of Me.' In like manner also the cup, after He had supped, saying, 'This cup is the new covenant in my Blood; do this as often as you drink it, in remembrance of Me. For as often as you shall eat this Bread and drink the cup, you proclaim the death of the Lord, until He comes.' "

Catholics take literally the Lord's words: "This is my Body, this is my Blood." In Holy Communion, then, we receive Jesus personally. His Body and Blood are now in glorified form; but the person is the same one who walked the roads of Galilee, the same one who is equal to the Father in all things. Thus in Communion we have personal encounter with Jesus.

The third requisite is unity. Because we receive the Eucharist in the form of a supper, like brothers eating in the same home, it is the supreme sign of unity among the people of God. Those who have openly broken this unity would be acting falsely if they joined in the supper of unity.

You are entirely correct, Mrs. Enyart, in saying that Jesus invited all to take and eat, to take and drink; and that He forgave sinners whom He came to save. The Church wishes nothing more than that everyone receive Communion, but only when they come to receive in a manner pleasing to God and fruitful for themselves. We might continue with our quotation from St. Paul: "Therefore whoever eats this Bread or drinks the cup of the Lord unworthily, will be guilty of the Body and the Blood of the Lord. But let a man prove himself, and so let him eat of that Bread and drink of the cup: for he who eats and drinks unworthily, without distinguishing the Body, eats and drinks judgment to himself."

There are some Christians who do not believe that Jesus is really, personally present in the Eucharist. These are not permitted to take Communion with us because of lack of faith. Their encounter with Jesus would be impaired because they would not see or recognize him. Many of them have their own Communion services which are sacred ceremonies comemorating the life and death of Jesus, recalling his love and forgiveness. They probably get much spiritual good from these, but should confine themselves to the services, not taking part in our Communion, whose full meaning they do not accept.

Then there are other Christians, like Anglicans, Lutherans, and Orthodox, who do believe that in the Eucharist we receive the true Body and Blood of Jesus, the true person. These are kept from our Communion because of lack of unity. We must not pretend before the Lord or the world that we are one family at table when we really are not. It is true that we are brothers in the same Lord Jesus, that in Baptism we have all been adopted as sons of the same Father, and that we hope in due time to share the same home in heaven. But here and now there are important differences between us. We hope to work them out, but until we do we should not deny them by false signs of union.

Then, finally, there are sinners. We are all in that class, and without the generous forgiveness of our Saviour none of us would be able to receive Communion. But forgiveness must precede the banquet of love. When forgiveness has taken place, Communion becomes the supper of joy and thanksgiving.

Of the seven sacraments, one is the effective sign of forgiveness. We call it Penance. It is better known as Confession. When Jesus was a dinner guest in the home of Simon the Pharisee, "a woman in the town who was a sinner" came to Him and "began to bathe his feet with her tears, and wiped them with the hair of her head, and kissed his feet, and anointed them with ointment." Because of these signs of love and repentance Jesus told her, "Thy sins are forgiven."

Our Confession is less spectacular. We simply kneel

humbly beside the priest, who is a minister of Christ, and through him we admit to Jesus our sins and our sorrow for them. And then the priest, speaking in the name of the Saviour, forgives us. It is a great sacrament: a sign and a mystery. And in it we encounter Jesus personally. He listens to us as He did to the woman of the town; He recognizes our sincerity, and repeats to us those ancient words: "Thy sins are forgiven."

Our encounter with Jesus in the sacrament of Penance is an embrace similar to that of the father who welcomed home his prodigal son. And the Communion that follows bears much resemblance to the banquet of joy prepared by this same father, who killed the fatted calf. But seldom is there a brother who grieves that the prodigal is so lovingly fêted.

I presume you know, Mrs. Enyart, that Catholics hold forgiveness of sins to be possible in anticipation of Confession. When we sin we need not remain in our guilt until we have opportunity for Confession. If our love for God, revived by his grace, is deep and honest, we have perfect contrition, sorrow from a perfect motive: the love of God. Here, too, is an encounter, but without any external sign. God reaches out to us to inspire repentance; we respond in love, and He accepts it with his constant love.

There is reconciliation in perfect contrition, but it is not enough, in normal circumstances, to prepare us for Communion. We go to confession first. There may be three reasons for this. 1) Because the Eucharist is the most sacred of all sacraments, it is fitting that we be doubly careful about our forgiveness before receiving it. 2) The Eucharist is a sacrament of the Church, and we need to be reconciled with the Church before approaching it. The sacrament of Penance is a sign of this reconciliation. 3) We should use the sacraments in due order, for the purposes our Lord intended: first the sign of forgiveness and then the banquet of joy.

So you see, Mrs. Enyart, that our Communion is not really closed to sinners. Their supper of joy is withheld only until they have received sign of forgiveness. And we should note that Confession is necessary preparation for Communion only when our sins have been serious. Our routine failures are readily forgiven in the encounter of love which is the Eucharist.

God does not hold past sins against us, and neither does the Church. But the prodigal must first return to his father's house.

21

Will We Ever All Get Together?

THE LETTER:

I am Lutheran married to a Roman Catholic. A few weeks after our marriage I was waiting in the neighborhood laundry for the wash to get done, and started doodling a list that I called *On Reunion of Roman and Lutheran Churches.* This was before the first session of the Vatican Council.

Now, less than three years later, looking down the list, I note that the Council took action on five of my 23 points (which were 50–50 between the two Churches) and has started action on several other points.

As unity talks increase I am firmly convinced that it must eventually happen. My personal hope is that the Lutheran and Anglican "rites" will be acknowledged by the Roman Church as the Orthodox Church was recently acknowledged. Could you discuss the possibility of this coming to pass? I realize that this may take ages, but once I thought that recent reforms would not take place in my lifetime and here in the matter of two years all kinds of welcome changes have come and gone and the Roman Church has not suffered from it (as most nonprogressive Romans thought that it would).

Robert W. Hohlmayer

THE ANSWER:
By J.D. Conway

My practical judgment inclines me to agree, Robert, that our reunion with the Lutheran and Anglican churches may take ages. As you well know, the question of rites is minor.

Some doctrinal differences between us, while not many in comparison with the beliefs we have in common, are so deep that agreement is beyond present human perspective.

However, my practical judgment has its limitations in face of the surprising activities of the Holy Spirit. You have seen the Vatican Council take action on 5 of your 23 points of difference between us. I have no checklist, but in both number and significance the changes in the past four years have been phenomenal. A few years ago I used to say that I was sure Mass would be said in English in another generation or so, but that I had no hope of living long enough to see it. Then suddenly Pope John called the Council, the Holy Spirit took charge of things, and our manmade timetables became obsolete.

Five years ago the Rev. Robert McAfee Brown, Presbyterian minister and professor, and the late Father Gustave Weigel, S.J. joined in writing a little book called *An American Dialogue.* In it, Dr. Brown gave his well-known "ground rules for fruitful dialogue today." About reunion he wrote, "And if we believed only in what is humanly possible, we would despair, 'but with God all things are possible.' "

We must offer our ecumenical efforts up to God, and leave the results in his hands. The fruits He has produced these past few years are beyond any expectations we had when the Council was called. Let me recall a few of them. They make your question seem realistic.

We Catholics, from Pope Paul on down, are openly confessing our guilt in the events that led to the disunity of Christians, and we are asking pardon from our separated brethren. Protestants are responding in the same spirit. We—Protestants and Catholics—who quit speaking to each other in the 16th century, are now engaged in frank, honest, charitable dialogue.

Catholics who shunned the religious services of other Christians as though they were idol worship are joining Protestants in prayer to our common Father, asking through his Son, Jesus Christ, that we may all be one, as that Son Himself prayed.

A good example of our changed attitude is in the solemn prayer we say for the unity of Christians on Good Friday. We used to pray for heretics and schismatics, asking the Lord God to tear them away from all their errors and call them back to Holy Mother Church, Catholic and apostolic.

We referred to them as souls deceived by diabolical fraud, and prayed that they get rid of their heretical depravity, that their erring hearts might come to their senses, and that they return to the unity of divine truth. Fortunately we said the prayers in Latin, and few of our separated brethren were fully aware of the insulting language we used in seeking their spiritual welfare.

Now we pray for all our brothers who believe in Christ (Catholic, Protestant and Orthodox) that God our Lord may gather and keep them in his one Church. They are sheep of the Lord's flock, sanctified by his one Baptism. May the completeness of faith and the bond of love join them all together.

In general, we have quit calling each other bad names like heretic and papist, and we have begun to greet each other with respect. Some who could never say *Father* are giving priests their proper title; and we try, sometimes a bit awkwardly, to use the preferred form of address for ministers and pastors.

We are beginning to work together for racial justice, and plans and discussions are extending to other fields. The clergy are getting acquainted and priests are joining ministerial associations. We are preparing to serve our brethren together rather than in competition.

We are coming to realize that we need each other as we confront modern secular society; our contrast with the new atheism makes us realize how much we have in common.

As a result of the Vatican Council there is in the Catholic Church a surging spirit of reform and renewal. The Church of Christ, divine in its origin and in its inner life and purposes, is made up of men who are fallible and often sinful. We are now determined to see our faults and purge them, to understand those human features of the Church that make it unattractive to many people, and to reform or eliminate them.

In this process of inner renewal we are examining many features of Catholic organization, procedures, life, and worship which we have simply taken for granted. The questioning is so thorough that some people are disturbed by it, fearing that we may even change our doctrines by way of compromise. Certainly nothing of divine origin can be changed. But we are restudying many of our traditional teachings to understand them better, make them more vital, and explain them in terms modern man can find pertinent. We are reemphasizing the role of Sacred Scripture in our lives. Catholic and Protestant scholars are working in collaboration. The inspired word of God which we revere together can do much to bring us back together.

The most easily seen results of our renewal have been in the liturgy, but attention has been given to the layman and his role in the Church; to Religious Orders; to the bishops and their place in the Church structure; to the operations of the Holy See and the prescriptions of Canon Law; to our relationships with the rich and the poor; to the pomp of our ceremonies and the elegance of clerical dress; to missions and methods of teaching and preaching; to marriage and the intricate problems of married life; to anti-Semitism and even to anti-Communism. Of primary interest has been the Council's concern with religious liberty, with the rights of the individual person and the sacred precincts of his conscience.

From these searching studies of inner Church life and relevant world problems may come results which will cancel out some more of the 23 points you listed, Robert. A similar spirit of examination and renewal is at work in many Protestant groups. From their efforts of renewal may come results which will cancel out more of your points. Those remaining may gradually disappear through our mutual dialogue, prayer, love, and cooperation. So, impossible as it may seem to us, counting on human forces, there may come a time when the careful study of various rites and liturgies will be practical—from the Catholic point of View—to see if we can accept them as valid methods of divine worship.

The Lutheran service of Holy Communion has external similarity to the Roman Mass. There is a general confession of sins, with absolution, an *Introit, Kyrie, Gloria in Excelsis,* Collect, Epistle and Gradual (with the Alleluia in proper seasons), the Gospel and the Creed (either the Nicene or the Apostles Creed). Then a hymn precedes the sermon. Next there is the Offertory, with appropriate hymn or recitation, followed by the Prayer of the Church.

Then comes Thanksgiving. It has a Preface, appropriate to the season, the *Sanctus,* and the Words of Institution, with a preamble and following prayer which may vary from one church to another. In some rituals the Lord's Prayer precedes the Words of Institution; in others it follows. The doxology, "For thine is the kingdom, and the power, and the glory . . ." is sung or recited by the congregation after the minister has finished the Lord's Prayer.

Then there is the *Agnus Dei,* and Communion is received under both species: "When the Minister giveth the Bread he shall say; 'The Body of Christ, given for thee.' When he giveth the Cup he shall say: 'The Blood of Christ, shed for thee.' " And the communicant often says Amen after each Element has been received.

The Missouri-synod churches use a longer and more explicit form: "Take, eat; this is the true body of our Lord and Saviour Jesus Christ . . . . Take, drink; this is the true blood of our Lord and Saviour Jesus Christ, shed for the remission of your sins. May this strengthen and preserve you in the true faith unto life everlasting." There follows an appropriate thanksgiving, including the *Nunc Dimittis,* and the minister gives his blessing.

The Lutheran calendar has Propers of the Service for the Apostles and Evangelists, the Presentation of our Lord and his Transfiguration, and Annunciation and Visitation, for All Saints day, and Reformation day.

The great difference between the Lutheran Communion Service and our Mass is that their rite carefully omits any reference to Sacrifice. It commemorates the death of the Lord, but does not seek to perpetuate and apply the redemptive and sanctifying benefits of the Passion and Resurrection except through the sacrament of Holy Communion.

Similarity of rites can have little meaning without doctrinal agreement about the sacrificial nature of the Mass. And another great impediment to union results from the fact that we cannot recognize the ordination of Lutheran ministers.

The Anglican rite resembles our Mass more closely than the Lutheran service does, and not all references to sacrifice are eliminated. Allowing for variations of belief within the Anglican community, their doctrines about the sacrificial nature of the Mass, and the manner of the True Presence approach more closely than those of Lutherans to our Catholic teachings. There remain notable differences.

You and I must keep on praying, Robert, that still more changes may come, not only in the Roman Church but among all Christians; and we must be sure that our own minds are free of prejudice, and our hearts filled with love, which is the bond of union.

22

Why Should Different Churches Tell Me Different Things?

THE LETTER:

I guess you would call me an agnostic; I'm still searching. What I would like to know is this: How can one church tell me I am saved and another tell me I am lost?

I was raised by a weak-Catholic mother and an atheistic father. Grandma sneaked me out of the house when I was three months old, and had me baptized a Catholic. On her deathbed she made mother promise to follow through. Father permitted me to receive the sacraments because of his love for mother, although she never attended church with me.

At the age of 10 I received instructions at the Catholic school for a few weeks on my way home from public school. This was deemed sufficient 30 years ago for me to receive Communion and Confirmation. Frankly, since I received no further Catholic education, these sacraments meant little to me, especially since I seldom went to Church afterward.

Later I married a divorced Catholic, and now I am said to be "lost" because I betrayed the true faith. Yet, when I attend a Protestant service with friends, they invite me "down the aisle, to be saved" if I will only do one thing: believe in Christ.

Please tell me what is it all about? Am I lost because I am a "fallen-away Catholic" or will I be a "saved" Protestant if I do as they ask?

Mrs. D. Berryman

THE ANSWER:
By J.D. Conway

Whether you will be lost or saved, Mrs. Berryman, depends on the honesty of your own conscience and your fidelity in following it. Your conscience seems honest, but by your own admission it is neither clear nor certain in its dictates. You must keep on praying for grace. How can I help you? Should I tell you to give up your marriage, learn the religion of your Baptism, and return to the sacraments? I think this righteous admonition would only alienate you.

You received the gift of faith in Baptism; it was nourished by Holy Communion, and you became a witness to it in Confirmation. But you were not instructed properly so that your faith might face the problems of life. This is not your fault, but I have to face it to answer your question.

I would first recommend that you and your husband consult a priest to see if there is a solution to this matrimonial problem that could permit your proper marriage in the Church. The way to faith could become easy for you if this enormous block can be removed.

Next, do not be fooled by the invitation to go "down the aisle, to be saved." Salvation is not that easy. You qualify because you must believe in Christ. If you went down that aisle as an agnostic, you would remain an agnostic. Your walk would be more than meaningless, it would be untrue.

If you get that faith in Christ, have you any idea of its implications? If your new faith is merely an acceptance of Jesus as your personal Saviour, it will have even less influence on you than your Baptism. It would be only a spiritual tranquilizer, lulling your worries. Christ is, indeed, your personal Saviour, but your acceptance of Him should mean a thorough commitment to Him.

If you are to believe in Christ, you must also believe in the Father who sent Him. You must accept the teachings of the Old Testament which prepared the way for the coming of the Messiah: that the Lord alone is God, and we must be his people; that man is sinful and needs redemption; that God's law must be fulfilled.

Belief in Christ means that we accept what He told us about the Father; that the Father sent Him to save us and to teach us all things needed for our life in union with God, here on earth and hereafter in heaven. Jesus is the Word of God; He came to revel God to us by his words and actions, by his life, death, and resurrection.

One who believes in Christ must accept his claim to be one with God the Father. He must believe what He said about Himself, and what the Father said about Him through his miracles and his resurrection.

If we believe in Christ, we must make the paradoxes of

his Sermon on the Mount, his teachings about humility and forgiveness, poverty and suffering, prayer and fasting, love and penance part of our lives. We must believe in the fatherhood of God, and the brotherhood of men.

You cannot believe in Christ until you know the history of his selection and training of the Apostles, his commission to them to announce the Good News to all men, to baptize, to forgive sins, and to "do this in the commemoration of Me." If you believe in Christ, you cannot ignore his words to Peter: "Thou art Peter, and on this rock I will build my Church and the gates of hell shall not prevail against it." Belief in Christ includes you and me and his presence and activity in the mystery of his Church.

It is not complete unless we accept the mystery of his sanctifying activity in his flock, by his word and his deeds. His word is found in Scripture, in his preachings of the Apostles' successors, and the example of his brothers one to another. His deeds are in the active mysteries of his sacraments and his sacrifice: effective signs of our union with Him.

My point, Mrs. Berryman, is that if you go down the aisle to be saved, you must go with faith in Christ. The partial faith of your youth was enough to sanctify you then, because you implicitly accepted Christ. But this implicit faith was not enough to carry you through the rugged realities of life. The belief in Christ now proposed to you is much less explicit than that which you once had. It will not transform your life, or commit you to Christ.

But it is not impossible for you to receive a gift of partial faith, implicitly complete, which could be the means of your sanctity. Your conscience will tell you whether joining a Protestant church, rather than returning to the religion of your youth, is prompted by your marital situation: an effort to escape the rigor of Catholic laws about divorce. You may be seeking an easy way into heaven.

Mrs. Berryman, what does your husband think about this? He is Catholic, too. You both are not completely out of the Church; you are still members, but not living in accordance with its teachings, and may not receive the sacraments. Your decision to join another church does not depend on him; but I am sure you are concerned.

The problem of divorce which keeps you from living an integral Catholic life has taken many people out of the Church. Only God knows what might have been the history of England if King Henry VIII had not divorced himself. Once two baptized persons are married and have lived together as husband and wife, only the death of one will sever their union.

This is firm, constant Catholic teaching, which conforms to the teaching of Christ. In particular cases, like your own, we may only hopelessly wish there were some way to change it. The choices are difficult: be heroic, or continue to face sin and dangers to salvation. Some wait the problem out, hoping that Providence will find a solution, or that they may be finally repentant.

23

Should I Follow My Family's Religion?

THE LETTER:

Yours is the richest magazine I have encountered in a long time. It's very interesting and instructive. Our Catholic neighbors give it to us when they are through with it, and then I take it to my Catholic girlfriend in Rockford. I am a Lutheran.

I am a young mother of two sons. For several years, I have been deeply interested in the Catholic Church. I have read quite a few books and completed the course of instruction offered by the Knights of Columbus. While some doubts remain, mainly about the office of the Pope and infallibility, I believe I would convert, were I responsible only to myself.

But I am not responsible to myself alone. I come from a very anti-Catholic family and married into an even stronger one. My husband would permit me to convert, but would not allow our children to be brought up as Catholics. Both sets of parents would go up in smoke, and as my husband works together daily with his father, he feels this would greatly hamper even their business relationship.

My question is this: With all these considerations, am I committing a sin in postponing a decision to become a

Catholic? It might even be that I would have to wait until
my children are grown and their grandparents are dead. I
always thought freedom of religion was guaranteed in
America but I don't feel very "free" at this point.

Mrs. T.

THE ANSWER:
By J.D. Conway

Your problem is difficult, Mrs. T. It is easier to offer
sympathy than to solve it. Your dilemma shows how hard
it is to be truly free amid the complex duties and relationships of our society.

It would be easy to criticize your parents, your husband,
and his parents for their prejudice, intolerance, and selfish
restriction of your freedom. But that would be unfair, because I know that, if they were all Catholics and you
wished to give up the Catholic Church and become Lutheran, their objections would be just as strong.

As I write, the 2nd Vatican Council is preparing to de-
bate and vote on a declaration of religious liberty that will
define the right of all men to practice their religious convictions without interference from governments. Faith is by its
very nature a free act of the individual. If anyone tried to
force faith upon you, he violates the meaning of faith.

It has always been a Christian teaching that each person
has a right and a duty to follow the dictates of his own
conscience. He is obliged to study God's teachings carefully, to seek guidance humbly, and to strive for a right
understanding of truth and goodness. But no one has a
right to force him to worship God in a way he honestly
considers to be wrong, or to prevent him from worshipping
God in the way he is convinced is right. Christian history
has seldom seen these principles applied logically. Catholic
or Protestant, Arian or Orthodox, our zeal for truth has
blinded our respect for the honest conscience. We have
tended to make heresy a crime, to stamp out error by
force, and to restrict religious freedom by law.

More recently we came to take pride in our Christian
tolerance, a broad-minded attitude of putting up with
things we know are wrong. But tolerance is a matter of
tactics rather than of principle. It is a gesture of love, but it

does not express the love of the Christian who has genuine respect for conscience. Tolerance is being replaced by an honest conviction that freedom of faith and worship is a right of every person. This new conviction implies no indifference to conversation to the Catholic Church. It means rather that our methods will be only sensible persuasion, example and prayer. The greater our reverence for the true faith, the more we must insist that those who embrace it be free.

Respect for freedom, reverence for a man's right and duty to carry out God's will according to his own conscience, should be the official law of every land and the honest attitude of human society. If this attitude were now prevailing, Mrs. T., you would have no personal problems. We are still a long way from practical esteem for freedom of conscience. The interference of government with religion is rapidly disappearing, but social conventions affecting conscience are still with us. Soren Kierkegaard claimed that in many ways a faulty faith held firmly was better than the true faith maintained by social convention.

Even if social conventions were to set you free, Mrs. T., you would still face a problem about your children. When you become a Catholic, it might weigh heavily on your convictions to have them educated outside the Church. But here you would need to respect your husband's conscience. His convictions would be equally perturbed if you tried to raise them Catholics. This conflict is not one of conventional pressures but of two consciences, each sincere. With honest and general cooperation, the two of you should be able to teach your children sound religious truths and guide them in Christian morality without causing confusion in their growing minds. If they are committed to Lutheran belief and practice, you could avoid any undue efforts to change their position.

Some Catholics may wonder at what I say compared to our teachings about the duties of the Catholic party in a mixed marriage. But there is a great difference: A mixed marriage begins with agreement between husband and wife regarding the religious education of their children. Your marriage began with an understanding that your children would be raised Lutheran. If you become a Catholic, you are not free to disregard the rights of your husband or to confuse the tender consciences of your children.

You live in a real situation with people as they are. Your

efforts to change their attitudes would be futile. They are not ready for new ideas; they are prepared rather to "go up in smoke." A theorist might tell you that when conscience points the way, you must follow that way promptly. But in a concrete situation we must weigh all the factors. Obligations can conflict. Conscience points in several directions, and religious prudence must seek a practical road. This statement is not situation ethics. It is an effort to apply sound principles in a practical manner to a complex situation. It advocates the careful meandering required to get out of a maze.

You have obligations to your husband and children, duties to your parents and to his. A mature person need not delay an important religious decision because of duties to parents. The children alone are not reason to postpone your becoming a Catholic, nor should the duties of husband or wife prevent one from embracing the religion which conscience requires. But when you entangle all these obligations into your own special maze, there seems to be no direct way out.

You may not create family conflicts that will threaten the happiness and stability of your marriage. You may not induce tensions that will endanger the welfare and education of your children. It may be that your husband's fears about his business relationship are exaggerated, but you must seriously consider your family's security.

My rationalizing may remind you of the Parable of the man who invited guests to his supper and found them offering various excuses: one his farm, another his oxen, and a third his wife. But you are not refusing the Lord's invitations; you are only delaying your acceptance of it, and you are delaying for reasons that meet with his approval: your duties as wife and mother.

However, your delay should be as brief as possible, and you should continue to study. You can pray fervently for faith and for God's help in solving your problems. It should be possible for you to assist at Mass on special occasions. You may be able to take part in Catholic social or parish activities, making Catholic friends and growing in your understanding of the religion.

In this way, without sudden conflict, your family will be gradually prepared for the step you plan to take, while you become more sure of your own decision. And as your intention becomes familiar to husband and parents, it may be that opposition will weaken and respect for your conscience will grow.

I am giving you all this advice without having had much experience in helping young people. Often university students face problems of violent parental opposition to their becoming Catholics. They seldom heed advice to go slowly. Their youthful zeal sometimes leads them to give up home, support, and inheritance, rather than renounce the demands of their conscience.

But youthful problems are simple compared to yours, Mrs. T. If the young people persevered, reconciliation usually resulted; most parents learn to accept the accomplished fact. While you might not worry about the opposition of your parents, you cannot fail in concern for your husband and children.

The delay of commitment is traditionally in bad repute in the Church. In early centuries of Christianity, cathechumens delayed their Baptism, often waiting until they were in danger of death. The Emperor Constantine was a notable example. These early converts wanted to delay their forgiveness until all their sinning was finished. For obvious reasons Church authorities opposed this practice until it was finally eliminated

Your delay, Mrs. T., is entirely different. You are already baptized, and when your Catholic faith is firm you can profess it quietly but effectively before God and confide it to your trusted friends. It is only public profession and practice that you delay for family reasons. And your delay is only for as long as family duties demand.

24

What Good Has Christianity Ever Done the World?

THE LETTER:

From the Jewish standpoint, the Messiah is yet to come. From the Catholic standpoint, the Messiah came in the person of Jesus Christ. Is there persuasive evidence that people are any "better" today, morally and spiritually, than people were 2,000 or 2,500 years ago?

What difference has it really made in the world that the Messiah came?

Samuel Rabinove

THE ANSWER:
By J.D. Conway

I had better start with the word *Messiah*. It is derived from a Hebrew word that means "anointed." It has the same meaning as the word *Christ*, which comes from the Greek. In the Old Testament the name *messiah* was given to many prophets, patriarchs, priests and kings: the anointed of the Lord. But in the later centuries of Jewish history it came to designate a great savior of their nation, a king of the house of David, who would restore the kingdom of Israel, liberate the Jewish people, and inaugurate the messianic age.

The rabbis often referred to this golden age as the reign of God or the kingdom of heaven. The Messiah was expected to set up a new heaven and a new earth, distinct from the existing order. In the new era God would manifest Himself in a startling manner and establish his dominion over the world. The Jewish nation would become a perfect theocracy. Men would be faithful to God and live in great sanctity and happiness. The Jewish nation would be the first to benefit from the messianic kingdom; the chosen people would then spread the benefits to other nations. In the messianic kingdom the people would be holy, happy, secure, and closely united to God. They would lead long lives in peace and harmony and would never be sick; they would become too numerous to count, and would enjoy all the riches of the earth. The harvests would be abundant; Palestine would be a paradise. The moon would be as bright as the sun is now; but the sun would become seven times more brilliant.

At the time of Jesus the kingdom of heaven was expected to come soon, but not to bring complete happiness here on earth, since man's true destiny was in the world to come. But the messianic age would see Israel triumph as a nation: the rule of the true God would be established, the Roman empire would be vanquished, false gods with their idols done away with.

In judging the messianic role, Samuel, we must keep it in mind that Jesus said his kingdom is not of this world. He did not come to bring paradise to earth, but to prepare man for heaven. In Him the messianic prophecies were fulfilled, but in such manner that the prophets themselves might not have recognized Him. He disappointed both popular and rabbinical notions of the Messiah.

However, I cannot evade your question, Samuel, by appealing to the spiritual nature of the kingdom established by Jesus Christ. Matter and spirit in man are united during his life on earth. He is redeemed and sanctified in this world. While the Christian's gaze has been fixed on heaven, he must sanctify himself by contributing to the sanctity of the world. The kingdom of Jesus the Messiah is not of this world, but it is in this world, and we rightly expect to find its effect on this world.

Morality, culture, and civilization are relative things; the perfect society exists only in dreams. Redeemed man keeps his nature weakened by original sin. The evidence of moral and spiritual gains resulting from Christianity is offset by the failings and scandals found in the Christian community.

We find evidence of the Messiah's presence in the brotherly love of the early Christian community, in the courage and sacrifice of martyrs, in the dedicated zeal of missioners, in the prayerful peace of monasteries and the generous service of other Religious Orders, in the multiple works of charity which have abounded in most ages, in the civilizing influences exerted on barbarians, and in Christian contributions to education, culture, and the arts.

We believe that the messianic influence is seen in these accomplishments, even while it is obscured by our tolerance of social evils and our intolerance of religious differences, by the straying zeal of crusaders and the cruelty of Inquisitors, by the worldly ambitions and ostentation of many prelates, the greed and ignorance of many clerics, and the constant wars of Christian kings.

You may rightly demand that the messianic influence show itself beyond the "chosen people." The entire world of today should be better because the Messiah has come; and I am convinced that it is better morally and spiritually as well as materially. And I say this without trying to cover up the obvious mess we are in.

Look back 2000 years! Slavery was an accepted social institution; today it is known only in one isolated nation or another, and it shocks the conscience of modern man. Despotic rulers and arbitrary judges were the general rule; today they still exist in some areas, but violate the moral sensibilities of most of the world. Human rights were hardly known; today they are formally recognized and increasingly respected. National freedom and autonomy are the modern ideal, replacing the glories of the empire. Social injustices are still rampant; yet many have been eliminated, and others cause us grave concern. Who worried about such things in the time of Caesar?

Today we are conscious of the solidarity of the human race, have formally declared the equality of all men, and are striving in an awkward way for peace. Such notions would have been foolish 2000 years ago. We have feelings of guilt today because we fall short of our ideals. In ancient times the ideals did not exist. Today standards of business ethics have been established, which, faulty though they be, are better than the anarchy which once ruled the market place.

The rule of law is the most notable characteristic of modern life. The ancient Greeks and Romans were interested in the law, but they were more concerned for order than for rights and freedom. Our great deficiency is the absence of an effective, enforceable international law; and it is a sign of our moral maturity that the development of such law is the concern of many nations.

Modern men have developed new kinds of courage in the air, in outer space, and deep under the sea. Ancient sailors were intrepid; early warriors were brave; but none of them would have dared what modern heroes accomplish with routine virtue.

In praising modern man we know that evidence to the contrary is often spectacular. We moderns sin in a big way and the glare of publicity is on us. Hitler's crematories broke world records for pogroms. Atom bombs make the ancient religious wars of total destruction seem like child's play. Our pornography rolls off the presses by the ton. Our racial discrimination is practiced in full view of the world. The defects of our legal system in apprehending and convicting racial murderers are glaring. Our racial riots are dreadful. Our juvenile delinquency is phenomenal. Television is our tutor, the Beatles our artistic norm. But we have a strong tendency to know our faults and deplore them. We aim to be honest. Even if you grant that there has been improvement, morally and spiritually, in the world generally, you may still ask how much of this can be attributed to the Messiah, and how much is the result of man's natural evolution or the work of social reformers without Christian inspiration.

Again my answer can be only comparative. Has advancement been greater in Christian nations than in other areas of the world? If so, can this progress be attributed to the spirit and teaching of Christ, to his moral example, his grace, his active presence in the world, and the zeal and example of the Christian people? Were I to assert flatly that Christian people have led the world in moral and spiritual growth for nearly 20 centuries, I would surely be accused of prejudice. We have no monopoly of truth or morality.

And yet I believe that a strong case can be made for the leadership of Christianity in the moral and spiritual growth of the world. It is not a case that can be made by facile arguments in a brief article; it requires profound study, complete honesty, and frank dialogue. We must not equate Western civilization with Christianity; the two have lived and grown in tension and conflict as often as in mutual support.

By his faith the Christian is aware of God's presence and is impressed by his pervading goodness. Divine love is the source of Christian activity and the goal of its striving. From the example and teaching of Jesus we learn the dignity of man; the love which is due our neighbor as a brother; the universality of the Redemption and the solidarity of the human race; the authentic freedom of grace and the equality of all men before God; respect for justice and law; and the necessity of sound virtue in our personal lives.

It seems hardly possible that a man can live with such ideals, principles, and motivations without exerting influence on the society of which he is part. Not all Christians are authentic, and few approach perfection, but the traces of sanctity must be discoverable. The message taught by Jesus Christ was focused on personal morality and sanctity; He taught social justice only as love of neighbor. During most of its history the Christian message has emphasized personal perfection and eternal salvation. We must give due emphasis to this in judging the success of the messianic mission. Its primary purpose is to bring men to life in heaven. But the perfection on this earth of God's kingdom cannot be ignored.

In the medieval days of Christendom the Church had keen but faulty awareness of its social mission. During the past 75 years Christians have become increasingly conscious of their duty to sanctify the world, of the enormity of social and economic problems, and of the glaring truth that personal faith and morality give little aid in solving these problems, but on the contrary may easily be engulfed in the morass of them.

As Christianity becomes more relevant to the modern world, Samuel, we can expect the temporal glories of the messianic kingdom to become more like those in the visions of the prophets.

25

Why Not Trim Our Dogmas to Achieve Unity?

THE LETTER:

As a Lutheran (and an ecumenist), I believe that in both my church and yours the way we use creed and dogma is doing the cause of oneness in Christ a disservice. That is, we make the acceptance of them a condition of membership in the Church.

The unfathomable riches of Christ should not be confined to the niceties and precisions of word formulas. For example, concerning the centuries-old confusion over trinity and unity, it seems to me that if we used the word *aspects* or *manifestations* for *persons,* many of our intellectual problems in these concepts might be solved. Thomas Merton has expressed his thoughts on the Trinity: that God is the Father, Christ is God's idea of Himself, the Holy Spirit is the love between the two. What I would ask of the Church is the freedom to think creatively in this way.

Let us draw all men to Christ through our love for Him,

the measure of our love to be shown by the boundlessness of our giving to Him of the resources (time, money, talents; mind, heart, soul), bestowed on us by the grace of God. Not through the exaction of a formula of words which are, after all, human tools confounded by the mysteries of time and space and, even at their most exalted best, inadquate to express the inexplicable grandeur of the Godhead. This is my question: Just how much creed must the Church insist that all Christians agree on? Can we not safely minimize the dogma so as to maximize the love?

Bob Bergh

THE ANSWER:
By J.D Conway

I am an ecumenist too, Bob, but I cannot agree with your proposal that we discount doctrinal differences to attain unity. I do agree that our love for Christ and for our brethren is supremely important because it provides the motive which urges us toward unity. But we can never truly love Christ while we consider his revelation unimportant; and we cannot fully love our neighbor if we are unconcerned about his lack of faith.

There can be no true and complete unity in Christ until we know Christ as He really is. The goal of ecumenism is reunion in both faith and love. Doctrine is important because it is truth, and love which is not based on truth will hardly endure.

We cannot minimize doctrine, but neither should we maximize it. For instance, we Catholics must not demand for our reunion with Protestants a greater unity of dogma than that which actually exists among the Catholics of various nations, cultures, and educational levels. If we follow this norm, we have considerable room for diversity. All Catholics say the same creed, but not all understand the teachings of the Church in the same way. Very often the faith that unites them is only implicit about some doctrines, and is muddled or distorted regarding others.

Consider your own case, Bob. You are a Lutheran, living in corporate unity with other Lutherans; yet few of the Lutherans I know would approve of your attitude about doctrine. Certainly Martin Luther would not.

The average Catholic and the average Lutheran today have little accurate knowledge of the doctrinal causes of our initial separation. But there is no need for average laymen to review them. They should rather seek the positive truths of Jesus Christ as we may be able to understand them today. We need not retrace the steps of division on our road to reunion.

So I agree with you, Bob, that we should not deliberately stir up new doctrinal problems by hair-splitting distinctions. We should rather look for the simple Gospel truths in our common Christian tradition. We should also keep in mind that the average Catholic and the average Protestant are kept apart less by doctrine than by external things like rituals and popular pieties, or by traditional attitudes and prejudices. Unless a Lutheran is well-educated, he is less concerned about the manner of justification than about indulgences, the Mass, the Pope, and the Rosary. And a Catholic of ordinary education is repelled by his image of Martin Luther, a married clergy, and two instead of seven sacraments.

We must admit that in the course of four centuries of separation we have developed doctrinal differences more difficult than justification. But recently we find oursevles coming closer on many points, like the meaning of the Mass, the role of Sacred Scripture, and the nature of faith.

And we must always be encouraged by the vast fund of basic doctrine we have in common. We believe in the same God, Father, Son, and Holy Spirit; in the same Lord and Saviour, Jesus Christ; in our redemption through his death and resurrection; in Baptism, and the true presence of Jesus in the Eucharist; in the inspired revelation of the Scriptures; in sanctification by God's grace; in the ten Commandments; and life after death. We say together the Apostles' Creed and the Nicene Creed.

The great mysteries, Bob, which you invite us to think and ponder and love, are for traditional Christians a sacred heritage on which they already agree. The Trinity, the divinity of Christ, and his incarnation are doctrines which our common ancestors, the Christians of the first five centuries, attained with much difficulty and conflict under the guidance of the Holy Spirit. In our efforts toward Christian unity we must keep truth and love in proper balance. We must not let our zeal for doctrinal integrity destroy the bond of love which should unite all of us to Jesus Christ and each of us to the other. And we must not allow our love to urge us to a compromise with truth, so as to bring us only a semblance of unity. I am certain, Bob, that you are familiar with the Decree on Ecumenism given us by the 2nd Vatican Council. It is one of the most inspiring of all the Council documents, the Catholic's charter for ecumenical hopes and activities. It points up the change in attitude required for those who would seek unity.

Our basic preparation for unity requires a change of heart and a sound holiness of life. There must be a recognition, admission and reform of human defects in the Church, and a continual reform of our individual lives. We must have humility and honesty to recognize our faults and those of our ancestors in the faith, to admit that we do not have all the truth in its fullness, nor others all the errors. We must frankly admit that we have distorted history and doctrine in the cause of polemics. Naturally we do not assume all the blame for our separation, but we must pardon the faults of others, even as we ask pardon for our own.

From the beginning of our ecumenical efforts we must be aware of our shortcomings and our limited abilities to achieve our goal. We can never reach unity by our own efforts; we can only strive, with God's grace, to conform ourselves to his will, offer our activities to Him, and let Him produce the results. That which is impossible for us He can do with ease. But He never forces our will. We must really desire unity or it will never be given to us. God does not will separation, but He permits it when we will it; and He knows how to derive good from it.

We will heartily desire unity once we recognize the sin and scandal of disunity: the false witness it causes us to give to Christ, and the harm it does to men, both Christian and non-Christian. We must clearly understand unity as the desire of Christ and the goal of his fervent prayer: "that they may all be one . . . so that the world may believe that Thou hast sent Me . . . that they may be one even as We are one, I in them and Thou in Me, that they may become perfectly one."

Only when we have these attitudes and convictions may we hope to engage fruitfully in ecumenical activities. But our first activity should still be prayer: public and private prayer for unity, sometimes separate prayer by each denomination, sometimes common prayer together. But we must always be honest about our prayers together, never pretending. Common worship implies unity; so we should seldom go further with it than the truth of our separation indicates. But there are times when our common prayer clearly indicates not unity achieved but unity desired. And when the desire for unity is true, we may worship together to obtain the graces we need for love and understanding.

As a result of our prayer we should receive the guiding and inspiring virtue of ecumenism, which is love. Its first effect is to eliminate our traditional hatreds, suspicions, and prejudices, our vituperative name-calling, our hostile polemics, and our dishonest arguments. Instead of devoting all our efforts to prove others wrong, charity prompts us to see all that is right with them, all that we have in common with them, all we can learn from them.

Now we are ready for dialogue: an honest, forthright exchange which should lead us to mutual understanding and respect, even when it does not lead to agreement. The dialogue is primarily a tool for theologians, but it can also be used in the layman's living room provided we keep ourselves well informed and do not go beyond our depth. It can help us to understand each other, our history, beliefs, practices, spirituality, and sincerity.

Our next step in ecumenism is our united witness before the world by our cooperative action in social work, race problems, community projects, education, relief, aid, justice, and charity, all inspired by the Gospel.

In all our common worship, our dialogue, and our common enterprises we must all personally seek to lead holier lives. There must be no watering down of doctrine, no false irenicism, and no dishonesty. Where differences are real we must face them frankly. We must accept our separation, at least temporarily, and learn how God wants us to live with it.

Each of these ecumenical steps produces greater unity. We are one in prayer, up to a point. We are one in the harmony and honesty of our dialogue. We are one in our manifestation of Christ's charity to the world, united in the works we do for love of Him, as we see Him in the person of his brother. Thus we hope gradually to come closer in doctrinal belief, as our dialogue leads us to better understanding of each other and of God's revealed word.

In many respects religious unity is a relative thing: we never expect or wish it to become rigid uniformity. The present unity of the Catholic Church allows for a variety of rites and languages, various popular beliefs, fantasies and devotions, divergencies in philosophy and theology, and some room for both credulity and rationalism. Many popular notions would be heresy if held by a theologian.

At what point can we say we are fully united, as Christ prayed we would be? Certainly there must be an acceptance of the Church of Christ in its essential features: a basic measure of organizational unity. There must be acceptance of all essential doctrines, and substantial agreement regarding morality. We must be able to participate in a common worship; have one priesthood which we share with Jesus; an effective remembrance of his sacrifice; and sanctifying encounter with Him in the sacraments, especially in the reality of the Eucharist.

In doubtful matters, and in those which are less than essential, great liberty may be allowed. A married priesthood, a shortened, simplified liturgy; austere churches devoid of statuary; Communion under both kinds, using leavened bread, and a wide choice in private devotions—all are possible, and only careful theological study and dialogue will tell us how much latitude may be permitted in other matters, like private auricular Confession.

Possibly the greatest diversity ever tolerated without breaking the bonds of unity was between the Churches of the East and the West regarding divorce. During the 16th century various Churches of the East were seeking union with Rome; some of them achieved it then and others later, but for a long time they retained their ancient custom of permitting divorce for reason of adultery. And the Fathers of the Council of Trent in defending the Roman Church's opposition to divorce framed their statement with great care lest they alienate their brethren of the East on this point.

Churches of East and West long remained united despite their disagreement about purgatory, and the procession of the Holy Spirit from the Father and the Son.

These examples of historical tolerances may indicate the limits within which it is possible to "minimize dogma," though I dislike that expression and would rather say "tolerate differences." There are no limits to maximizing love, Bob, as long as it is honest and true.

26

What Have You Got Against the Masons?

THE LETTER:

I would like to know why the Catholic Church does not accept the Masons. All I've ever been able to find out is it's something to do with a secret the Masons have. This is rather vague and I know there must be more to it.

Esther Rosenfeld

THE ANSWER:
By J.D. Conway

In a quick count I find 17 papal condemnations of Freemasonry, made by eight Popes, in various encyclicals, bulls, allocutions, and apostolic constitutions. Our present canon law states that those who enroll in Masonic sects or other associations of the same kind, which plot against the Church or legitimate civil powers, incur automatic excommunication reserved to the Holy See. If they died without repentance they are denied Catholic burial. If a cleric were to join the Masons he would be suspended, deprived of his office or benefice, and of any dignity, duty, or pension he might have in the Church.

The first paper condemnation of Masonry was made by Pope Clement XII in 1738. He accused it of naturalism which fostered religious indifferentism. He detected in it contempt for orthodoxy and for religious authority. And he objected to its inscrutable secrecy; its fallacious, everchanging disguise of its objectives and its "work"; and to the frightening oaths of secrecy and fidelity required of its members.

One of the strongest and most formal condemnations of Masonry was that made by Pope Leo XIII in 1884. This was a century and a half after the first condemnation, and during that time, on the continent of Europe, Masonry had become associated in the popular mind, and frequently in fact, with anticlericalism, liberalism, conspiracy, and revolution. At the time Pope Leo wrote, the 3rd Republic in France was only 14 years old, and it was strongly anticlerical. The Masons were given much credit for its establishment. Since 1880 it had suppressed the Jesuits, established free secular education, made civil marriage compulsory, and permitted divorce. Unified Italy, with Rome as its capital, had existed only 14 years; and the Popes were convinced that the Masons and their blood brothers, the Carbonari, were instrumental in stealing the Papal States from them, making them prisoners in the Vatican.

During the same 14 years Spain had undergone Civil wars in which atrocities had been committed by both clericals and anticlericals. There had been a short-lived Spanish republic which enacted anticlerical laws. Socialists, syndicalists, and anarchists were rampant. And the Masons were involved in much of this.

Anticlericalism was rife in Austria-Hungary, where the state had taken charge of seminary education and even of religious worship. The Kulturkampf had produced violent attacks on the Church in Germany, along with much anticlerical legislation, including the banning of the Jesuits. Again, Masons were blamed.

Socialism and secularism were seen as the great dangers of the times, threatening established social structures as well as Christian institutions. Liberalism and egalitarianism were associated evils. And with all of them Masonry was identified in the popular mind.

Just the year before Leo XIII became Pope, the Grand Orient, the supreme Masonic authority in France, abolished belief in God as a requirement of membership. This caused the United Grand Lodge of England and nearly all the Grand Lodges in the United States to break fellowship with the Grand Orient, but to the Pope it was evidence that Masonry was passing beyond its anticlericalism towards atheism.

Pope Leo first denounced Masonry for its secrecy, its severe discipline, and the slavish obedience demanded of its members. He said its main secrets were known only to its leaders and masters, who used members as tools: "As a matter of fact, if any are judged to have betrayed the doings of the sect or to have resisted commands given, punishment is inflicted on them not infrequently, and with so much audacity and dexterity that the assassin very often escapes the detection and penalty of his crime."

Pope Leo wrote that Masonry sought to overthrow the whole religious and political order. It fostered naturalism, sought to destroy the authority of the Church, and to establish a lay state devoid of Church influence. It attacked with impunity the foundations of the Church, and was guilty of detailed crimes of anticlericalism, such as banning Religious Orders, and confiscating Church possessions. Masons do not make their members attack Catholic doctrine, but that is only a ruse by which they entice them in their plots, and deceive them.

The encyclical said that they intend to ruin all forms of religion. They no longer require that their members believe in the existence of God or the immortality of man's soul. They promote religious indifference, seek to destroy the foundations of justice and honesty, threaten both domestic and civil society, seek only to be independent and free. They would abolish Christian education and destroy sound morality. They exaggerate man's natural virtues, forgetting original sin. They are responsible for the many evils found in journals, pamphlets, drama and art, by which they offer people the blandishments of pleasure, seeking with set purpose to satiate the multitude and dominate them.

They back civil marriage and divorce, promote the Masonic education of youth, and advocate democracy in which power is held by the people, whereas true authority comes from God. They defend the equality of all men, trying to destroy every distinction of rank and property. They advocate a community of goods, approve sedition, and delude the people by flattery. The Pope explicitly attributed to Masonry many of the doctrines and machinations of socialism and communism.

This is merely a summary of the Pope's indictments, and many of them were true as applied to the Freemasonry on the continent of Europe during the revolutionary turmoil of the 19th century.

To an English or American Freemason such charges are utterly ridiculous. The Masonry they know is nothing like that at all. They know Freemasonry as a fraternal organization which exists primarily for fellowship, benevolence, and mutual assistance. Since it accepts members from all religious groups, and does not require them to reject any denominational allegiance or belief, it restricts its own religious philosophy to fundamentals: a belief in God, the Grand Architect of the Universe; a life after death; and a sound morality that emphasizes justice, truth, and fraternal charity. In its rituals it seeks to inculcate the truths of such basic religion and morality by allegories and symbols based on the art of building and its tools, e.g., the compass, the square, and the plumb line. And, of course, it has secret signs, passwords, and handgrips.

Most fraternal organizations require members to take an oath to keep secret their rituals of initiation, private lodge business, passwords, and the like. But the oaths taken by the Masons are of fantastic severity, presumably borrowed from medieval formulas, or contrived to simulate ancient oaths. They are mostly spoofs, of course. As an example, here is an excerpt from the oath by which an Entered Apprentice binds himself before God: "All this I most solemnly, sincerely promise and swear, with a firm, and steadfast resolution to perform the same, without any mental reservation or secret evasion of mind whatever, binding myself under no less penalty than that of having my throat cut across, my tongue torn out by its roots, and my body buried in the rough sands of the sea, at low-water mark, where the tide ebbs and flows twice in 24 hours . . . ."

Modern Freemasonry traces its origins back to medieval guilds of masons, and especially to those of superior skill who worked in stone doing ornamental work. Their enemies were the cowans—masons who had never served a proper apprenticeship and did not even know how to use mortar in laying their stone. Many of their passwords and hand grips were used to keep cowans out of their lodges.

By the 17th century guilds of operative masons were dying out, and they began to accept honorary members, often men of some dignity or wealth, who were not masons. These were *accepted* masons, whence the name "Free and Accepted Masons"—F. & A. M.—so widely known in this country.

Freemasonry in the modern speculative sense had its origin in England in 1717, when four lodges in the London area, accustomed to meet in pubs, got together and formed a grand lodge. It spread through the world rapidly. It very quickly came to the United States, where is now has some 4 million members with a grand lodge in every state. It has three degrees: Entered Apprentice, Fellow Craft, and Master Mason, each with its own ritual of initiation, its charges, oaths, and passwords.

Speculative Masons did not remain content with the symbols and degrees derived from the craft of masonry. Almost from the beginning there was a Royal Arch degree which was a superstructure of Masonry, and during the 18th century many other degrees were developed. In the United States we have two distinct systems of higher degrees, built on Masonry: the York Rite, of which the highest degree is Knights Templar, and the Scottish Rite, which has a 32nd degree, with a 33rd conferred as an honorary degree. Both the Knights Templar and 32nd Degree Masons are eligible for membership in the Ancient Arabic Order of Nobles of the Mystic Shrine.

Other groups associated with the Masons are the Red Cross of Constantine, whose members are Royal Arch Masons; the Mystic Order of Veiled Prophets of the Enchanted Realm and the Tall Cedars of Lebanon, open to all Master Masons; the Order of DeMolay for boys; the Order of Job's Daughters for girls; the International Order of the Eastern Star; and many others.

The Masons have added to their basic masonic traditions and legends a wide variety of rituals, symbols, and legends by which they got involved with Noah's ark and the Egyptian pyramids; Solomon's temple and medieval cathedrals; Jehovah, Mohammed, and Baal; the Crusades, and the avowed enemies of the Crusaders.

It seems to be mostly in fun, though there is some serious emphasis on the lessons taught by the symbolism of the degrees. There is considerable religious ritual in degrees like that of the Rose Croix and the Knights Templar. It is noteworthy that the Popes in their condemnations refer to the Masons as a sect, the word used for non-Catholic religious groups. Yet it is a basic and well observed rule of Masonry in the United States that there must be no discussion of politics or religion in their lodges.

The only evidence of anti-Catholicism exhibited by Masons in America is that inveterate and virulent bigotry displayed by the southern jurisdiction of the Scottish Rite in its official publication the *New Age*. Freemasons generally, including the northern jurisdiction of the Scottish Rite, are friendly toward Catholics, and would like to reach a better understanding with them.

In these days of ecumenism there is great need for an honest, friendly dialogue between Catholics and Masons. It is evident that most of the reasons given by Leo XIII for condemning Masonry have no application at all today, at least in America and England. Honesty, justice, and Christian charity demand that we Catholics cease propagating calumnies, enmities, and misunderstandings.

IV

Questions About Catholic Practices

The largest group of questions was inspired by curiosity about Catholic practices that seemed queer, unreasonable or even antireligious to persons who had never before investigated them.

27

Is the "Infant of Prague" One of Your Idols?

THE LETTER:

My place of business was formerly owned by Catholics and, even after six years, I still receive Catholic literature addressed to the business. One of these contained offers of a statue of the Infant Jesus of Prague. To a non-Catholic like me this seems to be the worship of idols, pure and simple!

A Catholic employee could not explain this to my satisfaction and suggested that I write to you, especially as most of my Protestant friends feel the same way about this.

Ralph W. Shelton

THE LETTER:
By J.D. Conway

For various reasons which I will discuss later, Ralph, I am not enthusiastic about the popular devotion to the Infant of Prague, but we should not call it a worship of idols. My dictionary tells me that an idol is an image to which religious worship is given. But the statue of the Infant of Prague is not given worship for itself. Our worship is directed to the Child Jesus whom the statue represents. The Child Jesus was a divine person: God become man. Child is proper: it is the worship of God Himself—the Second Person of the Trinity in his human nature.

Catholics are generally well conditioned to the use of statues, pictures, relics, and the like. We may sometimes suspect a bit of superstition in the simple devotions of uneducated people, but it is possible that we judge them unfairly. Our theological knowledge is quite abstract: their devotions are concrete and confident. They know well that there is no divine power in their statue.

155

For centuries Catholic people have been taught the doctrine which the Psalmist expressed so well ages ago:

The idols of the gentiles are silver and gold,
*   the works of human hands:*
They have a mouth but do not speak,
*   they have eyes but do not see;*
They have ears and do not hear,
*   and there is no breath in their mouth.*
Those who make them become just like them
*   and so does everyone who trusts in them.*

The original statue of the Infant of Prague is not made of silver or gold, however, but of wax. And its replicas are made of plaster, porcelain, wood, or stone, usually designed to sell quickly.

My brief research on this statue and the wide devotion it inspires has led me to no serious historian. However, I found a pamphlet with an 1898 imprimatur, still being sold. To me it seems unfortunate that it did not go out of print years ago. I do not recommend it to you, Ralph. It might not confirm your opinion that this devotion is idol worship pure and simple, but it would surely give you the notion that there is some silly superstition involved in it. The title of the pamphlet is *Devotion to the Miraculous Infant Jesus of Prague*. It is fittingly anonymous; and I will not name the publisher.

A more recent pamphlet, compiled in 1944 by Father John A. Kalvelage, C.SS.R., is better and briefer. A little bit of this sort of history suffices.

The story begins with a prelude involving Emperor Ferdinand II, staunch patron of Catholic causes in the 30 Years' War. In 1620 his army was victorious in the Battle of the White Mountain, near Prague, and he attributed his success to the special intervention of the Infant Jesus. We may doubt, however, that the divine Child approved the subsequent executions, banishments, and confiscations Ferdinand employed in ruthless efforts to stamp out Protestantism in Bohemia and reinstate the Counter-Reformation.

In 1624 the emperor established a Carmelite monastery at Prague. Shortly thereafter a princess, Polixena von Lobowitz, gave the monks a statue of the Infant Jesus, which her mother, a Spanish princess, had brought from Spain. It was an old family heirloom treasured as miraculous. Its miracles continued with a sort of childish jealousy. When the Community was devout in its veneration of the little wax image it was very prosperous. When its fervor declined the Community fell on hard times.

After Gustavus Adolphus of Sweden landed in Germany in 1630 the trend of the war changed. The Carmelites went from Prague to Munich, seeking safety. In 1631 a Saxon army invaded Bohemia, occupied Prague, put Protestant preachers in its pulpits, and proceeded to eliminate the emblems of "Popish superstition." The little wax statue was thrown on a heap of rubbish behind the altar, both hands broken off by its fall.

The monks returned, probably after Bohemia had been reconquered by the imperial forces in 1632, but they left the miraculous statue unnoticed on its rubbish heap. Seven years it lay there, "forgotten by all, maimed, and deprived of all honor." Meanwhile, of course, the poor Carmelites were struggling in poverty and misfortune. It was not until they had rescued the statue and restored its hands that prosperity returned.

It was not long until the restored statue became famous. Devotion to the Child Jesus spread through Bohemia and thence to other parts of Europe, and miracles were abundant. About 75 years ago this devotion began its wave of popularity in the United States.

That is the skeleton of the story, Ralph. Many of the details are less edifying, especially as told in my 1898 pamphlet.

I suppose you are familiar, in general, with the traditional fondness of Christians for statues, icons, and religious pictures. We find first evidence of it in the catacombs, and from those earliest Christian days until the 8th century the number, use, and veneration of holy images increased everywhere in the Church.

In the Byzantine churches of the East, flat pictures called icons were preferred. They became excessively numerous. Many of them were very good; some splendid examples are preserved to our own day, especially in mosaics. It is possible that superstitious abuses accompanied their veneration. In any case, the Byzantine emperors of the 8th century carried on a vicious campaign of iconoclasm: image smashing. It produced many martyrs and did great harm to religion. A General Council of the Church, 2nd Nicea, was called in 787 to settle the conflict. This Council affirmed the propriety of icons and their religious use, and brought peace for a while, but complete harmony was not restored for another half century. Today the Byzantine churches, both Catholic and Orthodox, still revere their icons; and each year they celebrate the feast of Orthodoxy to commemorate the final vindication of holy images.

The quarrel about icons spread to the West, where Charlemagne became an opponent of image worship. He may have had good reason for his attitude in that his Franks were recent converts from paganism, and might easily be led back to idolatry. Three centuries later Charlemagne's empire began a great tradition which was to produce some of the finest statues of Christendom.

Apart from the convulsions of iconoclasm, the popular use of pictures and statues in religion went without serious challenge until the time of John Calvin in the 16th century. His followers in England were known as Puritans, and they were grimly determined to purify the English Church of superstition, meaning all images and decorations—most of its beauty, in fact. Spartan prayer halls were often the result, and religion tended to become cold and forbidding.

True virtue is often midway between extremes. By all means we should keep statues, holy pictures, icons, and decorations in the measure that they make our churches beautiful, create an atmosphere conducive to prayer, and help us to concentrate on the realities of mystery and worship. But we must limit their number by good taste, determine their quality by sound artistic norms.

Charity should keep us from being Pharisaical in our criticisms of the devotions of our neighbors. Just because our education guides our religious thought, we should not be scornful of simple people whose love of God expresses itself in a manner so concrete that we might judge it crude. Their faith is sound, their confidence explicit, and their discernment probably much clearer than it seems to us.

Nevertheless, Ralph, at the risk of alienating many of my readers, I must tell you some of the reasons why the statue of the Infant of Prague and the popular devotion it inspires do not appeal to me.

First, I believe it distracts from the essentials of religion. To this there will be the objection: what could be more central than devotion to Jesus Christ, the Son of God? I can only agree, of course. But it is very important that our devotion encompass Jesus in his entirety: his divine personality, which provides our only reason for worshipping Him; his personal relationship to the Father, through the loving action of the Holy Spirit in us, his mission as Messiah and Redeemer, his human life on earth in its totality; and above all his death and resurrection; and finally his continuing life in his mystical Body, in such manner that He lives in each of us, and we live in Him. To me it seems that the statue of a sweet infant in regal clothing is poorly designed to lead us to all these mysteries.

Secondly, both the statue and the devotion are cloyingly sentimental. The statue is better designed to serve as a doll than as a religious symbol. The prayers in my pamphlets drip with saccharine, though I must give Father Kalvelage credit—he has eliminated the worst ones, and has substituted some acceptable Catholic prayers.

We are not sentimental when we love little children, but we are sentimental when we want to keep them childlike for life. The statue of the Infant of Prague centers our minds on Our Lord as a perpetual baby.

I have never seen the original statue, but if its multiple replicas do it justice, it is abominable art. Wax is hardly a medium for great art to begin with; it is better fitted to the exhibits of Mme. Tussaud.

Another of my objections to the statue is its royalist character, which has little pertinence to modern times and democratic nations. It may, if we stretch our imaginations, convey the idea that Christ is the King of heaven and earth. But it serves better the needs of aged girls who wish to play with dolls.

The sweet statue of a royal Infant was fine for Spanish princesses and appropriate for a monastery established by the Holy Roman Emperor. But what message does it have for Czech Communists, or for the modern atomic world and its plebeian problems?

I do not assert, though I do suspect, that the popularity of this devotion is much enmeshed in superstition. There is far too much stress on its miracles. Indeed, the full name of the statue is the Miraculous Infant Jesus of Prague. We all believe in miracles, but a devotion that is miracle-centered is not healthy. It should be mystery-centered, concentrated on the three Persons of the Trinity reaching out to redeem, adopt, and sanctify us; and on the Son who permits us to join Him in worship of the Father through the Holy Spirit.

Not only should true religion be mystery-centered, but it

should be pertinent to our life in the modern world. What does a sweet, royal infant show that he knows of sin and suffering, of war and tyranny, of race and rights and riots?

At best the Infant of Prague is a refuge from reality.

28

I Thought Only God Could "Make" Saints

THE LETTER:

A few days ago I read an article entitled "Move to Make Pope John a Saint" in the *Courier-Journal*, Louisville, Kentucky. Why does the Catholic Church go through the procedures of beautifying and canonizing? What good can it do? The Bible gives us nothing as to beatification or canonization of a person. How can anyone know whether or not a person is a saint? The days of miracles and healing were over when the Apostles died. Miracles that have taken place in the last 50 years are in science, such as wireless telegraphy, telephone, radio, TV, and many others.

The article also said, "The Rev. Pietro Bosio, parish priest in John's hometown, Sotto Il Monte, said there has been no Church-recognized miracle for John. But he said there were stories of a girl recovering her eyesight and an elderly man regaining health, both through prayer to the Pope." How can there be any proof of this? Many other persons, I am sure, prayed for the girl and the man. Many times we take some medicine for a minor ailment. We get well and think the medicine cured us, when we might have recovered without any medicine.

Nina Alice Bowmer

THE ANSWER:
By J.D. Conway

To give any kind of satisfying answer to your letter, Nina, we will have to start with a lot of background. Beatifications and canonizations result from popular devotion of the Christian people, not only from the decrees of Church authorities. In fact, the authorities, in general, restrain the enthusiasm of the people.

From the earliest centuries of our era the People of God showed great reverence for the martyrs. They honored them as heroes who had willingly suffered death rather than deny their faith in Christ. The courage of the martyrs gave inspiration to the Christians, who collected their relics, built altars over their tombs, and used the altars for the Sacrifice of the Mass. Prayers directed to the martyrs asked that they, as favorite children of the Father, pray for their brethren still on earth.

There was no thought of making gods of the martyrs. The Christians were simply giving honor to those who had attained the goal of all: union with the Saviour in his kingdom. In those early days the martyrs were often called confessors, because of the words of Jesus: "Whosoever therefore shall confess Me before men, him will I confess also before my Father in heaven." The faithful had no doubt that the Saviour was keeping his word: confessing the glorious martyr by presenting him to the Father in heaven.

As early as the 2nd century, Christians celebrated the anniversary of a martyr's death as a feast day. St. Polycarp suffered death for the faith at Smyrna, in Asia Minor, in the year 155. His local church wrote a circular letter to neighboring churches to let them know about it: "We have at last gathered his bones, which are dearer to us than priceless gems and purer than gold, and laid them to rest where it was befitting they should lie. And if it is possible for us to assemble again, may God grant us to celebrate the birthday of his martyrdom with gladness, thus to recall the memory of those who fought in the glorious combat, and to teach and strengthen, by his example, those who shall come after us."

By the end of the 3rd century the custom of celebrating feast days of martyrs was in vogue in the entire Church, with each community venerating its own heroes. But as time went on the more famous martyrs gained wider recognition and some feasts became universal. Early examples, besides St. Polycarp, were St. Lawrence of Rome and St. Cyprian of Carthage.

Circular letters like that of Smyrna spread the fame of the martyrs. One church would send them to its neighbors, asking that copies be made and sent on to other cities. Often these letters described the acts (the heroism, suffering, and miracles) of one who had given his life for Christ. And many churches would keep the letters and read them publicly each year on the day of the martyr's death.

All this was an expression of popular faith and enthusiasm. For that reason Church authorities were concerned to keep the zeal of the people in the right channels. The bishops did not want any cult to develop until they were sure the person honored was really a martyr. Not every violent death of a Christian was martyrdom.

Around the 4th century another type of hero worship began. The times of intense persecution were over, and the people became increasingly aware that it was not necessary to suffer violent death to confess Christ before men. The hermits in the desert lived a sort of daily martyrdom as a witness to their faith, and some bishops and monks, as well as lay people, became famous for their heroic practice of virtues. Gradually the name of confessors came to be applied to saintly persons who had confessed Christ not by dying but living for him. The hermits Paul and Anthony captured the minds of the people. Athanasius, by his sufferings in exile, showed the courage of martyrdom. St. Martin of Tours became a fabled hero. The anniversary days of their deaths became feast days.

When public honor was given to this new type of confessor Church authorities became more careful and exacting than they had been regarding martyrs. Here there was greater opportunity for the people to be led astray. Bishops made careful investigation of each confessor and of his miracles.

But by the middle of the 11th century it was clear to some of the Popes that abuses were resulting anyway. Pious people were sometimes imprudent in their enthusiasm and could be misled by virtues more seeming than real, and by stories of miracles that were hardly reliable. And bishops were occasionally negligent in making the careful studies they should have made before permitting formal devotions to develop.

Three different Popes urged greater care, and recommended that pronouncements regarding the sanctity of a person be reserved to councils, and especially to general councils. Finally Pope Alexander III, in 1170, made it clear that all declarations of the sanctity of a servant of God were reserved to the Holy See, and he himself made use of the papal power to canonize King Edward the Confessor, Thomas of Canterbury, and Bernard of Clairvaux.

Even though Alexander's prouncement was reaffirmed a few years later by Pope Innocent III, the practice of individual bishops of approving the cult of local saints in their own dioceses did not quickly disappear. And it was not until the years 1624 and 1634 that Pope Urban VIII set forth our present rules for both beatification and canonization.

First there must be a wide popular appeal that a person be canonized. The bishop of the place where the person lived or died collects all the writings of the person, not only published books, but letters, diaries, notes and the like. Then he makes formal inquiry into the reality of the popular veneration of this person. It is sound and extensive? And thirdly he makes a careful study to see that there has been no *public* cult of this person. Such a cult would be an abuse. If the writings are all orthodox, the reputation for sanctity solid, and no unauthorized cult has been tolerated, the cardinals of the Congregation of Rites may recommend to the Pope that the cause be accepted for further study.

If the Pope accepts the cause, further studies are made under the Congregation of Rites. It delegates bishops to investigate first whether or not the virtues of the servant of God were real and truly heroic. Next comes investigation of alleged miracles. Sworn testimony must be taken in formal manner, and the depositions of experts have particular value. Usually miracles are cures, so doctors who treated the person or who are specialists familiar with the case are questioned.

All evidence is sent to Rome where experts and specialists review it. These studies may take many years, but if the officials and cardinals of the congregation are convinced that the person was an example of heroic Christian virtue, and that two unquestionable miracles have resulted from his intercession since his death, they may recommend to the Pope that the servant of God be beatified. If the Pope agrees, a solemn ceremony of beatification takes place in St. Peter's. It states that the Pope, guided by the Holy Spirit, finds no reason why this person should not be honored as a saint. Formal public veneration is still restricted to named places or religious orders.

Then the Church waits for further testimony from God. There must be two miracles after the beatification, and they must be investigated with the same thoroughness and established with the same certainty as the previous ones. Again experts, specialists, and consultors subject the evidence to minute scrunity and criticism. And again the cardinals study the matter and make recommendations to the Pope. If he, after prayer to the Holy Spirit, decides on canonization, there is another solemn ceremony.

Canonization is a declaration of the supreme authority of the Church that God has rewarded his servant in heaven for his life of heroic virtue on earth, that we rightly honor him as a close and blessed friend of God, and that his prayers for us can be very helpful. In other words, it is perfectly proper for us to imitate the early Christians in their devotion to their martyrs and confessors.

Your letter, Nina, used the word *miracles* in a sense different from ours. The achievements of modern science and technology are not miracles in our sense. They are wondrous, and many of them would have been hardly credible to a previous generation; but they are achieved in natural manner, by man's intelligence and ingenuity. A miracle for us, is something beyond the powers of man to achieve, contrary to known forces of nature, requiring the direct intervention of the Creator of nature.

Incidentally, no cure of a minor ailment is ever accepted as a miracle; nothing that might be cured by medicine or surgery can be accounted a miracle. Only things doctors know could not happen by any natural means are accepted in the processes of beatification and canonization.

As for your other point, I presume it is never possible to establish in scientific manner that no person other than the candidate for canonization prayed for the person who was cured. What must be established in the case is that the intercession of this servant of God was implored in obvious formal manner, and that prayers to him were not linked with prayers to other saints. In other words the evidence must permit a sound and prudent judgment that the miracle resulted from the intercession of the person in question. And great reliance is placed on the guidance of the Holy Spirit.

29

Why Should a Young Girl Shut Herself Away in a Convent?

THE LETTER:

My husband and I are non-Catholics. We receive the *Catholic Digest* because our 17-year-old daughter became a Catholic two years ago. Now she wants to become a nun.

She is a popular, intelligent, attractive girl, with all the advantages of a good home. We cannot understand why she wants to throw her life away, locked up somewhere doing God only knows what. Aren't nunneries medieval?

And taking a vow of obedience, being told what to do and what not to do, isn't that communistic? What possible advantage can a modern-day young woman receive from this type of life? We have nothing else against the Catholic Church, but we do not want to see our daughter ruin her chances for happiness by doing something foolish.

Mrs. R.S. Shaw

THE ANSWER:
By J.D. Conway

My dear Mrs. Shaw, I sympathize with you in your problem. It is easy to understand that the nature of a vocation to Religious life in a convent is strange to you. Many good Catholic parents share your very concern when their daughters propose to enter a convent. Many others, however, more familiar with the goals of a dedicated Religious life, are proud and happy at such a proposal. Usually the reluctant parents become aware of the nobility and satisfaction of their daughters' vocation.

Let me assure you that the Catholic Church would never want to see your daughter ruin her chances for happiness by doing something foolish. The laws of the Church are carefully designed to prevent that very thing.

Should your daughter try to enter a convent despite your strong objections, I believe that most Religious Communities would hesitate to accept her until she is a bit older. Besides, careful attention would be given to the fact that she has been a Catholic only two years. It is probable that she would be advised to wait awhile to be sure that the emotional fervor of her conversion is not making her impetuous.

Even if she is determined to enter Religious life now, and if a Community of Sisters is willing to accept her, she is burning no bridges of retreat. During her first six months in the convent she would be merely a postulant, a young lady living in a "nunnery" to see what it is like. She is free to leave at any time. I put the word *nunnery* in quotation marks because it is seldom used by Catholics, who consider it a term of ridicule. We use *monastery, convent,* or *Religious house. Monastery* is usually the correct name for the home of cloistered nuns. Other Sisters, the kind you see in schools and hospitals, are not properly called nuns, and they live in convents, where the doors, like those of your own home, are locked only to keep out burglars.

After your daughter has been a postulant for at least six months, if she firmly desires to become a member of the Community she may be "received," in a very formal and beautiful ceremony in which she exchanges a bridal gown for the habit of the Community.

During her postulancy she will be carefully observed and frequently interviewed by qualified members of the Community. They try to judge if she will adjust happily to convent living. They will advise her to leave if she is evidently out of place. She will have regular opportunity to consult a priest about special problems and for help in deciding if she has a real vocation to the Religious life. And before her reception, the bishop, or his representative, will have a private interview with her to make sure she knows what she is doing and really wants to become a member of the Community.

After her reception, she will be called a novice, with no vows. She is free, any day she wishes, to put aside her Religious habit, don her civilian clothes, and walk out the door. The only restriction is that her leaving must be final. She cannot change her mind and come back the next day, or the next year. As a novice your daughter will learn the problems, routines, and hardships of living in the Community. She will also learn some of its happiness and consolation. But in general those first two years are made more rigorous than any later years will be, especially in matters of obedience. It is a trial period, a time of learning and adjustment.

After two years of novitiate your daughter will be ready for "profession," provided she still wants to stay and the Community wishes to keep her. Profession is a ceremony more solemn than reception. The young novice professes publicly that she is dedicating herself to intense love and service of God by taking the vows of poverty, chastity, and obedience. But those first vows are taken only for three years. At the end of that time she is again perfectly free to leave.

It is only after five and a half years of trial and experience that your daughter would be able to take perpetual vows, adopting the convent as her home for life. There is little chance of her "doing something foolish."

Even if she left at this point she would still have much of her life ahead of her. The years would not have been wasted, because apart from the great spiritual advantages, she would probably have received an education, fitting her for some profession in her life outside the convent. I might add that even after final profession, if situations change in such manner that it is not good for a Sister to remain in Religious life, she can obtain a dispensation from her vows from the Pope and return to secular life. The Church will never keep her against her will, or even bind her in conscience to remain in the convent.

It is true that "nunneries" are medieval, at least most of those which are strictly cloistered, and in which the nuns devote their lives to prayer, meditation, fasting, and penance, performing the routine daily tasks of community housekeeping, and working at simple tasks of art or industry by which their monastery is supported.

Many things medieval were excellent in their day, and some of them remain useful in the modern world. There are a limited number of young women today, many of them popular, intelligent, attractive women, with the advantages of a good home, who are definitely called by God to the rigorous life of the monastery. There the intimate love of God becomes their full portion of life, and their Sisters their only direct contact with the world. These women are in the fullest sense spouses of Christ, content to live quietly in his home, to join Him daily in worship of the heavenly Father, and to join with Him and their Sisters in the daily Eucharistic banquet, the Mass.

Sisters today drive automobiles, watch television, and even go to occasional movies and concerts. They teach everything from atomic physics to art and religion. They are nurses, doctors, and hospital administrators. They write books and excavate ancient ruins. They are theologians and philosophers, social workers and missionaries, dramatists and dishwashers. Your daughter would not have "to throw her life away," but rather live it fully and happily in the dedicated, loving service of God.

While the practical world may admire the generous and competent work of modern Sisters, it is only in terms of faith that their vocation in life really makes sense. You ask, Mrs. Shaw, what possible advantages a modern young woman can receive from this type of life. The answer of faith is that in it she can give herself totally to the practice of virtue and the service of Christ's brethren; living every moment of her life in the love of her chosen spouse, Jesus.

What is life's goal, anyway? Is it only a few years of mingled happiness and sorrow here on earth before we are buried in the earth? Is pleasure our only gain, or suffering life's greatest failure?

Your married life has apparently been happy, and experience has made you see normal fulfillment in it. No one can guarantee your daughter complete happiness in the convent. But you know that many marriages are unhappy. As a pastor I see more problems of married misery than of frustrated or joyless life in Religion. Most of the Sisters I know are happy people.

As you suggest, obedience presents a special problem to modern youth, raised to idealize personal freedom. And I must admit that most of the convent difficulties I have encountered stem from it. However, when rightly exercised the authority in a Religious Community is domestic rather than communistic, and obedience is required simply for harmonious community life. The ideal of communism is for men to live together equally and peacefully without any authority. Today's dictatorships are proof that this ideal is impossible. The modern Religious Communities aim at rule which is material rather than dictatorial, and at obedience which is spontaneous rather than servile. Aims are not always achieved in any manner of living.

Probably I have not answered all your questions, Mrs. Shaw, or eased all your worries. But in summary I would suggest that you encourage your daughter to patience. She is young and her faith is new. She certainly needs good spiritual counseling. But if she persists in her intention you should not strongly oppose her. A trial of her vocation will do her no harm, and if it should prove real it may lead her to much happiness on earth, and to a union with God in heaven.

30

Shouldn't Priests Get Married?

THE LETTER:

I found out only in an embarrassing way that Catholic pastors aren't allowed to marry, and I am confused.

Recently I had our minister and his wife and two children as guests. Later in the week, I suggested to my Catholic neighbors that they invite their pastor and his family. Although a little shocked, they told me that their pastors have a rule against being married.

I don't see why, since a pastor, as the head of a church, should set an example of a good Christian family. Could you clear up this point for me?

Mrs. Jean Lewis

THE ANSWER:
By J.D. Conway

I hope I do not embarrass you even more, Mrs. Louis, by expressing surprise at your letter. I had taken it for granted that everyone knew that Catholic priests do not marry.

Catholic priests may not marry, but there are married Catholic priests. Now do I add to your confusion? No priest may marry after he has been ordained, but many men already married are ordained and continue to live with their wives and families.

The Catholic Church has two branches: the Latin, or Western Rite, and the Eastern Rites. They are under the same Pope, believe the same doctrines, offer the same Sacrifice, and receive the same sacrament; but they have different customs and languages. The Eastern Rites have always ordained married men; the Latin rite has never for nine centuries. I am of the Latin Rite, and what I have to say of clerical celibacy is affected by that fact. A married priest would treat the subject differently.

Recent Popes have granted a few dispensations from this law of the Latin Church. Protestant ministers who had become converts to the Catholic Church have been ordained as priests, even though they were married and had families. One man ordained in this manner was an American; but his ordination took place in Germany. No such ordination has yet been permitted in the United States.

Eastern Rite Churches are not permitted in the United States to ordain married men, though they do have married priests here. Some are here as refugees from Eastern Europe.

A person who remains unmarried is called a celibate. He lives in celibacy. So we speak of the celibacy of the Latin clergy, meaning they are unmarried men. Your concern, Mrs. Lewis, seems to be with our reasons for having a celibate clergy. They are historical, spiritual, and practical.

There is a rule but no doctrine of our Church which requires that priests be celibate. There is no directive for it in Sacred Scripture. But words of Scripture inspired its practice. Our Lord seemed to recommend celibacy for those who are able to accept it. St. Paul was unmarried, and expressed to the Corinthians the wish that all could imitate him, though he recognized the fact that not all were called to such a life. St. Paul also said to the Corinthians: "I would have you free from care. He who is unmarried is concerned about the things of the Lord, how he may please God. Whereas he who is married is concerned about the things of the world, how he may please his wife and he is divided."

To both Timothy and Titus, St. Paul laid down rules for

bishops. One qualification was that they should be "married but once." These words of St. Paul, though their meaning was sometimes disputed, and though they were not always observed, became a guiding principle for choosing bishops in the early centuries of Christianity. If a bishop's wife died he could not marry again. From there it was only a gradual step to require the bishops not be married at all.

In the first four centuries of the Church's history there was no requirement that either bishops or priests should be celibate. But the example of some who were had wide influence, later magnified by the inspiring celibate lives of hermits and monks.

Meanwhile, local meetings of bishops were making laws for some areas. A council held at Elvira in Spain about the year 300 imposed celibacy on bishops, priests and deacons. If they continued to live with their wives and beget children they would be deprived of their positions as clergy.

In the East, councils held a few years later forbade priests to contract new marriages after ordination. Those who did would be deposed. Another council forbade deacons to marry after ordination unless they had made known to the bishop at the time of ordination their intention of doing so.

About the year 400 the rules in the West became definite: bishops, priests, deacons (and later even subdeacons) must be celibate. These laws came from various councils and Popes. They were not observed or enforced everywhere, but the policy was established. While Charlemagne was emperor, enforcement was quite general. But as his empire disintegrated, there were no general efforts at enforcement until the great papal reforms in the middle of the 11th century. The Lateran Councils held in 1123 and 1139 made the laws of clerical celibacy very clear and general· no bishop, priest, deacon, or subdeacon could be a married man, and, if he tried to marry after he was ordained, his marriage was invalid.

In the East during the 5th and 6th centuries laws took more definite and general forms, sometimes dictated by emperors, especially by Theodosius and Justinian. The tendency was that bishops should not be married men, or at least should not live with their wives (though they had to support them); priests, deacons, and subdeacons could be married before ordination, but could not contract a new marriage after ordination. The Eastern discipline was put in final form in 692, at a time when the Churches of the East and the West were not speaking. It is still the rule in the Eastern Orthodox Churches and in many Eastern Churches united to Rome that bishops must be celibate; other clergy may be married; but none can marry after ordination to subdiaconate.

The spiritual reasons for the celibacy of the clergy are based on the ideal of virginity as exemplified in the lives of Jesus and his blessed Mother. The thought is that the priest is not only to bear witness to Christ, but to represent Him before his people: to be another Christ. It is the priest's ideal to be like his Master. Jesus was unmarried. The priest is to remain unmarried in a spirit of self-sacrifice, love, and dedication. In the words of St. Paul, he is undivided; has no wife or family to distract him from the things of God, or from the needs of his spiritual children, the people of God, who call him Father.

The highest ranks of sanctity have mostly been attained in the life of the convent and the monastery, where self-sacrifice and separation from the world are the rule. The secular priest cannot separate himself so completely from the world, but he can renounce the normal cares and pleasures of secular life.

There are many practical reasons for celibacy. One is the education of the clergy. For several centuries priests have been trained in seminaries: schools of strict discipline, prayer, meditation, and intense study. This rigid preparation could hardly be combined with the distracting influences of a family. Living expenses are also an important practical consideration. A pastor ordinarily shares his home in the rectory with his assistants. If every priest maintained a home and family expenses would be greater. Another factor is that the bishop must move pastors from one parish to another. This is difficult now, but what would it be if the pastor's wife were taken from her friends, the children from their schools, and the whole family from its home?

The Church is trying to follow the command of our Lord to go into the world and make disciples of all nations. In many primitive lands it is hard to transport and maintain a family. The Catholic missionary is concerned only about living from day to day, or about the cost of a church, school, or hospital. The needs of his family, education of his children, and demands of his wife would be a worry.

Priests are often chaplains in time of war. They are perhaps no braver than other chaplains, but they have less to lose. They have no concerns about wife or family. Martyrs must always be heroes, but a man would not be free to sacrifice his wife and family along with himself. This is a kind of reason for celibacy.

Pope John XXIII convoked the 2nd Ecumenical Council of the Vatican to bring the Catholic Church up-to-date. He proposed many reforms, and was most sympathetic with the problems celibacy may impose on many priests, but he made it very clear that he envisoned no change to his ancient discipline (as has Paul VI).

The Council has voted that the permanent diaconate should be restored: that men should be ordained deacons who do not seek to become priests or bishops. The Council Fathers decided that married men could be ordained to this office of deacon. They would remain married. But when the question was proposed of ordaining young unmarried men as deacons, permitting them to marry later, the Fathers of the Council opposed it 5 to 3.

As Pope John said, we should not abandon a celibate clergy, Mrs. Lewis, because it has so many historical, spiritual, and practical advantages.

31

What's the Best Way to Be Holy and Good?

THE LETTER:

My wife is a Catholic, and has a Catholic calendar illustrated with pictures of saints. The note on one of the pictures says that the saint deprived himself of essential things to help the needy.

Why does the Church hold up as examples persons who deprived themselves of even the necessities of life when, if they had striven to earn more, they could have kept their health, lived a longer life, and had more to give the poor?

Bradley Hall

THE ANSWER;
By J.D. Conway

You do not tell me your saint's name Bradley, so I will call him St. Askesis. That is a strange name, but many saints have odder names. I will tell you what it means later.

Popular stories of saints' lives are often exaggerations, especially those of earlier saints. But the saints were still extraordinary persons, and some of the stories are true. They give us inspiring examples of great virtues, even when their virtues were practiced so extremely that we ordinary persons can't use them as models. Few young women are called to become saints by leading an army as did Joan of Arc. Modern hermits are rare, and none of us would think of living atop a pillar, like St. Simon Stylites, although we have had nonsaint flagpole sitters.

St. Askesis, as you described him, showed two great Christian virtues: love and self-denial. We may agree that he was not very prudent. But it is easy to exaggerate prudence. We save for a rainy day so carefully that we miss the sunshine of generous love; and we take such good care of ourselves that we become fat and lazy. Askesis gave us an extreme example of Christian love. But Jesus, who gave his own life for us on the cross, told us, "This is my commandment, that you love one another as I have loved you. Greater love than this no one has, that one lay down his life for his friends. And Askesis quite literally laid down his life for the needy. When a man gives until it hurts, and, ignoring the hurt, keeps on giving until it kills him, can we doubt that he is filled with love and urged to extremes by it? He may lack prudence, but his charity has no lack.

Our most practical way of showing our love for Christ is through our love of our neighbor. You remember the description which He gave of the Last Judgment, when the Son of Man would come in majesty, the angels with Him, and He would gather all together, the good and the bad, the sheep and the goats. And to the sheep on his right hand He would say, "Come, blessed of my Father, take possession of the kingdom . . . for I was hungry and you gave Me to eat; I was thirsty and you gave Me to drink . . . ."

When the just asked when they had done these favors for Him, Jesus replied, "Amen I say to you, as long as you did it for one of these, the least of my brethen, you did it for Me."

St. Askesis saw Jesus in the needy, and the urge of his love was so great that it pushed prudence out of the picture. We are not expected to imitate him all the way. But we can learn from him to see Jesus in the beggar at our door, in the Black man who wishes to move next door, and in famine-stricken millions who have declared themselves our enemies.

Now a look at the self-denial of your saint. That's where I got the name for him. *Askesis* is Greek for exercise or practice; and it was used for the rigorous training of athletes. The ascetic (from *askesis*) Christian trains himself to reach spiritual perfection by denying himself things that might distract him from his goal. A true ascetic knows he can't attain holiness just by his own efforts. Holiness comes from God. But his works of asceticism are a practice of love which enable him to accept love more readily and to respond to it more generously. Asceticism takes two forms. First is renunciation: giving up pleasures and privileges, not in a casual manner, but with the determination of an athlete in training. This form removes the impediments of love. The second form is positive. It is the active practice of virtue so that love can respond promptly.

We need not worry about the excesses of asceticism of our friend Askesis. Our natural tendencies are in the opposite direction. We incline to pleasure, comfort, self-indulgence, luxury, and ease. We need prudence to keep these tendencies from leading us from sanctity to sin. We should be very slow to criticize the self-denial of another person. Maybe his practices are not for us. But a strong, willful person needs a different kind of ascetic practice than that good for a weak and fearful man. The lazy man needs a type of self-denial and control opposite to that of the man who is ambitious, proud, or vain. The fat and the lean, the critical and the indulgent, the hot-tempered and the placid, each needs his own self-discipline.

Asceticism has its dangers, even when practiced without excess. It can lead to the self-satisfaction of the Pharisee. It can make us too aware of our own virtue. A form of asceticism good for all of us is the acceptance of our lot in life, the daily annoyances we cannot avoid: the pain of arthritis;

or slights, snubs, and the general unfairness of the world. Groans, complaints, and a bitter sense of injury never light a candle or change a world.

Strong asceticism was common in earlier ages of the Church. Hermits had no monopoly on it; monks and nuns frequently flogged themselves and wore hair shirts. Even kings wore instruments of pain under their garments of glory. Probably the oldest form of asceticism is fasting, which once meant no food or drink from midnight until evening. Gradually custom mitigated it. The Church, aware of our softness and of the demands of modern life, has become lenient. Before 1957, the person receiving Communion or the priest celebrating Mass had to fast from every form of food and drink from midnight until after Communion, even though it might be past noon. Today, an hour is the norm, and you can drink water at will.

Self-denial is also a means of doing penance for our sins and of making reparation. As sinners, we deny ourselves, accept burdens, and practice special virtue to show sorrow for our sins. And, though we can do nothing by our own feeble efforts to repair our offenses against the infinite goodness and love of God, our Saviour is pleased to join our good works, our self-denial, and our sufferings to the infinite merits of his own reparation on the cross.

So I agree with you, Bradley, that Askesis was not a prudent man. We should not try to imitate his excesses. But the ardor of his love and the intensity of his sacrifice compensated for his failings. We are not asked to imitate him, only to learn from him.

32

How Can the Church Cut People Off From God?

THE LETTER:

After seeing the movie *Becket* and then reading "What Would You Like to Know About the Church?" in the November *Catholic Digest,* a question came into my mind.

Where does the Church get the right to excommunicate? Isn't that a form of judging others, which the Bible says we have no right to do? My husband is a Catholic and mentioned canon law. I still don't understand, for if these laws were written by man, they still don't give us the right as far as I can see.

Maybe you can explain this, maybe it is not considered judging others? And on what grounds can people be excommunicated?

Mrs. Judy Knapp

THE ANSWER:
By J.D. Conway

The word *excommunication,* Mrs. Knapp, has acquired a tinge of terror that it does not deserve. It is the severest punishment imposed by the Church, but it is strictly medicinal. Its first purpose is to bring a sinner to repentance. It also emphasizes the gravity of certain sins to deter people from committing them.

In most excommunications there is no question of one person "judging" another. The Church law simply states that a person who maliciously commits a certain crime incurs excommunication. The guilty person, knowing the law and its penalty, judges himself in his own conscience. If he is honest, he accepts the penalty; and if he is repentant, he seeks absolution from it.

Usually this can be obtained in the confessional, and not even the priest knows who the guilty person is. Some excommunications are matters of public knowledge, and absolution from them must be obtained outside of Confession. But even in most of these cases there is no question of "judging others"; the guilty person remains his own judge. It is only in cases in which the crime is evident and the criminal refuses to reform that the bishop or some higher authority publicly declares the excommunication.

When the Church excommunicates a person, she does not wish nor pretend to change the relationship that exists between him and God. She cannot remove the mark of adoption that God placed on his soul in Baptism. She passes no judgment on the status of his soul before God; and certainly she does not try to anticipate the eternal judgment that God alone can make.

In this sense the Church does not judge others, even when she formally declares a person excommunicated. But she is an organized society with definite membership, and when a person shows himself unworthy of membership, she excludes him until he reforms. This exclusion means that he loses the benefits of membership over which the Church has control. He cannot receive the sacraments, is not included in the official public prayers of the Church, loses any office, dignity, or pension he may have, and, if he should be a bishop or other person in authority, cannot exercise any jurisdiction.

The Church is the people of God. The members—chosen, redeemed, and baptized by our Saviour, Jesus Christ—are so intimately united to each other and to Jesus Himself that they form one living body. It is in this mystical Body that we join with Jesus in offering constant worship to our Father in heaven, particularly through the Mass, and it is in this mystical Body that Jesus gives his graces to us. The excommunicated person is a dead cell in this Body, not active or effective in its worship, receiving no sanctifying benefits from its life. However, he is not entirely cut off; the Body retains him, dead as he is, hoping to revive and reintegrate him.

You ask, Mrs. Knapp, where the Church gets the right to excommunicate. We believe that Jesus gave this right when He explained to his Apostles how they should go about correcting a sinning brother. The final step was to bring the matter before the Church, and "if he refuses to listen even to the Church, let him be to you as a Gentile and a tax collector." The Gentile and the tax collector were standing examples of exclusion from the Jewish community. Immediately after these words, Jesus gave his Apostles general authority to punish and to forgive: "Truly, I say to you, whatever you bind on earth shall be bound in heaven, and whatever you loose on earth shall be loosed in heaven."

There are many examples of excommunication in the Bible itself. When Ezra (Esdras) and the chief priests commanded all the returned exiles to assemble at Jerusalem, their proclamation was enforced by penalties: "If any one did not come within three days, all his property should be forfeited and he himself banned from the congregation of the exiles."

The Jews often excluded people from the synagogue. When Jesus had healed the man who was blind from birth, the parents of this man were evasive of questions, "because they feared the Jews, for the Jews had already agreed that if anyone should confess Him to be Christ, he was to be put out of the synagogue. St. John tells us that many of the Jews, even members of the council, believed in Jesus, "but for fear of the Pharisees they did not confess it, lest they should be put out of the synagogue."

St. Paul used terms as strong as any medieval Pope when he told the Corinthians to excommunicate the man who was living with his father's wife: "You are to deliver this man to Satan for the destruction of the flesh, that his spirit may be saved in the day of the Lord Jesus."

There is evidence that excommunication has been used from the earliest days of the Church. In early centuries it may have been the only penalty for laymen. But it was not until the canon law of the Church developed in the Middle Ages that excommunication became the dreaded weapon of Church government, a strong coercive means of enforcing law. It was between the 11th and the 16th centuries that the word *excommunication* acquired the bad reputation it retains in the minds of many people today. There is a tendency to link it with ordeals by fire and water; the Inquisition, with its rack of torture and its stake for burning; the mighty medieval conflicts between Pope and emperor; and the bitter animosities of the Reformation. We must frankly admit that excommunication justly earned its ill repute. It was frightfully abused at times. It was the Church's most extreme penalty, but it was often used for petty and tyrannical purposes; to enforce feasts and fasts, to force payment of tithes, to pry out information, or simply to compel obedience to a bishop's command.

A terrible feature of this penalty in medieval times was its carry-over from religious to civil relationship. The entire society was Christian, and a person excluded from the Church was excluded from society. He was to be avoided like a leper; Christians were not to talk to him, eat with him, write to him, or show him ordinary signs of friendship. They must not pray with him, do business with him, or give him any honor or respect. He was a pariah with whom all social contact was forbidden. Anyone who broke these rules incurred, in his turn, a minor type of excommunication. The person under major excommunication was called *vitandus,* a person who must be shunned. Minor excommunication did not make a person *vitandus;* it merely excluded him from religious activities.

Imagine the situation when major excommunications happened frequently. One scarcely knew whom to avoid. There was daily danger of incurring a penalty. But from such intolerable situations both the people and the canon lawyers found ways of escape. The people often ignored the penalties, which were gradually forgotten. And the lawyers found loopholes. You could speak to an excommunicated man if it were to help him spiritually or aid the community. His wife could live with him, his children, servants, and vassals could obey him. And best of all, if you did not know that a person was excommunicated or that association with him was forbidden, you incurred no penalty. Finally, any real necessity would permit social or business contact, and this could be widely interpreted.

So, in practice, excommunications were seldom as frightening as they were in theory. But they often created confusion in society and weakened respect for genuine Church authority. In the 6th century the Council of Trent began a reform of the whole discipline. The number of excommunications declined, and the number of those to be avoided civilly and socially became negligible. Today I doubt that there is a *vitandus* in the whole world, though that penalty is still mentioned in the law. Only the Pope can impose it.

Our present disciple in that matter dates from 1918, when Church law was entirely revised, updated, and made definite in our Code of Canon Law. There are still many crimes for which excommunication is decreed as punishment. In a quick count I found 43. But most of them are crimes which rarely happen, like assaulting the Pope, breaking the seal of Confession, or desecrating the Holy Eucharist. A great number are imposed on Church officials who abuse their authority. Others are designed to protect the rights and freedom of the Church from violation by conspiracy or by authoritarian regimes.

The average layman might incur an excommunication for deliberate heresy, schism, or apostasy; procuring an abortion; or fighting a duel. If he tried selling indulgences, seriously simulated the role of a priest in offering Mass, or carried on graft in Mass stipends he would incur the same penalty.

Our Canon Law is again in process of complete revision, and many of us hope that most of our present excommunications will disappear when the new code appears. It is highly questionable whether they serve any good practical purpose. They are relics of former ages which revive unhappy memories, and they complicate the studies of seminarians. In actual practice the confessor rarely encounters any problem with them; but, if he does, it becomes his problem more than that of the person under penalty.

We still need the authority to excommunicate in rare cases, but I doubt if we need it anymore for those who fight duels.

33

Can't the Church Be Reasonable About Mixed Marriages?

THE LETTER:

I long to become a Catholic but have been told that I cannot. I have been married to a fine man for 19 years and have a baby just eight weeks old. I would like to become a Catholic and have my baby baptized, but my husband does not wish to join the Church.

My husband has been married previously and divorced. He has never been baptized and he doesn't think his first wife was baptized. She is still living back in North Carolina. The Church says that because my husband was divorced I cannot become a Catholic and neither can my child. This does not seem fair to me.

I am being penalized for something I cannot help. The Baltimore Catechism question No. 169 says: "All are bound to belong to the Church and he who knows the Church to be the true Church and remains out of it cannot be saved." Am I to be sent to hell? Surely God cannot desire me to break up my good marriage of 19 years and take away a tiny precious baby from her living father.

Mrs. E.M. Pohl

THE ANSWER:
By J.D. Conway

Your letter puts me in the mood for argument, Mrs. Pohl. I disagree not with you, but with the person who told you that you cannot become a Catholic. I am quite sure that you can. The process will not be simple, and you will have to be patient while necessary investigations are made.

While I am disposed to argue with your advisor, I am not inclined to blame him. It is not generally known that marriage cases like that of your husband can receive favorable solution. Such cases are rare and present some interesting theological problems. But the fact is that the Pope has found happy solutions to problems so nearly identical to yours that I feel safe in assuring you. However, you must not accept my encouragement as a guarantee. My 30 years of experience in handling marriage cases have taught me that no decision can be given until all the evidence has been presented and weighed. And in a case like this the final decision is not made by me or by the bishop, but by the Pope, who is advised in such matters by experts.

Many people will say that the Church is unreasonable in not admitting you to membership right away. You are evidently honest, you have the gift of faith, and your desire to be a Catholic is ardent. Why should you be penalized for something your husband did?

The difficulty is that age-old problem of divorce, and the Church's steadfast strictness about it. I must be frank, even at the risk of offending you. The Church does not consider your present marriage valid. Your husband had a former wife, and she is still alive. The Church holds that she is still his wife. Catholics respect your good faith, the civil legality of your marriage, and your honorable social standing. But a priest giving you instructions in Catholic doctrine would find it necessary to disturb your good faith. Then you would either reject the teaching of the Church or find yourself living with a bad conscience. You could not be an honest Catholic.

I assure you that the Church wishes to have you as a member. We have many spiritual benefits to offer you and your fine precious baby. One of the frequent sorrows of a priest's life is a marital situation which prevents a prospective convert from entering the Church, or keeps a Catholic from receiving the sacraments. But one of his many joys is finding a marriage problem which can be solved for the benefit of all concerned.

If your husband and his first wife had both been baptized before their marriage to each other, your letter would cause me sorrow. Since it is certain that your husband, at least, has never been baptized, I answer your question with joy.

There is a great difference between the marriage of two Christian people to each other, and the marriage of two unbaptized persons. In Catholic doctrine the marriage of two Christians is a sacrament of Jesus Christ: an effective sign of union with Him. So a Christian husband and wife are not only joined to each other, they are mutually joined to Christ. His love and grace make the bond between them doubly strong, spiritual, and truly ratified in heaven. Only death breaks it.

Nonbaptized people are joined together by their own love and fidelity. Their marriage is natural, but not supernatural. It is legitimate but not sacramental. It is valid but not absolutely unbreakable. St. Paul was the first one to tell us that the bond of a nonscramental marriage can sometimes be dissolved. He wrote to the Corinthians, in effect, that divorce is possible when an unbelieving (unbaptized) spouse refuses to live with the husband or wife who has become a Christian.

Most Catholics know about the Pauline Privilege. We still use it today. Your husband's case, Mrs. Pohl, could be solved by this privilege if he had the gift of faith and wished to become a Catholic, but faith can come only from God, and it must be accepted by a will entirely free. It would be wrong for anyone to put pressure on your husband to join the Church so that your problem could be easily solved.

In saying that your husband could make use of the Pauline Privilege, as a convert, I am presuming that his first wife remains unbaptized and that this fact can be proven. But what if we find that she is a baptized person? Then, even as a convert, Mr. Pohl could not use the Pauline Privilege. But there would still be a solution available to him. We call it the Privilege of the Faith. In granting this privilege to a convert, or prospective convert, the Pope dissolves the bond of his previous marriage to favor his faith: so that he can embrace the faith and live by it in good conscience. "Dissolving the bond of marriage" is a euphemism of which we are fond. It means granting a divorce; but we dislike this word.

It is possible for the Pope to grant the Privilege of the Faith for the same reason St. Paul could grant his Privilege of Divorce to the Corinthians. A marriage in which one partner is unbaptized is not sacramental. Its bond is not unbreakable.

You may be impatient, Mrs. Pohl, because I keep discussing favors which suppose your husband's conversion. Let me come to the point. The Pope can dissolve the bond of Mr. Pohl's first marriage as a favor to your faith so that you can become a Catholic, be properly married to Mr. Pohl in the Church, and have your baby baptized, too. Ordinarily the Pope has neither the right nor the interest to break the bond of marriage between two nonbaptized persons. But when the faith and spiritual welfare of a Catholic or prospective convert is directly menaced by that bond, his power as Vicar of Christ permits him to remove this obstacle to faith, provided that all parties concerned are willing. He cannot do injustice.

In this case, Mr. Pohl will ask the Pope to dissolve the bond of his first marriage: to grant him in the Church the divorce he has long had in civil law, so that when you become a Catholic, he may contract a new marriage with you in the Church. You may complete your instructions in Catholic doctrine while the case is being studied in Rome, but you will not be baptized until a favorable reply is received.

Usually it is the bishop of your area who presents the case to Rome. Many documents and proofs will be required, but he will obtain these with the aid of his priests and the cooperation of bishops in other areas. Your husband will have to answer some questions which a priest will ask him. Conclusive proof is needed that he has never been baptized. Are his parents still living? Will they give their testimony? Does he have older brothers and sisters from whom evidence can be obtained? Has Mr. Pohl ever attended a church with frequency? It may be necessary to examine the baptismal register of such church. Marriage certificates and his decree of divorce will be needed. But you will not need to worry about many of these details. Priests will handle them. It will probably be necessary for a priest to contact Mr. Pohl's former wife. She could hardly have any reasonable objection to the dissolution of the marriage, since she has been divorced so long. But we cannot disregard her rights. And besides, we want to find out whether or not she was baptized. Don't worry about that, though. Even if she is baptized, it will not harm your prospects.

Let me give you a word of caution, however. No two marriage cases are exactly alike. You can be hopeful because cases similar to yours have received favorable solution, but you cannot be sure until your own case has been solved. Much depends on the recommendation given your case by the bishop when he sends it to Rome. He will restrict his recommendation only if he finds reason to question your sincerity or that of your husband, or if he finds proof of non-Baptism insufficient, or if he believes that scandal may be caused or religion harmed by your receiving this privilege. If I may pre-judge his decision, on the basis of your letter, I can see only good resulting from your conversion and Catholic marriage: spiritual good for yourself, your child, and your husband, and edification for your neighbors.

There will be charges for work done in preparing and studying the case. But they will not be unreasonable. And the priests who obtain testimony will do their work without cost to you. If favorable decisions are made in your case, an official will meet with the Holy Father and recommend that the requested favor be granted. After the Pope has given an affirmative reply, a Cardinal-secretary will send a letter to your bishop giving him the good news. Then you will be baptized and the bishop will grant a dispensation permitting you, as a Catholic, to marry a nonbaptized man in the Church.

I began my answer with an argument and I wish to finish it the same way. I cannot see why your child was denied Baptism, even if you could not be received into the Church. It seems evident that you intend to raise the child a Catholic. Nothing more should be required, except some Catholic godparents.

34

Don't You Make Children Think of Death Too Much?

THE LETTER:

I consider myself a Protestant, but I do not attend church or belong to any particular denomination.

Recently I attended a funeral ceremony for a Catholic friend. It was a great surprise to me when a nun brought a class of young children in for the service. Do you think it is good for quite young children to be made so conscious of a sorrowful thing like death?

Gerald P. Ritter

THE ANSWER:
By J.D. Conway

Death is not really a sorrowful thing, Gerald. Dying can be frightening and painful, but death is as natural as birth, the necessary result of living. For the Christian, death is less the end of earthly life than the beginning of a new life in eternity. It is the only gate to heaven.

The sorrow of death seldom touches us deeply until it happens to a relative or friend; and then our sorrow is less for the deceased than for ourselves, the bereaved. Reading the obituary column can leave us quite unmoved, and the sight of a stranger's funeral is seldom depressing.

I am not a child psychologist, but I think it is good for us to give children a casual attitude toward the realities of life and death while protecting them from shock, fear, and anxiety. We used to think that scenes of horror were harmful to them, but now they seem to thrive on a steady diet of terror on television. A child unscathed by the bogies, bugaboos, murder, and mayhem of daily TV is unlikely to be harmed by a funeral.

I do not advocate regular attendance at funerals for children of early grades. It would hardly do them any emotional harm, but it would bore them. In many Catholic parishes it has been customary for the children in the upper grades of school to attend funerals and sing at the Mass. They like it because they get out of a class.

From their early years we teach them about the happiness of heaven, that Jesus is God, became man to redeem them, that He died on the cross, and rose from the dead to forgive our sins and give us eternal life. Children understand their faith only in the measure that they comprehend natural realities. Their belief in life after death will be firm and fortifying only when they understand the reality of life and the truth of death. Such comprehension can be gained only gradually, but should start early, lest faith become fantasy, deprived of its realistic basis.

Having written this, I do admit that our present (1966) funeral Mass presents some problems. It will hardly have traumatic effects on little children, but it does tend to tinge Catholic attitudes toward death and judgment with hues of gloom and fear. Until recently the requiem Mass and funeral services were in Latin and their dreadful laments had less impact. But now our English translation of the hymn *"Dies Irae"* confronts us with expressions that may depress or alarm us. Here are some examples, referring mostly to the day of final judgment:

> *Day of wrath! O day of mourning!*
> *Heav'n and earth in ashes burning!*
> *O what fear man's bosom rendeth!*
> *Judge on whose sentence all*
>   *dependeth.*
> *Death is struck, and nature quaking.*
> *Lo! the exactly worded book, in*
>   *which all hath been recorded.*
> *Each hidden deed arraigneth,*
>   *nothing unavenged remaineth.*
> *Ere the day of retribution.*
> *Guilty now I pour my moaning,*
> *All my shame with anguish owning.*

These are random excerpts which describe the suppliant groaning, fires undying, the flames of woe, and the day of tears and mourning.

In the Offertory hymn of the Mass we are warned of the pains of hell, the deep pit, the lion's mouth, and the hell that swallows people up in darkness. Following the Mass there is a ceremony of absolution in which a hymn is sung about the day of terror, when the heavens and earth will be shaken, with fear and trembling at the judgment and the wrath to come. It predicts the day will be one of wrath, of misery, and of ruin, and of great horror. And there is again the threat of the heavens and the earth shaking, and of the Lord's coming to judge the world by fire.

We must keep things in proper perspective: most of the funeral Mass has words of hope, consolation, and encouragement. In the entrance hymn we ask that the Lord will grant eternal rest to the deceased and let perpetual light shine upon them. In the prayer of the assembly we ask God to send his holy angels to carry the deceased person to his home in heaven. In the first lesson we read St. Paul's words of assurance that the dead will rise again. They have fallen asleep, but the Lord Himself will come down from heaven when Gabriel's trumpet blows and will restore to life those who died in Christ; and they will be with the Lord forever. "Comfort one another with these words."

The Gospel recalls the death of Lazarus and the Lord's words to Martha, "I am the resurrection and the life. He who believes in Me, even though he dies, shall live . . . ." And Martha expresses her faith, and ours, that Jesus is the Christ, the Son of the living God, who came to our world that He might lead us to his own home.

The Preface of the Mass reminds us that in death life is changed for the faithful; it is not taken away: "When our earthly dwelling is destroyed an eternal home is made ready in heaven."

The Communion hymn repeats our plea that the dead may live in eternal light with the saints, because the Lord is merciful. And in our final prayer we ask that the soul of the deceased may be purified by the Sacrifice of the Mass which we have offered, and may receive both forgiveness of sin and everlasting life through Jesus Christ our Lord.

It is good that we Christians be reminded of the realities of sin and hell. The love and mercy of God and our redemption by Jesus Christ do not take away these awful realities; they only make possible our forgiveness and our escape from condemnation. But it hardly seems appropriate that when we are paying final respect to a good and holy person who died in Christ, and when we are seeking to console the sorrowing family of this person, we should evoke visions of the deep pit, the lion's mouth, heaven and earth burning to ashes, and a stern Judge seeking retribution amid anguish and groaning.

Christians should look forward to the end of the world with longing and hope, not dread it as a catastrophe. Possibly it is because the Gospel message of the Lord's second coming is often interwoven with prophecies of the destruction of Jerusalem, and the two events have become confused in our minds. The early Christians waited eagerly for the Lord to return; many thought He would come soon and were impatient with the delay. For them the end of the world meant the final victory and triumph of Christ, the establishment of his kingdom, and the revelation of God's glory. Their constant prayer was, "Come, Lord Jesus."

It is true that the Scriptures sometimes speak of the destruction of the present world. St. Peter says that the day of the Lord is coming like a thief, and when it comes: "The heavens will vanish in a whirlwind, the elements will be scorched up and dissolve; earth, and all earth's achievements, will burn away." But Peter immediately assures us that "we have new heavens and a new earth to look forward to, the dwelling place of holiness." And it is probable that the whirlwind and the fire are merely ways of saying that our present world of sin and struggle will be marvelously transformed into a happy and holy dwelling place for men risen from the dead with bodies glorified.

The present world will be destroyed only in the sense that its present status will end, and a new one of glory will begin. God created the world that it might attain its perfection. Jesus Christ redeemed the world to save it from sin and death, and to prepare it for life and glory. It is in Jesus Christ, the world's Saviour, that God's universe will attain the goal of its existence. And that goal is not annihilation. Glorified man must have a glorified world as the place of his dwelling. The early Christians did not fear the Lord's judgment. Jesus had told them that He would be their Judge, and they were confident of his love for them. He had died on the cross to prepare them for the judgment, and He had sent the Holy Spirit to enkindle in their hearts the love which would be the basis of judgment. In describing the final judgment Jesus had told them that they would be placed among the sheep if they had loved their neighbor; among the goats if they failed to love.

Modern Christians are afraid of books exactly worded in which all is recorded; we worry about being arraigned before a wrathful Judge seeking vengeance for hidden deeds. We stress too much the shame, anguish, and groaning. We should share with early Christians their awareness of the saving love of Jesus dying for us and raised from the dead, the sanctifying love of the Spirit kindling a responding love within us, and the forgiving love of the Father welcoming his prodigal son home.

Death is the gate to heaven; the end of the world is not destruction but glorious transformation; the Second Coming of Christ is the triumph of his redemptive mission; man's resurrection is joyous; and the judgment is the complete manifestation of God's goodness, justice, and love. If we are aware of these great Christian truths, and, if our funeral services described them, we would never need to worry about any harm a requiem Mass might have on children.

Death puts our faith to the test, especially when it is the death of one we love. Day by day a firm faith meets little challenge. God and his providence are taken for granted. Jesus and his redemption offer hope and consolation. The Mass, sacraments, and prayer become routine. We do not expect the indwelling of the Spirit to produce tangible effects. A future life is normal expectation. Then death shocks our tranquillity. Life is gone; the body cold. A painful void has opened in our lives.

Faith now enables us to see life continuing when it has evidently disappeared, to see a body ready for resurrection when it is clearly ripe for decay. He whose faith can carry him undoubtingly through the death of a loved one need not fear the spiritual consequences of his own death. Faith will not remove sadness, nor the natural fear of dying. But it provides hope, which gives consolation, and it inspires love which conquers sorrow and fear.

Such thoughts and challenges are the effects of death when it is viewed by you and me, Gerald. Children at a funeral are quite untouched by them.

35

Why Does a Grown-up Need Godparents to Be Baptized?

THE LETTER:

I would like to know why the Catholic Church insists that a convert have godparents when he is to be baptized in the Catholic faith. I have asked Catholics about this and I must say that the reasons given were unsatisfactory.

I was told that an adult convert needs godparents in case he might become lax in following his adopted faith, which implies that the convert is really not to be trusted. I was also told that there has to be someone to vouch that he is not a spy, as many times people have tried to get into the Church to spy.

It takes a great deal of faith and a great deal of agaonizing humility to get baptized again when one is an adult. And to ask some strange Catholic couple to be his godparents is a humiliating experience a non-Catholic would rather forego, even if it means remaining outside the Catholic Church.

Cpl. Kenneth Robinson (RCAF)

THE ANSWER:
By J.D. Conway

Your resentment is justified, Corporal Robinson, but it has been needlessly aroused. Your Catholic friends have been giving you faulty information. It is quite probable that you need no ceremony of Baptism to become a Catholic. You mention the faith and agonizing humility needed to "get baptized again when one is an adult." You must have received Baptism already. If it was valid, you cannot be baptized again.

Let us suppose for the moment, however, that you and the priest who is receiving you into the Church agree that you should be baptized conditionally when you become a Catholic. There is no need for you to have godparents, not even one, for conditional Baptism. So your problem vanishes. The law of the Church is very clear on this point. When, because of doubts, a Baptism is repeated conditionally, it is recommended that you have the same godparent who was present at your first Baptism, if this can be done conveniently. Otherwise, at your conditional Baptism no godparent is needed. I presume you were baptized in a Protestant denomination and had Protestant godparents. Catholic regulations do not allow Protestants to be godparents in a Catholic Baptism. So you may not have the same godparents you had in your previous Baptism. Consequently you need none of all.

The presence of one or more godparents or sponsors is required for any solemn Baptism which is not conditional. If a baby is baptized privately, in danger of death, either by a priest or a lay person, no sponsor is necessary, though one may be used. The custom of having sponsors in Baptism is very ancient, and Church law says that they must consider that their godchild is committed to them in a special way and not specially concerned about the religious education of the child so that it may live in accord with the promises they make for it.

In past centuries, and in some countries today, the relationship between sponsors and their godchild was quite close and affectionate. They were related to each other in God. In America today custom seems to be the main reason for having sponsors, though they also answer the questions addressed to the baby.

The functions of godparents may be seen in the Latin names given to them. They are *offerentes,* those who present the child for Baptism; *sponsores,* those who make promises for the child, *susceptores,* either because they received the child as it was lifted from the baptismal font, or because they contracted to look after the child's spiritual welfare; or *fide jussores* because they promised in the child's name that he would be a good Christian. The word most used is *patrini,* which is closely related to our word *patron,* a protector or sponsor. Two godparents are not needed; the law supposes only one, and permits two only if one is male and the other female. So a baby of either sex may have a godfather, or a godmother, or both; but not two godfathers or two godmothers.

Suppose, corporal, that you had never been baptized at all and wished to become a Catholic; then you should have a sponsor, preferably a man. He presents you to the priest for Baptism, and that is about all. If you should have difficulty finding a sponsor the priest could easily find one for you. For practical pruposes he assumes no obligations in your regard. You are old enough to take care of yourself, and if you become lax about your religion that is your own problem. Your godparent would exert no pressure on you, though, if he were a close friend, he might offer you help and encouragement.

Godparents have no duty to keep a spy out of the Church. Anyone who joins the Church to spy is wasting his time. We have nothing to hide, and there isn't anything he can learn as a member that he couldn't learn as readily by study from the outside.

Now, corporal, let us consider the case where you have been through a ceremony of Baptism, presumably in a Protestant church. You would need to be baptized conditionally only if there had been something wrong with the way Baptism had been administered to you. Did the minister use water? Did he say, "I baptize you in the name of the Father and of the Son of the Holy Spirit"? If you were properly baptized as a Protestant, you may not be rebaptized when you become a Catholic. The Church has always taught that Baptism can be received only once; it makes spiritual changes in your soul, marks it as a Christian soul, and those changes remain forever. However, about the end of the 2nd century a new problem arose. There were heretics in those days, and they baptized many people. Now some of those baptized by heretics wanted to become Catholics. What should be done? Should they simply be received into the Church and given a penace for their heresy, or was it necessary to baptize them? Were Baptisms conferred by heretics valid or not?

During most of the 3rd century this question was argued up and down. Most of the bishops of Africa and many of those in Asia Minor and the East were convinced that Baptisms conferred by heretics were invalid. For them there was only one Baptism: that given in the Catholic Church.

St. Cyprian, Bishop of Carthage, was the leading proponent of this theory, but he was strongly opposed by St. Stephen, Bishop of Rome. Pope Stephen agreed that there was only on Baptism: that of Jesus Christ. But anyone who baptizes as Christ commanded gives the sacrament validly, whatever his personal sins or errors. It is really Jesus who baptizes; the minister is only an instrument used by Jesus.

The Pope's opinion prevailed, and the doctrine was firmly established that Baptisms conferred by heretics were valid. In the 8th century a new controversy arose about the validity of Baptisms administered by pagans or Jews. Again the decision was based on the principle that it is Jesus who baptizes. If a pagan baptizes properly, using water and saying the correct words, he confers a valid sacrament.

Back in the 3rd century there was no question of conditional Baptism. This idea seems to date from the 8th century, but was first clearly expressed by Pope Alexander III in the 12th century: "If there is doubt whether certain ones were baptized, let them be baptized after these words have been pronounced: 'If you are baptized I do not baptize you, but if you are not baptized, I baptize you in the name of the Father, etc.' "

The principle of conditional Baptism was incorporated into the law of the Church by Pope Gregory IX in the 13th century. In modern times, especially in the United States, we have tended to use conditional Baptism much too freely and frequently. It is a lazy man's solution.

We believe, corporal, that Baptism is necessary for salvation. We accept literally the words of Jesus, "Unless a man be born again of water and the Spirit, he cannot enter into the kingdom of God." So we want to be sure that all those who join the Catholic Church are validly baptized. And we do know that some Protestant ministers, who consider Baptism only as a sign of faith, are not much concerned about details we consider important: using water on the person as a sign of washing, and speaking accurately the words of Baptism at the same time.

Rome has often stated that Protestant Baptisms are, in general, to be presumed valid, and that if we are doubtful about a particular Baptism we must make careful investigation before we baptize conditionally.

It does not matter what the minister believes or his church teaches about Baptism. A Methodist minister wrote to a lady he had baptized: "So far as I know, no one of our ministers believes that water washes away any sins. I am satisfied that you are a Christian, but I am also satisfied that my baptizing you with water did not make you that. The water was a *sign* that you had become a child of God.

It would be a peculiar and, to me, a foolish and immoral God who would want anyone to believe that anyone could save a soul by putting water on the body."

The lady sent this letter to the Holy Office, asking if her Baptism might not be invalid because of the minister's total rejection of the sacramental nature of Baptism. In reply the Holy Office asked for information concerning the time, place, and manner of her Baptism. Was water used? Did the minister pronounce the trinitarian formula? Was the fact of the Baptism noted in the record books of the church? They showed no interest at all in the minister's beliefs or his church's teaching.

Our recent 2nd Vatican Council made us have a greater respect for our separated brethren, to be careful to avoid offense. We know that our indiscriminate baptizing of all converts from Protestant Churches has long been a cause of great offense; and some ministers and bishops have protested strongly. If we are sincere about ecumenism we must take their protests seriously. We should find out, in friendly dialogue, just how various ministers do baptize. And we should be particularly careful not to question without serious cause the Baptism of Anglicans, Episcopalians, Lutherans, and others who believe Baptism to be a sacrament.

We must not confuse scruples with sound, reasonable doubts. Only when doubts of this kind exist and cannot be cleared up by investigation should we baptize conditionally.

36

What Is That Ceremony Over the Mother After Childbirth?

THE LETTER:

While passing time in the waiting room on a visit to a friend who was a patient at the Good Samaritan hospital, I picked up a *Catholic Digest* and glanced through it. I became absorbed, especially in the article which answers questions concerning the Church. I have long pondered one and hope you can answer it. I attended, several years ago, a Catholic ceremony that aroused my curiosity.

What is the significance of the new mother, kneeling with her child in her left arm and a lighted candle in her right hand, being met at the rear of the church by the priest and led to the front—I believe to the altar of the Virgin Mary—where certain prayers are said by the priest? Inquiry has confounded me.

Before this ceremony, I was told, the new mother is not supposed to leave her home, but after it she is allowed to come and go. Is this tradition, or something? Is it in practice everywhere or peculiar to this religion? The ceremony I mentioned happened in the Polish church, although I've seen it in the German Catholic church also. I am taking a course in the Catholic faith with tests and questions to be written out and mailed back. (May I add, I am doing quite well with the tests.) However, I have not yet discovered anything about this in the books sent me to study. I am deeply interested in the Catholic religion and honestly hope this question merits a ten-year subscription. I could not afford it myself, but if I visit my friend or discover a copy of the *Catholic Digest,* I ask them to save it for me when they have read it. I have learned so much, and am very interested.

Clyde L. Meyers

THE ANSWER:
By J.D. Conway

The ceremony about which you inquire, Clyde, is commonly called the churching of women, but its proper name is the Blessing of a Woman after Childbirth. It is called churching because the woman comes to church to give thanks to God for the birth of her child, and because the priest meets her at the door and leads her into the church, where she receives his blessing.

In some countries there used to be a supersitition that it was unlucky for a woman to leave her home after childbirth until she went to the church for this ceremony. And some people have had the idea that a new mother was not supposed to go into the church until the time of her churching ceremony.

This latter idea probably comes from a false association of churching with the ancient rate of purification prescribed by the Mosaic law to remove the legal uncleanness a woman incurred through the birth of a child. We read about it in the 12th chapter of the book of Leviticus. A woman who has given birth to a boy is unclean for seven days, but if her child is a girl she is unclean for 14 days. Then after the boy's birth she must wait an additional 33 days (a total of 40) before she goes through the rite of purification. After a girl's birth the mother waits a total of 80 days. In the Mosaic rite a mother was purified by offering for sacrifice a lamb and a pigeon or dove, but a poor woman who could not afford the lamb could offer two pigeons or doves.

The Jewish law also specified that the first-born son of any Jewish woman belonged to God. He had to be brought back by his parents. At one time the offering for this redemption was five shekels of silver. St. Luke describes for us the purification of Mary, the Mother of Jesus, but he does not mention the price paid for His redemption as her first-born son. "And when the days of her purification were fulfilled according to the Law of Moses, they took Him up to Jerusalem to present Him to the Lord—as it is written in the Law of the Lord, 'Every male that opens the womb shall be called holy to the Lord'—and to offer a sacrifice according to what is said in the Law of the Lord, 'a pair of turtledoves or two young pigeons.' "

Probably our churching ceremony comes from this Jewish rite. In some times and places the custom was common to have the churching done on the 40th day after birth, in commemoration of Mary's visit to the temple. However, the Church, from the time of St. Paul, has never admitted in any official way the notion of legal uncleanness or the need for purification. The ceremony of churching has never been obligatory, but it has often been popular, and must have been a very early practice since it is observed in the Churches of both the East and the West.

The basic ceremony for churching is found in the Roman Ritual, and while it is entitled the "Blessing of a Woman after Childbirth," it is not found in Title VIII of the Ritual, which deals with blessings, but in Title VII, the "Rite of Celebrating the Sacrament of Matrimony." In former days this rite was performed in Latin, and I will translate part of the rubrics (instructions printed in red) and the prayers found in the Ritual: "If a mother after the birth of her child wishes to visit a church, in accord with a pious and laudable custom, to give thanks to God for her good condition, and if she should ask a blessing from a priest, he shall vest in surplice and stole, and accompanied by a minister carrying a holy-water sprinkler, he shall go to the door of the church, where he shall meet the woman who is kneeling at the door sill and holding a lighted candle in her hand; he shall sprinkle holy water on her and recite Psalm 23 [24], which praises God's power over the universe, lays down the moral requirements for assisting at divine worship, and calls on the gates of the temple to open that the king of glory may come in.

"Then the priest offers her the end of his stole and leads her into the church, inviting her to enter into the temple of God to adore the Son of the Blessed Virgin Mary, who gave her the privilege of bearing a child.

"Then the woman kneels before an altar and prays, giving thanks to God for the favors He has shown her. And the priest prays to almighty God, who by the childbearing of the Blessed Virgin Mary has turned the pains of birth into joy, that he look with kindness on this servant of his who has come to this sacred temple with happiness to give thanks and that He grant her that after this life she and her child may attain the joys of eternal blessedness, through Christ our Lord.

"Then the priest sprinkles holy water on her and says: 'May the peace and blessing of God Almighty, the Father, Son, and Holy Spirit, descend upon you and remain forever. Amen.' "

The pastor is required to give this blessing if a woman asks for it, and any other priest may give it on similar request, in any church or public oratory, provided he lets the person in charge of the church know about it. In some times and places it has been customary to give the blessing in the home. Now the entire ceremony is in English and it is found in a book called *Collectio Rituum* (a collection of rites) published in 1964 with the approval of the Conference of Bishops of the United States, and the endorsement of the Holy See. It has been changed to include a blessing of the child the woman brings with her. This blessing is found in Latin in the Appendix of the Roman Ritual. Here is its present approved translation:

"O Lord Jesus Christ, Son of the living God, begotten in

eternity, you willed to be born in time. You love the innocence of childhood, and lovingly embraced and blessed the little children who were brought to You. You anticipate the needs of this child with your tender blessings, and grant that no evil may corrupt his (her) mind, but that, advancing in age, in wisdom, and in grace, he (she) may live so as to please You always. You who live and reign with God the Father in the unity of the Holy Spirit, God, forever and ever. Amen."

There is another change: in place of Psalm 23 [24] we now say the *Magnificat*: the hymn spoken by the Blessed Virgin Mary to give thanks to the Lord that she had been chosen to be Mother of the Saviour.

Both the Roman Ritual and the *Collectio Rituum* have a blessing for a woman who is expecting the birth of a child, and the *Collectio* also has a blessing which I do not find in my edition of the Roman Ritual: For a woman whose child has died, its prayer is:

"Almighty, everlasting God, lover of holy purity, in your kindness You called the child of this woman into your heavenly kingdom. In your kindness also, O Lord, be merciful to your servant, so that strengthened by the merits of your passion and by the intercession of the Blessed Virgin Mary and all your saints, she may triumph over her sorrow, bravely resume her duties, and rejoice with her child forever in your kingdom. You who reign, God, forever and ever. Amen."

Joined to prayer and symbolism the essential feature of churching is the blessing. All through the Sacred Scriptures we find blessings or benedictions. Often men bless God. Such blessings are prayers to God, expressions of adoration, praise, thanksgiving, and petition. In patriarchal times fathers often blessed their sons, conferring upon them certain rights and privileges. The priests of the Old Law had the privilege of blessing the people. Speaking through Moses, God told Aaron and his sons "Thus will you bless the children of Israel and you will say to them: May the Lord bless you and keep you! May He show his face benevolent towards you and have mercy on you! May the Lord turn his face towards you and give you peace."

Jesus Christ often blessed persons and things. The women of Galilee brought their children to Him that He might lay his hands on them and pray for them. To multiply the loaves, He lifted his eyes to heaven, blessed the bread, and broke it. In similar manner his blessing multiplied the fishes. At the Last Supper He blessed the bread and wine before changing them into his Body and Blood. Jesus gave to his disciples the power to work miracles by giving blessings, and they used it often to heal the sick and to drive out devils.

From earliest days blessings have been used by the Church. They are rites accomplished by the ministers of God, to bring favors from God, or to dedicate persons or objects to the service of God. They are held to be much more effective than simple prayers, because they are an exercise of definite power which the Church has conferred on her ministers: the power to bless in God's name and thus to obtain through the public prayer of the Church certain benefits.

God alone can produce the effects of benediction in men and things, but He has communicated a measure of his power to those who represent Him on earth. The priests of the Mosaic covenant had it; the priests of Jesus Christ have it. They use it every day at the conclusion of Mass, and they use it frequently at other times.

The blessing of a woman after childbirth is not often requested in my own part of the country. Those who do ask for it usually receive it right after the Baptism of their babies. That is probably the reason that the two prayers, for the mother and for her child, are not combined in one ceremony. And because the mother is already in church for the Baptism, there is no need to meet her at the church door. Sometimes the priest accompanies her from the baptistry to the altar, reciting the *Magnificat* with her. Sometimes she simply kneels at the altar, with her baby in her arms, and a lighted candle beside her, and there receives the blessing.

37

Why Do Catholics Kiss the Pope's Ring?

THE LETTER:

During the Pope's visit to the United States I noted that many kissed his ring. I know that Catholics do this, but being a Protestant, I have never known why. Would you please explain this for me?

Does each new Pope have his own ring or is the same ring handed down from one to the other? And, what is the insignia on it?

Virginia M. Whitling

THE ANSWER
By J.D. Conway

Those who knelt to kiss the ring of Pope Paul, Virginia, were not venerating the ring but giving a sign of respect for the Pope. The ring now receives the kisses, but the original gesture was to kiss the hand of the person.

There is quite a bit about such kissing in the Bible. In the Book of Sirach we read of the borrower who kisses the lender's hand. Four times in his Epistles St. Paul tells his brethren to greet one another with a holy kiss. And St. Peter gives the same advice.

The Fathers of the Church warned that this kiss must be given with modesty and reserve, and Tertullian mentions a pagan man who was not pleased to see his Christian wife "meet one of the brethren with a kiss."

The kiss of peace was from earliest times a part of Christian liturgy before Communion, at Baptism, and in the absolution of a penitent. And gradually ceremonial kisses were given to relics, the book of the Gospels, the cross, blessed palms and candles, the hands of the celebrant at

Mass, many of the utensils and vestments used in the liturgy, and especially to the altar of sacrifice. Today most of these kisses are eliminated from our ceremonies, but the priest still kisses the altar during Mass, and he also kisses the book of the Gospels after the Good News has been announced to the people.

The old Romans at times actually worshiped their emperor; so kissing his hand was not enough; they kissed his feet or the hem of his garment. This mark of veneration thus became a custom of the papal court. The Emperor Justin paid respect to Pope John I in this manner when he visited him early in the 6th century. Even the great Justinian knelt to kiss the feet of Pope Constantine.

When St. Leo IV was elected Pope in the middle of the 9th century, this custom of kissing the Pope's foot was ancient. In principle it is still observed liturgically by the two subdeacons—one Latin and the other Greek—in the solemn papal Mass; and it is the formal salutation the cardinals give to a new Pope after they have elected him. The Pope may, of course, dispense with the formality.

Even into the present century it was customary for those received in private audience to kiss the foot of the Pope as a sign of reverence. I believe that recent Popes have rejected this custom, as foreign to the spirit of the 20th century.

In the middle of the 15th century, after long and delicate negotiations, Joseph, the venerable patriarch of Constantinople, was persuaded to visit Pope Eugene IV to work out a reunion of the Churches of the East and the West, separated for 400 years. The patriarch and his bishops were given a glorious reception at Venice and sent by river boat to Ferrara where the Pope awaited them. And there the whole program was nearly wrecked over a kiss.

Pope Eugene insisted the patriarch must kiss his foot at the public reception, as protocol required. Emperors, cardinals, and bishops had done it, but the Greeks would not permit it. They would not start negotiations for reunion by having their patriarch admit his inferiority to the Pope. Poor Joseph remained on his boat all day while prelates raced back and forth to work out a compromise. Eugene finally called off the public ceremony and received the patriarch privately with friendship and courtesy. Thus they began a year of cooperative and hopeful negotiations at Ferrara and Florence.

But, Virginia, your question is concerned more with the ring than the kiss. The story of rings goes back to the ancient Egyptians. Some of their rings were made of pure gold, simple in design but quite heavy, and many of them had the owner's name and title inscribed in hieroglyphics. Poor Egyptians wore rings of silver, bronze, glass, or pottery, sometimes brilliantly colored. Important Egyptians wore scarab rings. They were designed so that the scarab (beetle) could be used to make an impression in a drop of wax sealing a letter or document. All through ancient and medieval times this signet ring was used by persons in authority, including the Pope.

In ancient Rome the average citizen wore only an iron ring, and even this was forbidden to slaves. The use of a gold ring was regulated by law. Ambassadors were the first allowed to wear them, but only for public duties. Later, senators, consuls, the priests of Jupiter, and other officials acquired the right of the gold ring. The Emperor Severus extended this right to soldiers, and later all free citizens acquired it

In the Bible, when the prodigal son returned home, his father commanded that his servants "fetch quickly the best robe and put it on him, and give him a ring for his finger and sandals for his feet." St. James directs that the man in mean attire be given the same treatment as the "man in fine apparel, having a gold ring."

Clement of Alexandria had suggested that Christians mark their rings with symbols of the faith, like a dove, fish, or anchor. Other Fathers held that such show of luxury was unbecoming for a Christian, but there is evidence that Christian rings were worn in the 4th century. It seems that bishops began using rings about the same time, but they were not yet symbols of office, probably only signet rings for sealing their personal papers.

In the year 610 Pope Boniface IV indicated that the bishop's ring was a sign of his sacred office. A few years later a council at Toledo, in Spain, directed that when a deposed bishop was restored to his office, his crosier, stole, and ring should be given back to him. These became the inseparable signs of the bishop's office; and later, in the 11th-century fights over lay investiture, the point at issue was whether the king had the right to give a bishop the crosier and ring, and thus confer the Episcopal office upon him. Popes like Gregory VII and Innocent III insisted that the crosier and ring were symbols of spiritual authority and could not be conferred by the state, but only by the Church.

From the 8th and 9th centuries we have a book of Church ceremonies called the *Gregorian Sacramentary*. In it we find these words, still used in giving a bishop his ring: "Receive the ring, that is to say, the seal of faith, whereby thou, being thyself adorned with spotless faith, mayst keep unsullied the troth which thou hast pledged to the spouse of God, his holy Church."

In early centuries the transfer of a bishop from one diocese to another was strictly forbidden. The bishop was "married" to the church (diocese) for which he was consecrated, and if he should desert that church to take another he was guilty of "conjugal infidelity." One decree read like this: "A bishop deserting the church to which he was consecrated and transferring himself to another is to be held guilty of adultery and is to be visited with the same penalties as a man who, forsaking his own wife, goes to live with another woman."

In modern times the western Church is less strict about the transfer of bishops. Modern fidelity need not last until death, but the bishop still continues the ancient custom of wearing a wedding ring on the fourth finger of his right hand. Cardinals came to wear rings in imitation of bishops even though they might be only laymen, deacons, or priests. All modern cardinals are bishops. When the Pope names a new cardinal, he gives him a modest ring set with a sapphire. But the cardinal may lay it aside for one that pleases him more, and probably costs more. Before the bishops of the 2nd Vatican Council left Rome last December, Pope Paul gave each of them a plain gold-plated ring. Possibly in the future simple rings of this kind may replace the precious ones with large stones that many bishops now wear.

For many centuries it was held improper for a monk to wear a ring, but in due time abbots acquired this privilege. The highest ranking monsignors, called prothonotaries, may wear rings, as may doctors of theology and canon law. Most Sisters wear a simple gold ring as a sign of their betrothal to Christ; and in times past an occasional abbess acquired a jeweled ring like that of a bishop.

The most famous papal ring, though it is never seen by those outside the Vatican, is the Ring of the Fisherman. In early centuries it was used by the Pope as his personal seal;

now it is used on those official documents called briefs. This ring is etched with a drawing of St. Peter in a boat, drawing his net from the water. It is broken when the Pope dies. Then, for the conclave which will elect a new Pope, a new ring is prepared, with the space for the Pope's name blank. This new ring is placed on the finger of the newly elected pontiff, who then declares the name he has chosen, and gives back the ring so that the name can be engraved on it.

In some paintings of Popes of Renaissance times we notice a large ring worn on the thumb. These were seldom precious, sometimes made of gilt or bronze and set with glass or crystal, and had the Pope's name and coat of arms engraved on them. They were so heavy they were seldom worn, but were sent with envoys as objects of identification, or used in ceremonies of investiture.

Custom seems to prescribe that when a layman or a cleric of inferior rank meets a bishop, a cardinal, or the Pope, he should kiss his ring; and in most cases, especially for your own bishop or the Pope, a genuflection is in order. However, many bishops now lift you up if you try to genuflect, and twist their ring hand away from you if you try to kiss it. Possibly you noticed Pope Paul doing this when he received diplomats and dignitaries at the United Nations.

38

Isn't Confession Against Human Dignity?

THE LETTER:

One of the greatest obstacles to many joining the Catholic Church is the auricular Confession that must be practiced by Catholics. I am told this is a late introduction into the Catholic Church, one not practiced by the Apostles, and not enforced for centuries after the time of Christ. How can a practice introduced so late and felt by so many as revolting to personal human dignity be essential to Catholic belief? As God knows the heart, cannot absolution be ob-

tained by sincere repentant approach to a priest, without
subjecting oneself to the indignity of having to reveal one's
wretched deeds to another?

T.G. Thomas

THE ANSWER:
By J.D. Conway

To the average Catholic, Mr. Thomas, auricular Confession hardly presents the dramatic difficulties that you suppose. It is scarcely pleasant for most of us, but can give us
joy when we are properly through with it. And we are convinced that it is good for us.

However, I know that some converts retain an aversion
to Confession long after becoming Catholics. I usually advise a new convert to go to Confession frequently right at
the beginning, so that custom may blunt his aversion. It
usually works.

The Jewish-Christian tradition is that there is need for a
confession of sins to obtain divine forgiveness. Adam began
it, though he tried to put the blame on Eve. The Lord directed Moses: "Say to the people of Israel: when a man or
woman commits any of the sins that men commit by breaking faith with the Lord, and that person is guilty he shall
confess his sin which he has committed."

The books of the Bible, *Judges, Samuel,* and *Kings,* have
the sins of Israel and the people's confession of those sins as
a theme. The prophets were sent to show the people their
sinfulness that they might confess their guilt and be forgiven. In the Psalms we find many examples of confession,
both personal and corporate; the best known is Psalm 50,
[51] the *Miserere:* "For I acknowledge my offense, and
my sin is before me always; against You only have I sinned
and done what is evil in your sight."

The public ministry of Jesus was prepared by the preaching and Baptism of John: "And they were baptized by him
in the Jordan, confessing their sins." There is no reason to
believe that the confessions made to John the Baptist were
detailed or specific, any more than those of the *Miserere.*
Indeed, there is no explicit command in the New Testament that we must confess our sins to a priest. The later
Christian practice of detailed confession is based on the

manner in which the power of forgiving sins was given to the Apostles. They were to exercise judgment, which could be reasonable and fair only if it were based on the facts. And only by confession could they obtain knowledge of all the facts.

Jesus first told Peter, "Whatever thou shalt bind on earth shall be bound in heaven, and whatever thou shalt loose on earth shall be loosed in heaven." And later He gave the Apostles the same power: "Amen I say to you, whatever you bind on earth shall be bound also in heaven; and whatever you loose on earth shall be loosed also in heaven." The powers given here are quite general, probably referring to the power of Peter and the other Apostles to receive men into the Kingdom of God. But they have been interpreted traditionally with reference to the particular power of forgiving sins, which was given explicitly after the resurrection when Jesus appeared to the Apostles, breathed on them, and said to them, "Receive the Holy Spirit; whose sins you shall forgive, they are forgiven them; and whose sins you shall retain, they are retained."

That the Apostles—and their successors—might use this power which Jesus gave them, the power to forgive or to retain, it was necessary that sin be submitted to their judgment. Many of these sins they could know only by a detailed confession. For this reason the Council of Trent declared anathema those who denied that sacramental Confession was divinely instituted, or those who say that "the Confession made in secret to the priest alone is foreign to the institution and the precept of Christ, and is a human institution."

Trent also affirmed that this sacramental Confession has been in use in the Church from the beginning, and in proof of this it appealed to the testimony of the Fathers. We must admit, however, that this testimony is not very abundant during the first four centuries of Christianity. There is no real evidence that the Apostles ever heard confessions. The Ephesians did make confessions (Acts, chapter 19, verse 18) but we are not sure that these were part of the sacrament of Penance. St. James advised the early Christians to confess their sins to one another, but the context would indicate the sacrament of the sick rather than that of Penance. St. John wrote, "If we confess our sins, He is faithful and just to forgive us our sins. . . ." But the context gives us no certainty that he is referring to sacramental Confession made in detail or to a priest.

Among the earlier Fathers of the Church there is just enough reference to private confession to indicate that it was not unknown. St. Cyprian, who died in 259, wrote of the African custom of confessing sins and receiving forgiveness from the bishop. Tertullian, a bit earlier, exhorted the faithful to overcome their human respect by a sincere avowal of their faults if they wish to obtain pardon of them. Origen, about the same time, gave evidence that the Christians of the East sought a remedy for their sins in penitence which was preceded by confession to a priest.

After the 4th century, and especially after the time of Pope St. Leo the Great (440–461), there is evidence that the practice of secret Confession was becoming widespread. Pope Innocent I, about 416, gave advice to confessors about judging the seriousness of sins confessed to them. About the same time St. Jerome said that the sinner must confess his faults to the priest even as the sick person must confess his wounds to the doctor, who cannot heal that which he does not know.

Most of our knowledge of the penitential system of the early Church indicates the practice of public confession, which presumably included only sins of a public nature and may have been made in general terms rather than by name and number.

Another peculiarity of those early centuries was that only the bishop heard Confessions, gave absolution, and imposed penances. Furthermore, the notion was general that the sacrament of Penance could be received only once. A man's sins were forgiven once by Baptism. Then if he fell into sin again, he could be forgiven through Penance; but then if he relapsed again, the Church seemed to offer him no further help.

During part of the 4th century we find that the Bishop of Constantinople had a priest-penitentiary to aid him in administering the sacrament of Penance. This is possibly the first clear evidence we have of priest replacing bishop in hearing Confessions. But Socrates, a 5th-century historian of Constantinople, tells us that priest-penitentiaries were appointed from the earliest times, because bishops decided that "it was too much of a burden to announce one's sins as in a theater with the congregation as witness."

In the Church of Rome in the 5th century it was customary to hear Confessions at the beginning of Lent and to give absolution to the penitents on Holy Thursday. Gradually the practice grew of granting absolution immediately after Confession, and before the prescribed works of penance were performed. By the 11th century only the more notorious sinners had to wait until Holy Thursday to be forgiven.

Our modern confessional came into general use only after the Council of Trent, in the 16th century. Before that the priest usually heard Confessions seated in a chair somewhere in the church. The penitent would stand or be seated beside him, and would kneel for the absolution, which the priest gave while laying his hand on the penitent's head.

The fact that Confessions are usually heard in church lets the sacrament of Penance retain a measure of the public character it had in the early centuries, when the bishop or priest evidently acted in the name of the Church to bind sinners to penance and then to loose them and reconcile them to the community. But the enclosure of the confessional, with its screen between priest and penitent, gives modern sacramental Confession a secrecy and anonymity the priest is under gravest obligation to respect.

Since you speak of obtaining absolution by a sincere repentant approach to a priest, Mr. Thomas, it is evident that you have an understanding of the sacramental manner in which God has chosen to come to us, forgive us, sanctify us, and join us to Himself in fatherly embrace. Sacraments are the signs of God's activity. To redeem us He sent his Son, the visible, living sign of his redeeming love for us. To continue his sanctifying activity among us, Jesus gave us the Church, a sign of his living presence among us, a sign of the Holy Spirit dwelling in our midst. And the seven sacraments administered by the Church are seven effective signs of the sanctifying activity of Jesus, ministering to our various needs.

In recent years some pastors, to deepen the religious fervor of their people, have developed ceremonies of collective penitence, at which a priest helps the community make an examination of conscience, and leads them to an awareness of guilt and to an expression of repentance. In March, 1965, the bishops of Holland issued a pastoral letter in which they pointed out the advantages of such ceremonies, which encourage the people to make humble admission of their faults and to profit by the example of their neighbors

who join them in avowing guilt. There is also opportunity
for the priest to help them form right consciences and to
become more deeply aware of their responsibilities.

However, the bishops point out that these public ceremonies should be a preparation for a private Confession by
each individual: "A general intercession asking God's
mercy and pardon finds its place, indeed, in the framework
of the ceremony of penitence. We are not justified, however, in using it for the formula of absolution which is reserved by the Church for private Confession." The obligation of private Confession must be insisted upon for "all the
faults which conscience recognizes as grave."

The bishops also say that "the sacramental value of the
ceremony of repentance is to be considered as a theological
problem not yet resolved. It should remain clear that, before there can be a sacrament in the strict sense of the
word, there must be a decision of the Church authority
responsible for doctrine."

Church authorities may some day permit collective penitence and general absolution for those who are guilty of
only minor faults, without obliging them to a confession of
devotion. But traditional theology and practice indicate
that grave sins cannot be forgiven in this manner, except in
urgent circumstances, as military chaplains do before battle.

39

Doesn't Forgiveness Encourage More Sin?

THE LETTER:

My question regards absolution of sin by confession. If
the worst criminal can become "sinless" merely by confessing evil deeds to a priest, does not this doctrine actually
remove any moral or conscience-based restraints to
wrongdoing? If I have misunderstood this matter, I would
truly appreciate having it clarified and explained.

Barry Best

THE ANSWER:
By J.D. Conway

I believe, Barry, that there are two ways to answer your question. I have to talk about the nature of Confession and true penance, and about motivations in moral matters.

First, Confession is not a simple, automatic wash job. It must involve a real conversion, a sincere change of heart; otherwise it does not result in forgiveness. Some Catholics do have the wash-job concept. If they make a careful, detailed confession, say a fervent Act of Contrition, and perform the penance assigned them, they think their slate is washed clean, ready to be marked up by next week's sins! They think that if they get their sins cleared away regularly, they are leading a good Christian life.

It is a bad concept. But may I ask you, Barry, what is your own concept of forgiveness? Do you believe that Jesus Christ merited forgiveness for us? Do you believe that God is merciful and will forgive us when we honestly repent? Or do you believe that there is no forgiveness? That leads to despair. If God won't forgive me the sins I have already committed, what do I have to lose by committing more? If we have the slate-and-sponge concept of Confession, we must rid ourselves of it. The concept might apply to Baptism, which can be received only once. But it could destroy true morality if applied to the sacrament of Penance.

Someone has called the sacrament of Penance a Baptism in tears. The penitent is healed of his sins only through a bitter cure in which he has an active part. There is no such thing as a passive receiving of the sacrament of Penance as there is of Baptism. The penitent is not a minister nor even co-minister of the sacrament but he is an associate cause.

This active role was more apparent in the early Church. The penitent's role was liturgical; he even had special robes for it. He fasted, wept, publicly proclaimed and deplored his sins. In those days the sacrament of Penance could be received only once. We get the impression of a big sinner repenting in a big way, strongly admitting his guilt in public, forcefully declaring his total change of heart and life.

By contrast, our present liturgy of the sacrament gives us the impression of the poor little sinner, ashamed of his weakness, coming to admit his guilt secretly and anonymously. But in making this comparison, each of us should judge in his own conscience, honestly, which method fits him better. Do I have enough confidence in my own fortitude, strengthened by God's grace, that I will never need forgiveness more than once? If so, I may be a proud, self-deceived fool.

We do not merit forgiveness by the depth of our contrition and the perfection of our confession. Our forgiveness comes totally from the mercy of God through the merits of Jesus Christ. Perfection of detail in the telling of our sins is not needed. What we need is truthfulness and honesty. Soul-shaking sorrow is not required. What we need is an honest facing up to the evil of sin, an awareness of the love of God which we have violated and lost. Monumental resolution may be deceptive. We need an honest attitude toward the future and a confidence in God's grace. If a person honestly tries to make a good Confession, he cannot make a bad one.

Now, Barry, let us take up the second part of your question. What restraints does a mature person need to deter him from evildoing? The child is stopped by fear of a spanking. A criminal by fear of the police. An uneducated and poorly motivated Christian by threat of hell or loss of heaven. For an immature person the slate-cleaning Confession may be a momentary deterrent from sin, and a routine hope and consolation. The Christian who is simply running to escape hell will never achieve much positive goodness. He expends all his energies in conquering the negative. Until he becomes positively motivated he cannot be an authentic Christian. It is hard to say how much a routine Confession keeps him from sin, or how much it encourages him in sin by promising him an easy way out.

The truly moral Christian is not primarily concerned with sin and forgiveness. He is motivated by love and a sense of responsibility. He realizes that he is the adopted child of God, invited to love the Father who already loves him. He realizes that he has been redeemed by the love, sacrifice, and obedience of Jesus Christ, and endowed with freedom and grace through the Saviour's resurrection. He is aware of his responsibility as a child of God to open up his soul and his conscience to the demands of the Spirit.

The mature Christian sees the men about him as his brothers. He knows that all men are endowed by their creator with certain rights which must be fostered, not violated. He recalls the words of Jesus: "I tell you solemnly, insofar as you did this for the least of these brothers of mine you did it to Me."

The mature Christian loves his neighbor in daily practice. He realizes that each man is a person, resembling God in the very core of his personality. He respects the dignity of all persons, never treating them as impersonal members of a race, sect, or nationality.

The mature Christian's morality is not imposed on him by taboo or social restraint. It is a function of his own soul, a product of his personal freedom, formed under the responsibility of his own conscience. It guides him to the realization of his vocation as a man, a son of God, and a brother of Jesus Christ.

To the mature Christian, Confession is less a sponging away of sins than a means of personal encounter with his Saviour. If he is conscious of sins, he seeks their forgiveness because they hinder him in loving God. If he has failed in loving his neighbor, Confession challenges him to check up and make plans to see that he doesn't fail again. Then it frees him from hindrances, so that he may love more.

The mature Christian goes to Confession that he may receive from God, as a renewed gift, the freedom and grace to continue to grow in love. Genuine love is hurt when it has given offense. It hastens to deplore the injury, to seek forgiveness and reunion with the loved one. The repentant Christian seeks and finds in the sacrament of Confession the love that he has lost.

A timid and weak man seeks protection in negative law. It tells him not to cross this or that line or he will sin. He feels hemmed in by all the Thou-shalt-not's. He is protected from the dreadful challenge of personal responsibility. His sins are measured by the footsteps over the lines. Then he goes to Confession, wipes out the footprints, and starts over, watching the lines more carefully for awhile. If he ever reaches the point where he can stay within the lines, he is on the straight and narrow way. Confession now becomes for this man a routine devotion.

A mature morality does not ignore the law. It uses the law as its guide to develop personal responsibility. But at moral maturity, the force of love, guided by a well-formed conscience, pushes the person toward the good without conscious reference to the law.

A mature morality never loses awareness of sin. It is, however, free of any subconscious feelings of guilt, despite its clear consciousness of sin, and it is not preoccupied with sin. Its aim is positive virtue, Barry, of which love is the uniform source and basis.

The worst criminal can become sinless through God's forgiveness because Jesus Christ died for his sins and for him rose from the dead. But it is not enough that he merely confess his sin to a priest. He must turn away from sin, repudiate it, and seek God's grace and love that he may never sin again.

40

Why the Unusual Garments at Mass?

THE LETTER:

I am a 16-year-old girl, from a family of eight, and I have wondered why priests, when saying a Mass, wear a certain colored cloak—green, white, or some other color.

My question is: Is there a reason for this?

Teresa K.

THE ANSWER:
By Kenneth Ryan

Yes, Teresa, there is a reason for it. The basic reason for vestments is just to clothe the person wearing them. Like the joke you remember from childhood—the chief use of cowhide is to hold the cow together. And that answer is not really as smart alecky as it sounds.

Most people think the robes of the priest are full of mystic meaning. Yet historically, clothing very close to that which the priest now wears over his street clothes was worn as street clothes by the citizens of 4th-century Rome. The basic garment for both sexes, worn day and night, was just a long roomy shirt made of two flaps sewn together with openings for arms and head. Any further clothing was just wrapped on. A rope or a belt around the waist made things secure. Some had an outer garment against wind and rain contrived like the present-day Mexican serape or poncho, a blanket with a hole in it worn with the head through the hole.

The direct answer to your question, Teresa, is that the Church is so old-fashioned that priests at Mass still wear this 4th-century clothing. I don't suppose the ordinary man had so fancy an outer garment as the priest wears now, but what happened over the years was this: people began to wear their best clothes to Mass and, of course, saw to it that the priest and his ministers on the altar were dressed up.

The next step was that these better clothes were saved for wearing only at Mass. (We know that in 257 A.D. Pope Stephen I forbade the clergy to wear the Mass clothing for every day.) When an old priest or bishop died, the clothes often would not be worn out yet and would be used by his successor. When this sort of thing went on for hundreds of years, of course, the clothing became way out of style; but from reverence for the previous wearers it was copied rather exactly when it was worn out. What people were then wearing finally became so different that they began to think the vestments must have some hidden meanings. So meanings were invented. Such "explanations" of the vestments were not all to the bad; many were devotional and highly poetic.

The belt or ropelike cord, now called the cincture, was thought in the devotional interpretation to symbolize the ropes that tied Christ to the pillar for his scourging. In the poetic interpretation, it was a symbol of the restraining chastity to which the cleric vowed himself. But, of course, these vestments, like others, the amice and maniple, were in the first place just ordinary clothing. The amice was a cloth tied around the neck to protect the elaborate outer garment from perspiration. The maniple was a cloth tied to the arm and used to wipe the brow and, I suppose, to blow the nose. One famous scholar says the maniple was used as a napkin. People brought it to banquets and used it to wrap up and take home what they couldn't eat—the original doggy bag.

The priest now wears a stole at Mass. It is a long strip of decorated fabric. You don't see it when he has the outer

garment (chasuble) on and not everybody in 4th-century
Rome wore one. But certain magistrates and public officials did, and so it was adopted by the clergy as their token
of office. It, too, was utilitarian.

About 20 years ago we carried a joke in *Catholic Digest*
to the effect that if St. Thomas Aquinas could come back to
earth and go to Mass in our time, he would recognize the
theology preached in the sermon. (This filler dates from
1950.) The punch line was to the effect that if Adam came
back, he would recognize the jokes in the sermon. We
could now add that if St. Augustine came back, he might
be unfamiliar with the theology and humor but he would
recognize the clothing of the priest as being of his own
time.

In the reform of the Mass since the Vatican Council
there has been considerable modification in the rules about
what vestments are to be worn. Of course, there were extremists who wanted to do away with all formality in worship,
including vestments, and you still hear outraged stories
from people who have seen priests sit down on someone's
living room floor and celebrate Mass wearing sport shirts
and checkered pants.

Church rules have now made the wearing of the maniple
and amice at Mass not of obligation, and such odd garments as a chasuble with a sewn-on stole have made their
appearance. There is also a form-fitting alb which does not
need a cincture. I hesitate to suggest it, but the implication
seems inevitable that the wearer is guilty of a Freudian slip,
exhibiting a subconscious desire to put aside chastity, along
with its symbol, the cincture.

So we get this far, Teresa, but I have not answered why
the priest wears a *colored* cloak. He changes the color according to the season of the year (violet for Advent and
Lent, white for Easter and Christmas, red for Pentecost,
green for the rest of the year) or the kind of saint honored
on a feast day (red for martyrs, white for others). This is
all symbolism and in the very early days the color did not
matter. Basically, the priest wears the vestments now because the Church rules call for them, despite the pressures
from the revolutionists. The Church requires them because
of her long tradition and because they lend dignity and distinction to the wearer and contribute to the reverence and
awe the congregation should display at Mass. If Mass were

really only a game-room indoor picnic, as the extremists seem to think, play clothing would be in order.

It is true that our Lord wore no distinctive clothing at the Last Supper, which was the first Mass, but those sensitive enough will feel the force of his parable in which the man not wearing the special-clothing wedding garment was cast out of the banquet.

I never, Teresa, could see the point of going back to antiquity and its discontinued customs. We do not necessarily have to give up wearing Mass vestments now because our Lord didn't have them. The ostentation that worked its way into the papal and episcopal apparel has been very much toned down by recent regulations, but the Church did not do away entirely with special vestments for divine worship. They were a natural development, I suppose. Their innovators were not under divine guidance, but the investments still served the purposes of religion: awe and decorum at the Sacrifice.

In the good old days apologists for the Church used to explain that pomp and circumstance of the papal court was a kind of teaching tool; that people could learn the true dignity of the Pontiff from the outward display accorded him. They further argued that the honor shown the Pope gave him face in the sight of those who did not follow him.

On the purely practical level these arguments are still sound, though on the idealistic level they should not allow "triumphalism," the kind of thinking in which the Church becomes a conquering army. Secular army officers are distinguished by their better uniforms. In modern hospitals you can tell whether the woman employee is a maid, nurse, or doctor by the uniform she is required to wear. It all makes for more efficient operation, whether of army, hospital, or Church.

It may even be that our Vatican Council thinking was affected by the memory of our enemy Hermann Goering, the Nazi second-in-command, who wore medals the size of soup plates, and of Comrade Stalin, who wore workingman's garb. The Nazis have affected us in other ways. It is really the memory of their midnight knocking and arresting that has led to the elaborate protection our jurists have built up for the man arrested by the police. So we can account for some of the present-day opposition to many old cultural practices such as uniforms. Some of it took the form of toning down the apparel of the clergy.

The Church at present seems to be trying to strike a balance between the regalia of the Renaissance Pope and the near nudity of the holy Hindu saddhu. It seems to me a sensible effort and that the priest should continue to wear the vestments prescribed by the Church.

Teresa, at age 16, you don't remember the old High Mass. Most people didn't go to it because it took longer than Low Mass, the singing and organ playing were usually those of volunteer amateurs, the celebrant was not always up to the simple chant melodies and invariably talked longer because the High was the last Mass.

But come Christmas and the church was never big enough to hold all who wanted to come to the midnight Solemn High Mass. The choir had practiced diligently and with the advantage of singing familiar music was unquestionably always beautiful. The celebrant knew he must not preach too long because of the many Communions; he even practiced the Preface. But the real splendor came from the vestments. The assistants to the pastor wore the dalmatics, special vestments for the deacon and subdeacon used only for Christmas and Easter. There were lots of extra altar boys, the best of whom bore torches and filed in and knelt for the Consecration. The lights and music and golden vestments, the careful solemnity of every move in the ceremonies, the wafted clouds of incense made as fine a public tribute to the glory of God as we mortals were capable of.

Every Christmas season my confessional saw someone who had been away from the practice of the Faith for 20 or more years come back. They may have had other reasons, but I'm sure the attraction was attending that glorious Midnight Mass as an insider. The vestments were at the core of the visual appeal, though I must grant reluctantly that an occasional egghead may have been attracted by the abstractions "brotherhood" and "participation."

Dear Teresa, whether the colored cloak of a lone priest, attended by lectors and schoolboys in their street clothes, will ever bring you the sense of awe you should have at the Holy Sacrifice, is doubtful. But, so far, the Church insists that the priest wear it, and at least we have not taken the final backward step.

41

How Often Should I Go to Confession?

THE LETTER:

I am a Sister and have taught in elementary and high schools for 40 years. Outside the educational field, I have contacts with many relatives and friends, some of whom have been expressing their concern about changes in the Church.

A few elderly persons and others have manifested regret at the manner with which they were received by the priest in the confessional. Some were told quite bluntly that, since they had no sin to confess, they should not take up the confessor's time.

I have always felt there was value in frequent confession. My question is: Does the Church still approve of weekly and biweekly confession, or does she discourage it?

Sister Marie

THE ANSWER:
By Kenneth Ryan

The immediate reaction to your question, Sister, is to answer that the Church still approves, but that a great many priests do not. Having said that, so many observations occur to me that I have to pause and make a choice of what to say first.

So let's say first that no understanding, well-informed, sincere priest would ever tell an elderly person to discontinue frequent confession. If he is understanding, he knows that the lifestyle, habits, mental stability, and even creed of the penitent along in years are all likely to be involved. In the past, frequent confession has been preached universally as the foundation of the spiritual life and, in the excess zeal of some preachers, as practically necessary to salvation. It is not, of course, but countless people still alive are inclined to think it is. To drive such people away from confession is, to say the least, to be lacking in understanding, presently the prime requisite for with-it clergymen.

Of course, impatience has always been the besetting fault of confessors, and from my inside view I would say, who could blame them? After an hour or two of hearing Christmas or Easter confessions in the old days, tension would grow. On First Fridays, God forgive me, to get a real sinner was often a relief from boredom. But in the holiday seasons, I would get so many real sinners to whom I repeatedly would give the same reasoned, constructive advice that it seemed like it was the same sinner coming back instead of the same old sins. This hallucination usually brought on impatience in the confessor and, unfortunately, sometimes an excess of righteous anger against everyone. So, if you come innocent to your confessor at the end of a long line of penitents and are told in effect, "Scat!" forgive him. If he has just been sitting there in a nearly empty church, as is so often the case now, I don't think he merits such ready pardon.

If he is well-informed, the confessor will be acquainted with the Catholic doctrine of grace. Going to confession is an occasion of grace as going to certain other places can be an occasion of sin. Just for coming, so to speak, the penitent is rewarded with actual grace, the kind that helps him in his daily struggle to stay on the side of God.

Sanctifying and sacramental grace used to be assured by the priest asking the presently sinless penitent for a "sin of his past life." Despite the fact that most penitents thought he was probing for a sexual sin (and usually told him one), he was only trying to get "matter" to make up the complete sacrament. Like the Nixon pardon—absolution required something to absolve. The reconfession of sin allowed the reabsolution, which brought a rebestowal of grace. For a priest to tell a penitent simply to go away because he has no new sins to confess is to disregard the Catholic doctrine of grace.

If he is sincere, the priest will regard the provision of the sacraments as a duty second only to offering the Sacrifice. I can't help but believe that a priest who tells people not to come to confession is something like the satirical De Quincey's criminal, who started with murder and progressed through the stages of thievery and lying to arrive at the ultimate crime of procrastination. Telling people not to come to confession is (let us be honest) usually done in the somewhat mistaken expectation of awakening them to a deeper religion. This mistake may be put on a par with procrastination, but just like De Quincey's procrastinator, such an instructor must surely have begun with something much more important, like insincerity about his real duties as a priest.

All I have said so far, Sister, is just scolding. I am sort of passing on to inconsiderate priests what one of my old professors used to say, "If the shoe pinches, put it on!" Of course, not all priests are inconsiderate, and not all understanding, well-informed, sincere priests want to restore the sacrament of Penance to its pre-Vatican II glories and disabilities. Its rite has had various forms in the past and the hope of the present reformers is to contrive a new one that will bring back the popularity the sacrament once had but now has not. The thought is inevitable that maybe it is the people and not the rite at fault, but anyway the Holy Father himself has noted the advisability of frequent confession in the Apostolic Constitution *Poenitemini* which permitted meat on Friday and reduced the number of potential sins.

As a matter of fact, Sister, the whole thrust of the Penance reform is to increase the frequency of its reception. I think it fair to say that the emphasis in the reform is on repentance rather than the exactness in the confession of sins, and on some kind of public ceremony in addition to the private admission of sins.

There is a lot of talk about community forgiveness and asking pardon of the community which reactionaries regard as a gargoyle rather than a foundation stone of the new theological cathedrals. They say it is still God who must not be mocked, though they also say the community deserves some respect. In point of fact, except for quasi-maniacal blasphemy, sin against God is nearly always committed through sin against a neighbor. The new term *reconciliation with the community* is supplanting the older *forgiveness from God*. This change stems from the same cast of thought that appears at Mass now, where ideally everybody (the community) goes to Communion, not just individuals who go out of private devotion.

So, Sister, you may use different terms while retaining

the old essentials: 1) Examine your conscience. 2) Tell your sins. 3) Have sorrow for them. 4) Determine to give them up. 5) Get absolution. 6) Perform the good works the priest imposes on you. If different terms will bring more people to the sacrament, that is all to the good.

So far, of course, the reforms in the Mass have not brought any enormous increase in Mass attendance, and reform in the rite of Penance faces very many of the same difficulties in acceptance. In the old Mass the emphasis was on the transcendence of God and the need at Mass to be awestruck by his majesty and omnipotence. In the new, the emphasis is on God's immanence and the need to see Him constantly in our midst as we go about ordinary activity.

In recent but now rejected devotion, the best frame of mind at Confession was to be psychologically in the same spot as you would be if conscious on your death bed—personal and final judgment at hand! In the new rite you are preserving your membership in a holy community and, so to speak, deal with your God through its membership.

You might say that the people in the old days wore tight shoes because it felt so good when they took them off; in the new reform people do not have the pain of psychological crisis, but neither do they have the pleasure of relief from tension, which kept them coming to confession in the old days. Sitting in the box in those times now past, I would often hear the sigh of relief, sometimes too soon—after the recital of the sins; but often enough at the right time—after the bestowal of absolution.

Maybe there was a touch of the neurotic in all this but at least in those sighs of relief there were echoes of jubilant songs of faith in a certainly forgiving God. Real sinners walked home on air. Something of the same type of religious "moment" came at the Elevation in the old Mass in that hush of utter adoration of Christ newly present. Now the rubric writers of the new Mass canons have found it necessary to instruct the celebrant to pronounce the words of consecration distinctly. The new breed priests were so anxious that the people know Christ was there *all* the time that they were discounting the words that changed the bread to the Body of Christ to make Him newly present.

But when you point out the psychological joys of the old ways of Penance, you open the door to the objection that the sacrament was being used as a kind of do-it-yourself psychoanalysis and that people were finding in it the same type of relief. Of course, this was not true. The differences between confession and a spell on the analyst's couch are patent. The priest is a judge; the analyst is a doctor. The subject matter of confession is sin, in analysis it is memory. The purpose of confession is to be rid of sin, of analysis to be rid of mental disorder.

If people did indeed find the same kind of relief, it was still distinguishable into remedy for soul *versus* remedy for body. Incidentally, all the old writers on spirituality condemned any feeling of relief after confession, but this reproof only underlines the fact that many people liked it and went to confession on account of it.

Eventually the new rite of Penance will prevail. The rite of the sacrament has been changed often before this and to update an old joke, St. Joseph, though a carpenter, never built confessionals. But Christ did institute the sacrament of Penance. "Whose sins you shall forgive. . . ." He implied a judgment before forgiveness and as long as this consideration and other essentials are preserved, good Catholics should go fearlessly and more frequently to the sacrament no matter how the old jots and tittles be disturbed.

42

Can't the Church Allow for Mistakes in Marrying?

THE LETTER:

From time to time lately I read of the relaxation of the Church with regard to divorce and annulment—just slight reference and no detail. My question: What are the Church's current rulings on annulment and divorce? Are they really any different from what we have always been taught?

I am a happily married wife and mother and I do not ask for myself. But a first cousin of mine insisted upon marrying a boy who was still in the service. My aunt and uncle gave their permission because they were afraid they would run off and possibly go to a justice of the peace.

When he was discharged, they came to live with my aunt and uncle, but he was unfaithful.

My cousin learned of his affairs but because of the condition of my uncle's health (he had had a second serious heart attack and the family was advised absolutely no shocks) she never spoke of what was going on. Almost a year went by. Then my aunt answered the phone one day and a female voice said, thinking she was talking to his wife, "Keep your rotten husband away from my daughter." Of course, the whole thing came out and he was almost thrown from the house. My cousin was urged to start annulment proceedings and went through the entire procedure. But an annulment could not be gotten because of the impossibility of proving that he never had the intention of remaining faithful before the marriage.

My cousin eventually "married" the man she was working for during all of this time. Before this "marriage" her husband met her outside the office building one night and gave her a severe beating and this was the only time she has ever seen or heard from him to this day.

Eighteen years have passed. My cousin attends Mass every Sunday. Her present husband is a wonderful husband and father and their two girls are active Catholics who (one is 17, the other 14) still ask why Mother doesn't receive Communion. She is tearing herself apart because she has been excommunicated. Thank God I've never been faced with this temptation so I'm certainly not going to judge her. Since we started to subscribe to *Catholic Digest* and I discovered your "What Would You Like to Know About the Church," I've wondered if this might be the source of further information.

By the way, I and my family love the magazine—I really didn't realize that published questions mean a ten-year subscription until I read the fine print for your address today. I'm not looking for an easy way out for this girl, but I'm convinced that she had a rotten deal. She was headstrong and very young; but she is paying a terrible price, and I wonder if the good Lord in his mercy would help us find a way for her to return to the sacraments.

M.C.

THE ANSWER:
By Kenneth Ryan

Letters like yours and situations such as the one you describe, Mrs. C., are very moving and disturbing. They make nearly everyone wonder why the rules can't be changed. Just before your letter arrived, it was reported in the secular press that three priests' senates in the Eastern United States had petitioned for the readmission to the sacraments of divorced and remarried Catholics whose original spouses were still living, with permission to continue in their second marriage. They were undoubtedly thinking of persons who really wanted the sacraments again.

We can begin by taking up your question about the relaxation of the marriage laws. The answer is that there have been administrative changes which in some cases can speed up annulment procedures by eliminating automatic appeals and by delegation of authority to lower levels. But in the Church's doctrine of sacramental marriage there has been no change.

What you, judging from your letter, have been taught still has the force of law. Civil divorce, agreed to by both parties, of itself does not prevent the guilty or nonguilty from seeking absolution and Communion. It is remarriage, which is *prima facie* evidence of a determination to remain in what the Church declares to be a state of disobedience, that makes canonical reconciliation with the Church impossible. Strict law makes the official Church seem cold and inhuman to those who really suffer from its enforcement. Relatively few people can by themselves understand the need for it or have the ability to "take it."

My one-time best friend and worst golfing partner was deserted by his bride within hours of the wedding ceremony, yet waited 14 years for a Church annulment. It came through, but by that time he had lost all desire for another marriage, and considered that life had passed him by. Church legal procedures then seemed slow to the point of injustice, but he never questioned the basic law. He got the point that the Church really doesn't have a choice between being "strict" and "permissive."

A presentation of lawmakers' difficulties will not be as

moving as the recital of the difficulties of your cousin, Mrs. C., but before any final attitude can be reached, the Church's dilemmas must be considered. As an example, take her stand on the validity of Protestant marriages, or, to be more exact, marriage between validly baptized non-Catholics. Because of the Baptisms, the Church holds these marriages valid and a Catholic may not marry the divorced party to such a marriage. To change the rule would be a grave insult to millions of sincere Christians because it would amount to calling their happy marriages less than Christian, and their children illegimate. Yet the same rule must seem outrageous to a divorced non-Catholic who wants to marry a Catholic. It must seem to him that the Church is trying to exercise authority over a nonmember. It's easy to say "Brush away all the technicalities" but brushing away technicalities would harm as many people as it would help. The Church has only the choice of saying "This is the law" or "Anything goes!"

In civil law, failure to live up to a contract can be established by the usual rules of evidence and the case settled. The trouble with Church law cases, so to speak, is that they so often involve the mental intentions of the litigants. The Church holds that conscience (a judgment here and now about the morality of an action about to be performed) is supreme. The Apostles choosing a successor to Judas said only that he had gone "to his own place," not that the betrayer of the Lord had gone to hell. The Church has no ceremony of condemnation that is the opposite of canonization. She excommunicates (or rather, used to) by bell, book, and candle, but does not imply anything more than a judgment on the morality of the excommunicated person's action. She does not declare him lost forever. Even if he does not outwardly repent, he may have been acting according to his conscience.

In practice, of course, if every man were allowed to follow his own inward conscience without being required to accept outward legal consequences, the abolition of law and complete anarchy would result. So the Church, while for matters of eternal import, such as heaven and hell, insists that conscience is supreme, for matters of temporal import such as Christian marriage, must enforce laws. She could not exist in anarchy.

This is all in the face of compassion for those to whom the enforcement of her laws is painful. The priests senates which petitioned for readmission to the sacraments of re-married divorcees were asking the Church to abandon law. It may have seemed to individual members that they were only asking for a change in law but *de facto* they were asking that the Church give up all sanctions, allow individual conscience to rule temporal as well as eternal affairs, and surrender herself to anarchy.

At this point I imagine myself presiding over a joint meeting of the three priests' senates and hearing the cries that this wasn't what was meant at all. Some hold that the Church can dissolve marriages as well as witness them; that marriages can die of themselves and that the Church can be witness to their dissolution. If the new moralists are talking about the dissolution of marital love, common purposes, and so on, marriages certainly do die of themselves. But there can be no dissolution of the original contract in which the parties agreed to a Catholic marriage.

If the parties can prove in law that that was not their intention, there never was a Catholic marriage and the supposed marriage can be annulled. If it was the intention of the parties to contract a lifetime union, the new moralists, to declare their marriage dead, would have to deny the plain meaning of the contract. That way lies chaos. As an aside, I suppose the new moralists are proposing a conditional marriage contract for future use in the Church.

But that would take us into the metaphysical realms of the natural law on the question of whether a conditional contract could be the basis of a true marriage. The standard Catholic teaching is that marriage *as a sacrament* comes under the regulating power of the Church. But because marriage *as an institution* is based on the natural law, the Divine revealed law, and Apostolic law, mere ecclesiastical law cannot change the elemental requirements of monogamy and indissolubility: one man—one woman—till death.

By this time, Mrs. C., I can hear you saying something like "I know all that, but what can be done for my cousin?" I don't know. I have to admit there is no comfort in telling anybody "That's the law" whether you are talking about an overtime parking ticket or a life lived out in agony of conscience. Sympathy for a man on trial for his life, sympathy for the man imprisoned, sympathy for the good cause a criminal represents can all make the administration of justice and the enforcement of law painful to enforcer and enforcee alike. But abolishing law to do away with law-breaking makes no more sense than abolishing hospitals to do away with disease.

In such painful cases as that of your cousin, Mrs. C., the only "out" would seem to be reliance on the Catholic doctrine of conscience. Whatever disobedience caused her present status, her conscience may tell her that it is morally impossible to leave her partner. God's judgment will be the same as any sincere judgment she makes of herself. But the doctrine of conscience must be properly understood. Most people take it to mean that you can follow your own will (they think that is their "conscience"). The doctrine does not mean that. It does not allow going to confession and "not mentioning." It does mean being so certain of your position that you take your chances in not going to Confession or Communion and being willing at death to face God without having made use of the sacraments He has provided for you.

Technically, that is the sanction of the law: obey—or no sacraments. Honestly following your conscience means weighing your judgment against that of the teaching Church, which is based on the studies of learned theologians, and deciding that you are right and that they are wrong. It can be done but it is not simple. It would seem to require the same degree of heroism as fully obeying the law. Conscience is an "out" but not an easy one.

To abolish the law and its power to bring ordinary people into obedience to God and Church, to allow the disobedient to go to Communion, which is the symbol of unity of discipline as well as belief, would be to destroy the whole concept of the Church as a governing institution. It would be unreasonable.

To raise all this to a more philosophical plane we have to admit that the opponents of reason are in the ascendant now. They do what they please, shout "Why not?" and refuse to listen to the answer. This attitude accounts for the popularity of birth control, abortion, euthanasia, disbelief in dogma, irreverence in worship, and a lot of lesser things I could think of. I do not accuse, Mrs. C., your cousin, nor anyone caught in the toils of the law of being against reason. I can only offer my unworthy prayer that the trend toward unreason in our present society may be reversed and obedience to the Author of all good law be resumed on a world scale.

43

What's the Connection Between Communion and Feasting?

THE LETTER:

I understand the reason for the one-hour fast before Communion, but I am confused about the application of it in my own life. One weekday I desired Communion very much and was planning to go to Mass. But without thinking I took a sip of coffee and suddenly realized I had broken the fast and couldn't go to Communion.

There are other times when I keep the fast and receive Communion. But I have to say that the actual desire for Communion was greater that day when I had broken the fast. In conscience, I felt that my partaking of Communion that day would have been more devotional than usual. Shouldn't I have gone to Communion anyway?

Sheila A. Mellick

THE ANSWER:
By Kenneth Ryan

No, but yours is a good question, Sheila. It was chosen because nearly everyone has had that experience at one time or another and because it leads into discussion of a much larger subject: *mortification,* a good old Catholic word meaning deliberate nonfulfillment of legimate desires.

From your letter, you didn't go to Communion "anyway." But when I was in parish work many persons confessed to me that they had gone to Communion after breaking their fast and didn't feel right about it afterward.

I also remember from seminary days the case of Martin, the brother of the late Father Eddie Doherty who was on the *Catholic Digest* cover in June, 1970. In the long wait for a late Mass, Martin forgot and drank water the morn-

ing he was to be ordained deacon. He would have to receive Communion at the ordination Mass. He caused a lot
of inconvenience because he did not show up with his class
and an irascible bishop and ceremony crew had to make a
special trip later in the week just for him.

We young seminarians all thought Martin had acted the
only possible moral way. (This was in 1928, when more
things seemed to be mortal sins.) We were dumbfounded
that Martin was bawled out by the priest who was master
of ceremonies. He told him he should have "formed his
conscience," received Communion, and been ordained deacon on schedule. It was a beautiful case in moral theology
of a situation from which it was possible to escape by
"forming your conscience." This phrase, we found out,
meant making a definite judgment and a decision at the
time of difficulty and abiding by it later without further
story.

People used to confess to me that they had gone to Communion after breaking their fast. I used to explain, on the
basis of Father Martin's experience, that if it were an occasion socially requiring their reception of Communion (their
own Nuptial Mass or the First Communion of one of their
children) they could "form their conscience" and receive
Communion after unthinkingly breaking the fast. If it were
a case where they were going to Communion privately or
in cases where no one would notice whether or not they
went to Communion, they should not.

I don't think that any sin was committed in any of these
instances of confessing the past because usually, and as you
imply, Shelia, the motive in receiving was the plain love of
God. But note that there is no justification for deliberately
breaking the fast and then deliberately going to Communion. That could indeed, just as in 1928, according to one's
intention, be a mortal sin. Such a bad intention could be
that of showing how up-to-date, liberated, freethinking, and
independent a Catholic one was.

You see, Sheila, all these considerations go back to what
I said first, that your question opened the way for a discussion of mortification. It can be voluntary or obligatory.
Most people just ask, "Is it a sin?" about such things as
swearing, gambling, and—God save us all—in these days,
even abortion.

When the Church sets up rules about going to Communion, these same people overlook the main purpose and just

ask again, "Is it a sin to break the rules?" For people that simple there has to be the simple answer: Yes. For people who understand that the Church is just not offering us another way to commit sin, the answer would be longer, involving "mortification."

As I said, mortification is giving up the satisfaction of wholly legitimate desires. We might add that giving up the satisfaction of sinful desires is only obedience to law and that the two "giving-ups" must not be confused. The Church ties Communion and mortification together: one must either fast for an hour or give up the joy of Communion. The Church's purpose in imposing the fast was to encourage mortification, not to provide a new way to sin. The sin is really in despising the rule, not in the eating of food or reception of Communion. In that sense the law is no new occasion of sin, since God has always left people free to despise his law (for the time being, that is).

Mortification, Sheila, has always been an essential part of Christianity and even of religions like Hinduism. You have to take it out of context, but I suppose the thought behind it was poetically best expressed by Robert Browning, "A man's reach must exceed his grasp, or what's a heaven for?" If we routinely satisfy all good or bad desires in this life, how can we reasonably expect praise or reward in the next life?

The people who just ask, "Is it a sin?" missed, I am sure, the point of the Vatican II reforms. When meat was allowed on Friday and Lenten fasting practically abolished legally, it was with the provision that alternate but unspecified mortifications be undertaken. The shift was from obligatory to voluntary mortification; the thought of doing away with mortification was not entertained. The people who really shifted to voluntary mortification increased their merit and that was the purpose of the reform. Too many people, of course, just said, "It's not a sin anymore to eat meat on Friday or to break the Lenten fast."

I remember from our fourth-grade catechism that wonderful mouth-filling phrase "works of supererogation" which I childishly but correctly understood to consist in doing more good things here on earth than were strictly necessary to get me into heaven. Sister used to explain that if *some* people did not do them and pile up these heavenly treasures, there would not be enough of them to buy the way of the rest of us into heaven. She didn't go into the infinite merits of Christ in this particular matter, and her theology might have been a little incomplete, but it was a wonderful, workable idea for us children. The more I think of it the sounder it seems. It was the doctrine of the Communion of Saints adapted to our childish understanding. It is that doctrine that people forget when they refuse to mortify themselves or insist on checking first on whether it's a sin not to give up candy in Lent, not to put a coin in the Sunday collection and so on.

As a matter of individual practical spirituality, mortification has always been considered a shield against sinning: the more mortification, the less sin. So when you or the society or Church you live in decide to forgo mortification you don't exactly decide to sin, but you certainly change your moral direction. Mortification is readily seen to work and even be necessary in such things as athletic fitness or winning a war (meatless days). There are always some who won't make the effort to excel athletically or to help in winning their country's war. Their spiritual counterparts are those who exclude everything but joyous celebration from their religious lives.

When the kids come home from school and say that Sister or teacher said there was no need to learn the Ten Commandments, parents need not conclude that the devil is on the loose. But they ought to realize that the teacher has confused the "giving ups" (sin and legitimate pleasure) and what is voluntary and what is obligatory. In making *all* mortification voluntary there is danger of implying that *all* morality is voluntary, whereas there are and should be laws of God and Church about both. It's a path many heretics have followed: They start by being too strict or expecting motives to be too high and end up by being against all rules and commandments.

All this must seem quite a digression from your plain question, Sheila, and I just noticed that you began by saying you understood the reason for the fast before Communion! I just ask that you also understand my tendency toward setting the world right.

44

May I Be Cremated If I Want To?

THE QUESTION:

I am a senior sociology major at South Carolina State College, a native Southerner, Afro-American, and convert to Catholicism. I converted at the age of 13 and have never regretted my decision. I am presently 21 years old.

I have always enjoyed reading the *Catholic Digest*. It was partially through such good Catholic literature that I discovered the Faith.

I often contemplate death and the hereafter and often feel a desire to be cremated after death. My question is "What is the Church's official position regarding the cremation of Catholics?" If the Church does not allow cremation, then why not?

Ronny A. Baston

THE ANSWER:
By Kenneth Ryan

The Church doesn't forbid cremation anymore, Ronny, unless it is done to symbolize denial of the Catholic belief in the resurrection of the body.

Cremation was common in ancient Rome, but the Christians didn't practice it. The great Christian Emperor Charlemagne forbade it under pain of death (and burial) and there was little or no cremation in Europe for a thousand years. The convenient modern process was invented in 1869, and cremation was thereupon taken up by the anti-Catholic masonic societies as a symbol and forbidden by the Holy office in 1886. The new Code of Canon Law continued the prohibition in 1918, but the anti-Christian symbolic use had pretty well died out (excuse the unintended pun) by 1963, and an Instruction was issued, permitting cremation except when it was symbolic. Since then the Church attitude has progressed or regressed, according to your viewpoint, so that the new Rite of Christian Burial makes provision for the burial ceremonies being performed in the crematorium itself.

But while your question, Ronny, makes these snatches of history necessary, it turns my mind to the newspaper obituary column. That feature is one of the prime reasons why so many people still buy the paper, filled as it is with news even more disturbing than that of the tolling bell. I was taught in my college journalism classes that as people grow older, they get more and more addicted to reading the "obits," and that a good many people turn to them first of all. I took up obituary reading rather early in life and have always indulged in the usual speculations about relationships and in gossipy checking out of who was buried in, and who out of, the Church.

I think I give the column a more thorough reading than necessary, and perhaps that is why I have lately noticed the growing number of nonfunerals. I find not only the time-honored requests to omit flowers, but statements that there will be no reviewal, and no visitation. This means no wake, no prayers, no farewells, and most likely cremation, or donation of the remains to medical science. If Catholics are not involved, I don't suppose it makes any difference. But sometimes I think they must be, since there is a notice of a commemorative Mass to be offered later. But Catholic or not, cremations and donations for transplants are increasing in number. There is no right and wrong to be argued out here. It is a good thing to receive the full rites of Christian burial, and a good thing to give them up so that someone else can live a longer life. In point of fact, though, not all cremations are necessary, and not everyone's body is needed for transplants. So there is room to evaluate the traditional Catholic final rites and their place in the total framework of the Faith.

Catholics believe not only in an afterlife but in the resurrection of the body. About all we know about that resurrection we have learned from the resurrection of our Lord. His risen Body was palpable; it could be touched and felt, as the doubting Thomas learned. But it was unaffected by space and time. The Lord did not have to walk up to Galilee to meet his Apostles there after He rose from the dead;

but He ate food with them after He rose; He used his tongue to speak to them in their ordinary language; his face was recognizable. This aspect of the Lord's risen Body gave rise to the Church's traditional respect for the bodies of the faithful departed. The human body was not a piece of clothing to be discarded by the immortal soul. It was part of the Risen Christ. It will be part of the faithful follower of Christ in the final resurrection.

Just how this is to be accomplished remains one of God's mysteries. The story is somewhere in the old Roman breviary about the martyr who proclaimed his faith by pinching the skin of his hand and declaring that he expected to rise again with that very flesh. That would seem unlikely. To use a mechanical term, the turnover in material in the human body is such that, at the end of an average life, the organism will have used many times the amount of material needed for the fabrication of one body.

And then there is the question of the constitution of matter. The solidest stone is ultimately fashioned of elusive energy particles. So when we pass beyond this realm of space and time and our bodies have reached their ultimate dissolution, it would seem that God would have at his disposal pure energy from which to reconstitute our bodies.

The average human being, however, does not think of such possibilities; he thinks of the body he now has. Christian devotion has tended to take this unsophisticated approach. In its extreme form I suppose it is best seen in the famous Capuchin Catacombs of Rome where the mummified, unburied, religiously robed bodies or skeletons of long-departed monks wait patiently for the last day. The elaborate embalming procedures of modern Western society are based at least partly on respect for the remains, although health laws certainly play their part.

The very existence of cemeteries, tombs, and grave markers attests to a natural human reverence for the dead. I can remember Sister telling us in grade school that China was poverty stricken because it had so many well-tended cemeteries that good, straight railroads could not be built. Maybe, maybe not. But even around New York City the enormous burial grounds that you pass on the way to the airport show the prevalence of this human instinct.

I think it would be safe to say that people who have this respect for the dead are people who believe in God. Some of those who do not believe nevertheless use death and burial symbolically. I am not to sure of its truth, but I have heard the story that the French statesman of the 1st World War, Clemenceau, insisted on being buried in a standing position. Apparently he meant that this resumption of the standing position was the only one he expected for his body, a kind of joke or play on the word *resurrection*.

In the last century, in the days of the "freethinkers," cremation was a symbol of the same kind for them. Somehow the immediate fiery return of the body to its elements symbolized for them man's identity with the material earth better than the Christian "dust to dust" and the slower process of burial. This pagan or materialistic symbolism is generally acknowledged to be the source of the Church's previous prohibition of cremation (Canon 1203), although certainly the expectation of resurrection entered into it.

But the modern popularity of cremation arises not so much from denial of God or immortality as from the ordinary pressures of life. Those who spend time convincing others of the universal feasibility of cremation say we are running out of space for cemeteries. In many modern cities there is truth in the statement, although I have read that all living and dead members of the human race could be contained in one cubic mile of space, a minute percentage of the earth's volume. Other considerations are those of expense, though again the saving is minor.

Funerals, despite the cliché, "This is the only time we relatives see each other any more," are no longer social occasions. Obviously no one any longer has time for the leisurely all-night wake afforded our fathers and grandfathers. There is no question but that cremation and "donation to science" is the coming fashion in disposal of the dead. In England in 1971 more than 55% of all the deceased were cremated, and the percentage has surely increased since then. Besides the inclinations to save space, money, and time by cremation, many famous people, romantically or pantheistically inclined, have requested that their ashes be spread over the place they loved most in life, or the sea or the mountains or the desert. Now all these factors have considerable, not to say determining force in the decision for cremation on the part of pagans. But, Ronny, I don't think they completely outmode the traditional Catholic practice.

When I was chaplain at the county hospital, I dutifully went along with the resident doctors on the matter of autopsies. That is, when the survivors of a medically unsolved death would refuse the routine request for an autopsy, the doctors would ask me to ask them again. I would, but my heart wasn't in it and I can't remember ever changing a decision. Of course, an autopsy is not the same as cremation, but the same sense of reverence for the human remains is involved. Nowadays if the request was for organs for transplant I suppose in special cases I could work up more enthusiasm. But I'm still glad I don't have such problems anymore.

In the face of cold scientific reason, it still seems to me that I will keep bodily integrity and identity if I eventually attain that glorious risen body St. Thomas Aquinas writes about (everybody a perfect 30 years old, constant physical ecstasy, freedom from the limitations of space and time: all in participation in the Beatific Vision).

I suppose the beautiful words of the *"In Paradisum"* ("May the angels lead thee into paradise, may the martyrs receive thee at thy coming") can be just as appropriate in the crematorium as in the church. They will not, though, ever be as consoling to me as when they accompany the slow procession with the casket down the center aisle, even though they are followed by the devoted local soprano quavering "Nearer My God to Thee." The difference is in the reverence of an act designed to preserve instead of destroy the human remains.

Your letter, Ronny, didn't say why you felt a desire to be cremated. Any consideration of a private nature can now justify a decision for cremation. But the Instruction of May 8, 1963, encourages Catholics to follow the "old and better" custom of burial. That is the "official" and, may I add, my personal attitude.

V

Inquiries on Doctrine

Inquiries on the doctrines of the Catholic Church did not form the most numerous group of questions but did show that the correspondents knew that what was believed was at least as important as what was done in the Catholic Church.

45

If Jesus Was God, How Could He Learn Anything?

THE LETTER:

I am a Methodist, but very interested in the teaching of the Catholic Church. My college classes frequently raise points of Christian doctrine that leave me with many questions. The latest one arose in my course in "Understanding Christianity."

The professor made the statement that Jesus Christ first learned about his Messiahship at his Baptism in the Jordan by John the Baptist, for it was here that God the Father made this known to Him.

This puzzles me for I had always thought that Jesus knew He was the Messiah even from the time He was a boy in the temple.

Perhaps this question is part of a larger problem, that of the presence of both divinity and a humanity in Jesus. Just how did this dual presence affect his knowledge of Himself and his work? Our professor lays great stress on the humanity of Jesus, so much so that it frequently seems to be a problem to reconcile, theoretically at least, the humanity and the divinity in Jesus.

To sum up:

1. When did Jesus first learn of his Messiahship?

2. Did He have both a divine and a human knowledge of this fact?

3. How do we reconcile this double presence of humanity and divinity in the single Person whom history records as Jesus of Nazareth?

Sharon Hayden

THE ANSWER:
By J.D. Conway

You are quite right, Sharon, in suggesting that the knowledge Jesus had of his Messiahship is part of a larger problem: the presence of both divinity and humanity in Him. This joining of two natures in one Person is the great mystery which produces our salvation, and many minor mysteries result from it.

Your professor is right in laying great stress on the humanity of Jesus. So did the writers of the New Testament, especially Matthew, Mark, and Luke. But he makes a mistake if he ignores the divinity of our Saviour in his teaching.

St. Luke wrote his first two chapters to stress the divine origin of the Saviour; and his final chapter attests the resurrection and the return of the Son to the Father. Luke indicates Jesus' knowledge of God and of his own mission when he writes of the boy Jesus in the temple, causing amazement by his knowledge, as He went about his "Father's business." Yet this same Luke tells us, at the end of that story: "And Jesus advanced in wisdom and age and grace before God and men." He is surely speaking of real growth, progress in knowledge, even in virtue.

We see no special problem about Jesus' growth in height, weight, and age. But how can a Person who already knows all things learn new things? And how can the same divine Person who is the source of all sanctity advance in grace? These questions, Sharon, are only part of the problem of reconciling the double presence of humanity and divinity in the single Person, Jesus.

How could God all-powerful become a helpless human baby? How could the same Person on whom all created things depend become a created thing Himself, totally dependent on others? It is not easy to reconcile these seeming contradictions. The earliest Christians apparently did not try. They simply knew by faith that the Son of God became man, preached God's word, died on the cross, and rose from the dead. He was equal to the Father in all things; and He was a real man who had lived amongst them.

But soon Christians began to seek explanations, and the

answers they found often led them into difficulties. The Docetists decided that the human nature of Jesus was not real. It merely had the appearance of reality. Or, if there was anything real about it, it was not of earthly origin, but came down ready-made from heaven.

The Adoptionists, on the contrary, held that Jesus was only a man who was adopted by the Father to be his Son. At the Baptism of Jesus, they said, the Father communicated divine powers to Him. We could make a long list of such conflicting errors in the first five or six centuries of Christian history. But the faithful continued to believe that Jesus of Nazareth was true God, Son of the Father, and that He was true man, subject to human needs and limitations in everything but sin. The one divine Person had both natures complete and distinct.

Even when we have accepted this mystery as beyond the limits of our understanding, Sharon, your question about the knowledge of Jesus still offers special problems. As God, Jesus knew all things from eternity. As man, Jesus learned new things. It proves how real and distinct his human nature was from his divinity. He had eyes to see the beauties of nature, ears to hear the teaching voice of his mother, and a mind capable of learning from what He saw and heard.

And yet Jesus was God. He could not simply ignore his divine knowledge. In the measure that a human brain could hold it, there must have been some of that knowledge transferred. We call it infused knowledge, knowledge poured into Him. He had it as a man from the beginning. And yet it did not seem to interfere with the normal learning process of boy and man. Seldom did Jesus use or display his infused knowledge. His preachings reflected his background in Nazareth: He spoke of fields and animals, of wheat and weeds, of vineyards and fig trees, of the hen with her little chickens, the crowing cock and the foxes, the pastor and his sheep, the laborer and the fisherman.

And yet there were times when He evidently went beyond the range of his acquired knowledge. He amazed the doctors in the temple when He was 12. He had no master, and had attended no schools, except maybe for Saturday sessions in the synagogue at Nazareth. No ordinary boy, with such lack of training, could have known so much. The people of Nazareth knew that He had received no special education: "And coming to his own country, He began to teach in the synagogues, so that they were astonished, and said, 'Where did He get this wisdom and these miracles? Is this not the carpenter's Son?' "

Even in Jerusalem his unusual knowledge was recognized. St. John tells us that "Jesus went up into the temple and was teaching. And the Jews marvelled, saying, 'How does this Man come by learning since He has not studied?' "

Jesus' answer was: "My teaching is not my own, but His who sent Me."

When his divine mission required it, He made use of the knowledge He had from divine source. Otherwise He spoke the humble Aramaic dialect which He had learned in Galilee, with maybe a bit of Greek which He might easily have picked up there, and some liturgical Hebrew acquired in the synagogue. His education came from experience, and probably from reading the Scriptures, but for the most part He was his own teacher, which means that God was his teacher. His mother and St. Joseph contributed their share, no doubt. "He was subject to them." But the ultimate cause of the intellectual formation of Jesus is to be found in his divine nature.

Your professor's statement, Sharon, was that "Jesus first learned about his Messiahship at his Baptism in the Jordan by John the Baptist." I would be inclined to disagree with him. Matthew, Mark, and Luke give us accounts of Jesus' Baptism, and John makes clear reference to it. But none of them intimates that Jesus learned anything special from the event. We read that into the accounts only by supposing that Jesus had not previously known that He was the Messiah, the beloved Son of the Father, the Chosen One.

If your professor were talking about the temptations of Jesus, which follow immediately after the Baptism in the first three Gospels, I would be inclined to agree that there was a learning process. The temptations are all Messianic in nature. They seem to imply that Jesus, by a rugged process of human experience—combined with divine wisdom— could see through the materialist concepts of the Messianic kingdom then current, and perceived the true spiritual nature of his mission and a kingdom not of this world.

Maybe, Sharon, a few of our readers, who have not had courses like your "Understanding Christianity" may be a bit confused by our references to Messianic mission and Messiahship. Most of the religious history of the Jewish people was inspired by a hope in the Messiah, a great king who would be sent by God to establish the Kingdom of God, save his people, and bring them glory. Their ideas of this kingdom were not very clear, and their pictures of the Messiah diverse. In the time of our Saviour dreams of power, wealth, and splendor often characterized the Messianic hope. In the temptations the devil is shown presenting these dreams to Jesus, the true Messiah, one by one, while He in turn pushes them aside and staunchly pursues his true mission, which leads to the cross, on the way to glory.

Now returning to the Baptism of Jesus, the opening of the heavens, the voice speaking from heaven, the coming of the Spirit, and the dove as a symbol of Israel, were no doubt revelations to St. John the Baptist. As he himself said: "I have seen and borne witness that this is the Son of God." For Jesus it was not a revelation, but a solemn attestation to the knowledge He already had that He was the Messiah. And to the early Christians, who learned of it later, it was the solemn consecration of Jesus to his Messianic mission.

Apparently Jesus and John were the only ones who witnessed the heavenly manifestations. To the rest of his disciples Jesus revealed only gradually that He was the Messiah, and still more slowly the startling fact that He was God's own Son. None of them seem to have grasped it fully until after the Resurrection. Peter proclaimed it much earlier, of course, and Jesus blessed him for his act of faith. Peter, James, and John saw Him transfigured. And all the Apostles heard Him say that He came forth from God, was one with the Father, would soon leave the world and go to the Father. But these truths were so astounding that they sank in slowly. Even after the resurrection Thomas was able to doubt for a while.

Jesus the Man was the means God chose to reveal Himself to men. The divinity is perceived through the humanity. As men we are not able to see the divine directly; we see it reflected in Jesus Christ. In studying the Gospels we do well to look for the normal development of his human nature: in body, mind, and soul. St. Paul says, "Son though He was, He learned obedience from the things He suffered." And we know that this obedience led Him to accept death on the cross, canceling out the disobedience of Adam and all his sons.

We need not be afraid to say with Luke and Paul that Jesus acquired knowledge by experience, and made real progress in the external exercise of moral virtues. We are simply saying that He was truly man. But we must not stop there, as your professor seems to do. We must look for the divinity which frequently shows itself in the words and deeds of this Man, the divinity which is always there, even when it does not show. If we keep in mind that Jesus was truly the Son of God, then the answers to your three questions are not difficult:

1) As God, Jesus knew of his Messiahship from all eternity. As man, He knew of it from the beginning of his life on earth, by infused knowledge. But by contact with the realities of life, with the social, intellectual, and political ideas and conditions of his time (in other words, by his temptations) He acquired an acute, strictly human, experiential knowledge of his mission, its nature, and its import.

2) He did have both a divine and a human knowledge of his Messiahship; and those two types of knowledge were as distinct as his two natures.

3) Only the omnipotent God could make one person both divine and human; and our human minds can only speculate on how He did it. But we owe the flame of divine life within us to the fact that He did it.

46

Just How Is the Eucharist the Body and Blood of Christ?

THE LETTER:

Although I am not a Roman Catholic, I do believe very strongly in the Real Presence of Christ in the Eucharist. My problem concerns the doctrine of transubstantiation.

My present understanding is that Aristotle formed a theory about the nature of matter, saying it consists of "substance" and "essence." On this theory is based the present doctrine of transubstantiation. This clearly states that when the host is consecrated, the substance, or accidental part of the bread, remains while the "essence," or actual part of the bread and the wine, is changed into the actual

Body and Blood of Christ. The instruction book accompanying the inquiry class I am attending states explicitly that upon the consecration of the host, the actual bread and wine cease to exist.

However, in light of modern knowledge of the atomic structure of matter, Aristotle's explanation of matter seems as outdated as the ancient theory that the universe travels around the earth. How, then, is the doctrine of transubstantiation still seen as a valid explanation of Christ's words?

Fred Teichert

THE ANSWER:
By J.D. Conway

Your question introduces a subject of intense current interest, Fred. Pope Paul VI issued an encyclical letter about it and some newspapers have confused the issues and created controversies.

The first two Latin words of Pope Paul's encyclical are *Mysterium fidei* (the mystery of faith); so that is the title of his letter. These words also express the truth about transubstantiation: it is a mystery, a divine activity and reality which we cannot understand; but it is a truth which we accept by our faith in God and in his word to us.

May I begin, Fred, by correcting the names which you use for Aristotle's categories of being? He held that existing things are composed of substance and accidents (not essence). Substance is the reality which exists in itself and is a subject or support of accidents. Substance is something which we cannot see in itself or detect by experimentation. We can know it only through its accidents, which are realities also, but do not exist in themselves; they inhere in the substance. They might be called modes of being. Aristotle taught that there are nine accidents: quantity, quality, relation, action, passion, where, when, posture, and state. These are relative things; they have being, but not independent being. They exist only in the substance they modify.

St. Thomas Aquinas accepted Aristotle's theories of being, and when he tried to explain the real change which takes place in the bread and wine at the Consecreation of the Mass, he quite naturally used the terms *substance* and *accident.* The substances of bread and wine cease to exist and are replaced by the living substance of the Body and Blood of Jesus Christ. All the accidents of bread and wine remain, however, just as they were before, except that they no longer inhere in a substance, but are maintained by divine power.

St. Thomas was not the first to use the notion of substantial change to explain the mystery of the Eucharist. Even the word *transubstantiation* had been in fairly common use for a century before he wrote, and so it was not strictly tied to Aristotelian concepts. Rather, it expressed a common, unphilosophical notion of those days; that there was a substance or hidden reality underlying the appearance: the color, shape, and size of a thing. In nontechnical, non-Aristotelian language these appearances were called the *species,* a more appropriate and meaningful word than *accidents.*

I am explaining all of this, Fred, as background for the definition of the doctrine of transubstantiation by the Council of Trent in 1551. The Protestant Reformation had produced a diversity of views regarding the Eucharist. Luther was a strong defender of the true Presence. He claimed to assert it more forcibly than the Catholics, but he rejected the traditional notion of transubstantiation.

Zwingli, the Swiss reformer, saw no mystery or miracle in the Eucharist. It was just a plain symbol helpful to our faith: a souvenir reminding us of the sufferings and death of Jesus. The breaking of bread recalled his broken body, and the wine reminded us of the blood shed on the cross.

Calvin took a stand midway between Luther and Zwingli. He did not believe in the real presence as the Catholics or Luther understood it. He thought we would be inflicting an unworthy humiliation on Christ to bring Him from heavenly glory and tie Him to earthly creatures. However, Calvin rejected mere symbolism. There was a certain presence, an ineffable presence, which has truth only for faith and cannot be grasped by the mind.

The Fathers of the Council of Trent wished to condemn these and all other errors regarding the reality and manner of our Lord's presence in the Eucharist. They were familiar with Scholastic philosophy, and naturally used its ideas to explain the true Presence. They did not intend, however, to canonize any one philosophy or any one theological system. A number of the Fathers speaking in the Council made this quite clear. It may have been for this reason that they chose not to use the word *accidents* which Aristotle and St. Thomas had made a technical term in philosophy. Instead, they stated that when the entire substance of the bread is changed into the Body of Christ, and the whole substance of the wine is changed into the Blood of Christ, the *species* of bread and wine remain.

Any philosophical system can be reconciled with the dogma of transubstantiation and used to explain it as long as it leaves room for a distinction between the appearances of a thing and its underlying reality. The great problem for modern thinkers is that few of them accept a philosophy of this kind. Like yourself, Fred, they are familiar with the subatomic, atomic, and molecular composition of matter and see no sense in a metaphysics which seeks a deeper, purely rational explanation of being without experimental evidence.

In view of this, many theologians appeal to what they call common sense and designate as the ordinary manner of thinking of the average person. In these terms transubstantiation means three things:

1) It is a marvelous, admirable, mysterious, and singular change, in which one thing takes the place of another.

2) It is a change of substances, of realities. After the Consecration of the Mass, if I hold up a sacred Host and ask you what this is, you tell me it is the Body of Christ.

3) It is a change which allows the appearances of bread and wine to remain. To sight, touch, taste, and to any laboratory experiment it seems to be bread and wine.

This appeal to ordinary thinking also presents the problems you have indicated, Fred. We just do not think this way about material things. We need only basic studies in physics and chemistry to set our minds in a scientific groove. Once we have accounted for all the atoms and molecules of a thing, we have explained the whole of it: its entire being, its substance as well as its appearance. If no molecule or atom is changed, we are at a loss to imagine what is changed. The trouble may be that we do not have an adequate notion of being: that we do not rightly understand substance. But we find it hard to remedy our thinking.

Possibly our most useful modern concept of transubstantiation comes from theology. What God does to the bread and wine when they become the Eucharist is a great mystery. We can find no physical explanation of it; and the traditional metaphysical explanation seems unreal. But God, who made the bread, somehow changes it so that it becomes the Body of Jesus Christ, man and God, living and glorified. And God, on whom the wine depends for its existence, somehow changes it into the reality of our divine Saviour, present to sanctify us.

Some modern theologians, recognizing our problems of thought, have sought ways of explaining the true presence of Jesus in the Eucharist in terms that may be more meaningful for us. Their concern is concentrated on the personal relations of religion. They find little meaning in things; only persons count.

They say that in the Eucharist, Jesus Christ—living and glorified—comes to us personally, makes Himself known to us through the signs of bread and wine, gives Himself to us in a union so intimate that it is symbolized by food and drink, shares his divine life with us, and thus unites us to his Father. They fear that, instead of leading us to greater personal love and intimate devotion, our contemplation of the quasi-physical changes in the Eucharist may lead us to a mechanical concept of the Mass and holy Communion. They do not want us to get the idea that the Body of Christ is put into us automatically, and that we are passive recipients of grace.

Our modern theologians seek to divert our attention from the mechanics of substantial change and concentrate it on our personal encounter with Jesus Christ. They see the Eucharist as a sign and a signal of God's invisible approach to us, inviting us to meet Him with faith and love. He is really there, alive and active, and we see Him in the host and the chalice. In ordinary human encounter there is the visible approach of one body to another, the audible voice and the tangible embrace. When Jesus approaches us in the Eucharist, the form of bread reveals his presence even while it screens His reality from our gaze.

Various theologians have sought different words to explain the personal action of Jesus through the Eucharist as a sign of his presence, a symbol of his sanctifying union with us, and an expression of his sacrificial worship of the Father. Possibly the best known is *transignification,* which means that the reality of bread and wine has changed for God and man. Before, they were human food and drink; now, they bring us Jesus Christ, our friend, our brother, our Saviour, and our God. They have a divine value, a spritual and personal meaning.

Others prefer the word *transfiguration* (or *transfinalization*). Every created being has a finality of purpose which God the Creator gives to it. Bread and wine were given us for food and drink; but when they are changed into the Eucharist, they receive a new finality, a religious purpose. They bring Jesus to us, and bring us to Him.

In his new encyclical *Mysterium fidei,* Pope Paul showed some concern about these new terms. He praises the efforts of modern theologians to investigate the mystery of the Eucharist and to give it greater meaning for men of today. However, he warns that these new explanations are acceptable only in the measure that they do not deny or detract from the doctrine of transubstantiation as defined by the Council of Trent.

He reminds us that the sacramental presence of Jesus in the Eucharist "surpasses the laws of nature and constitutes the greatest miracle of its kind. As a result of transubstantiation the species of bread and wine undoubtedly take on a new meaning and a new finality, for they no longer remain ordinary bread and ordinary wine, but become the sign of something sacred, the sign of a spiritual food. However, the reason they take on this new significance and the new finality is simply because they contain a new reality which we may justly term ontological."

An ontological change, Fred, is a change of being, of essence or substance. The Eucharist certainly has sign value; it is the gesture of Jesus as He comes to meet us, to join us in worship, and to give Himself to us. But it is also a reality. The bread becomes his Body, and nothing else. How it is done God only knows. That it is done He has told us; and we believe.

47

How Could the Last Supper Be a Sacrifice?

THE LETTER:

I have taken several home study courses to learn about your faith. But I do not understand how or why the Last Supper was a sacrifice. It is easy to see how the Crucifixion was, but not the Last Supper. If I could see through this, I could tie together the Last Supper, the Crucifixion, and the Mass.

Edward B. Casson

THE ANSWER:
By J.D. Conway

May I begin, Edward, by quoting a paragraph from the Constitution on the Sacred Liturgy of the Council? It presents our notion of the Mass concisely and rather completely:

"At the Last Supper, on the night when he was betrayed, our Saviour instituted the eucharistic sacrifice of his body and blood. He did this in order to perpetuate the sacrifice of the cross throughout the centuries until he should come again, and so to entrust to his beloved spouse, the Church, a memorial of his death and resurrection: A sacrament of love, a sign of unity, a bond of charity, a paschal banquet in which Christ is eaten, the mind is filled with grace, and a pledge of future glory is given to us."

The Last Supper, Crucifixion, and Mass are tied together: 1) by their common element of religious sacrifice, 2) by their unity in the paschal mystery, 3) by the intent of our Lord as shown by his words, and 4) by their simultaneity in time.

1) If we are to understand the Mass, we must know the

meaning of religious sacrifice. In common terms, a sacrifice is the offering or giving up of something, and we make a great sacrifice if the thing we offer is dear to us. Sacrifice is made for a purpose: it is senseless merely to give up something or destroy it. A religious sacrifice is made to show our love for God, to offer praise to him, and to seek his forgiveness of our sins.

In more technical terms a religious sacrifice is an action, usually performed by a priest, by which a creature is withdrawn from the profane realm and placed in the realm of the sacred, and is thus dedicated to God in the hope that He will accept it with benevolence. And in many sacrifices there is the further hope that after God has accepted and sanctified our gift He will share it with us, very often in a sacrificial meal of the community, as a sign of his willingness to enter into communion with us.

History reveals man's natural tendency to offer sacrifice to the Deity as he understands it; and the revelation of the Old Testament shows that God is pleased with the sacrifices men offer in truth and sincerity. For all Christians the voluntary death of Jesus Christ on the Cross of Calvary is the one perfect and enduring sacrifice, the means of our redemption from sin, and the source of our sanctification. The victim of this sacrifice was completely acceptable and pleasing to the Father, something He needed and loved and wanted, his own Son. The priest who made the offering was without defect. And the offering was thorough and generous; no man can give more than his life. Jesus represented all of us on the Cross, and his perfect love and obedience reconciled all of us to the Father, who gave proof of his pleasure by raising his Son from the dead. The death of Jesus on Calvary was a unique historical event. It can never be repeated; its value is everlasting. But it is remembered and can be commemorated. In the Mass we have such commemoration.

2) The Last Supper had a definite paschal association. Either it was the sacred meal of the Passover, or it was a ceremonial meal celebrated close to the Passover, filled with its spirit and its theme. At the time of Jesus the Passover was not a sacrificial meal, but there had been many elements of sacrifice in its history: the killing of the lamb that its blood might be smeared on the doorpost as a sacred symbol; and the Deuteronomical custom of killing of the

lamb in the sanctuary of the temple and eating the paschal meal there.

In any case, the Passover recalled the exodus of the Jews from Egypt, which had become a figure of messianic expectation; and for the Christian it came to signify liberation from the slavery of sin, and hope for the promised land of God's kingdom. Jesus was the paschal lamb of the new covenant; his blood saved not only the firstborn, but all those who accepted its redemptive graces. So the Mass has become the paschal meal of the new covenant, sealed in the blood of Christ. And the redemptive theme of the Passover links it to Jewish tradition, to the Last Supper, and to Calvary.

3) The words which Jesus spoke in giving us the Holy Eucharist show how closely the Last Supper was joined to his sacrificial death on the Cross: "This is my blood of the new covenant which is being shed for many unto the forgiveness of sins." "This is my body, which is being given for you; do this in remembrance of me. This cup is the new covenant in my blood, which shall be shed for you." "This is my body which shall be given up for you; do this in remembrance of me. This cup is the new covenant in my blood; do this as often as you drink it, in remembrance of me. For as often as you shall eat this bread or drink the cup, you proclaim the death of the Lord until he comes."

It is evident that Jesus, in instituting the Eucharist, was making an offering of himself to God, an offering which He completed the next day on Calvary. And in giving us the Eucharist He gave us a way of remembering Him and proclaiming his death. We do this in the Mass, and our remembrance is not only in memory, but in the reality of his presence; and our proclamation of his death is not by mere words or empty signs, but in the effective sacramental sign of his real body and blood.

4) The Last Supper and Calvary were closely joined in time, in overlapping action, and in historical unity. Even before the breaking of the bread, Jesus knew of the plans that had been made to take Him prisoner that very night; and the presence of Judas, the traitor, caused the first deep sufferings of his passion. St. John relates the words of Jesus at the Last Supper as a last will and testament. As soon as the supper was over, Jesus went directly to the garden at the Mount of Olives where He began to suffer intensely. His enemies seized him there, and his close friend Judas be-

trayed Him; they interrupted the anguish of his prayer to drag him off to trial.

There is no intermission between the Last Supper and Calvary. After Gethsemane came a nightmare of accusations, questions, denials, and condemnations, followed by trials before Pilate and Herod, the scourging, the crown of thorns, and the mockery of the soldiers. Then there was the torture of the road to Calvary, the nails, the thieves, and the taunting crowd; and finally the sacrifice begun at the Last Supper was completed with death on the cross.

The signs and symbols of the Mass recall Calvary almost as well as the Last Supper. The setting is that of the Upper Room, with its table for a meal. But that table is also an altar of sacrifice, and the victim on it is that same body which was nailed to the cross, and that same blood which soaked into the soil of Golgotha. The essence of Calvary was separation: the blood from the body, and the soul from both of them; and yet there remained the inseparable union of the divine nature and the human nature. Even in the temporary separation of death, the body and soul of Christ remained those of a divine person.

In the Mass there is separation, too. The priest takes the bread, and speaking for Christ says, "This is my body," and after adoring and elevating it, he places it on the altar. Then he takes the chalice and speaks the words of the Lord, "This is the cup of my blood"; and the host and chalice remain separated in space. And yet there remains in each of them an essential and vital union. The living Christ, his humanity inseparable from his divinity, his soul now inseparable from his glorified body and blood, is present in his entirety under the form of bread and under the form of wine. Christ is not divided; only the species of bread and wine are separated. But their disjunction is an effective sign of the real separation of Calvary, and continues its reality in a sacramental way through the true presence of the risen Saviour.

In the Mass the sacrifice of Calvary is continued and projected; it is not repeated. The Mass is much more than a mere memory; it is a reality expressed in signs. The Mass is offered each day in many parts of the world; but the risen Christ remains alive and glorified, never to die again. The Mass is a true sacrifice, but not a new sacrifice except in its ritual repetition. In the Mass the Church repeats what Jesus did at the Last Supper when he accepted in free obedience, the real death by which he gave himself to the Father, and when he proclaimed the saving power of his sacrifice and applied it to his disciples.

It was at the Last Supper that Jesus gave his death the significance of a sacrifice of himself to the Father for all of us; and when we celebrate the renewal of the Last Supper, we ourselves take part in that sacrifice, in remembrance of Him. The redeeming sacrifice Christ offered at the Last Supper and consummated on the cross was an historical fact, but it is also a continuing, sanctifying reality.

At Mass we all join Jesus in the worship, love and obedience that he showed to the Father on Calvary and that he continues to show in heaven for all eternity; we offer ourselves to the Father with Him. And the Father is pleased with our offering because it is bound up with the sacrifice of his Son; and He shows his pleasure by giving us the glorified body and blood of his Son to be the food of our souls, the source of our grace and the nourishment of our love for Him and for each other.

48

What Is an "Immaculate Conception"?

THE LETTER:

What is the meaning of the Immaculate Conception? I would like a greater understanding on this subject, for while I do not deny a Catholic his beliefs, still I do not understand this teaching and would appreciate a full and clear explanation. There are many who ridicule it.

James Ringler

THE ANSWER:
By J.D. Conway

This doctrine is so frequently misunderstood, even by Catholics, Mr. Ringler, that it is best to say first what the Immaculate Conception is not.

Immaculate Conception has nothing to do with the manner in which the child Mary was conceived. She had natural parents, named, according to a venerable popular tradition, Joachim and Anna. The Church venerates them as saints, presuming that the grandparents of Jesus received special graces from God. However, this does not imply that their lives differed in any notable way from those of other holy people of their day. They conceived their child Mary by normal sexual relations, and they may have had other children.

Popular traditions are that Joachim and Anna were childless before Mary was conceived, that they were far advanced in age at the time of her birth, that they consecrated her to God, and presented her in the Temple when she was three years old, leaving her parents childless in their old age. These are improbable fantasies found in apocryphal writings. St. John says the Mother of Jesus was at the foot of his cross, and that her sister was with her. We are not sure who her sister is, but this testimony of John is worth our belief. The Church has always insisted that the brothers and sisters of the Lord, often mentioned in the Gospels, were not the children of Mary, but her cousins, probably children of Mary's brothers and sisters. My point in saying this is to emphasize that Mary's Immaculate Conception does not mean that she herself was conceived in a virginal manner.

We must know about original sin before we can understand the Immaculate Conception. The first man was created in sanctifying grace, which means that he was given a marvelous and mysterious share in God's nature, so that he could be a personal friend of God and share in his eternal happiness. But the first man, by free decision, turned away from God in disobedience, and lost sanctifying grace. We call this the fall of man. It was a fall from the state of original justice in which he was created. The fact of man's fall is told us in a symbolic story in Genesis. He was expelled from the Garden of Eden where he had lived in happy familiarity with God and in reach of the tree of life which promised him immortality.

St. Paul, by comparing Adam and Christ, tells us that Adam's sin and loss of grace had an effect on the whole human race, of which Adam was the head and representative. Through one man, Adam, sin came into the world, and through sin death; but through the one Man, Jesus

Christ, divine grace came into the world, and through grace life. St. Paul says: "As one man's fall brought condemnation on everyone, so the good act of one man brings everyone life and makes them justified."

In the first phase of God's plan for man's salvation, Adam was to pass on divine grace to his descendants. But Adam failed in his role as mediator; he lost the grace he was supposed to pass on. So God chose his own divine Son as mediator. The Son's total obedience to the will of his Father repaired the disobedience of the first man and that of all men. Adam's sin had left us alienated from God. Christ's redemptive death and resurrection restored us to God's love and friendship. Even more, it made us adopted brothers of Jesus, and so adopted sons of the Father.

And then St. Paul continues: "You have been taught that when we were baptized in Christ Jesus we were baptized in his death; in other words, when we were baptized we went into the tomb with Him and joined Him in death, so that, as Christ was raised from the dead by the Father's glory, we, too, might have a new life." Baptism is the effective sign of our sanctifying union with Christ, by which the original sin we inherited from Adam is removed from us.

The Council of Trent, in 1546, gave some definitions regarding original sin: 1) Adam by his sin had lost holiness and justice; 2) the sin of Adam had sad effects on all his posterity, depriving them of holiness and justice; 3) it is only through the redemptive merits of Jesus Christ that original sin can be removed from us; 4) these merits are applied to us in Baptism; and 5) Baptism really takes away the sin itself, and makes us sons of God.

While the Fathers at Trent were preparing their decrees about original sin, a Spanish bishop, Cardinal Pacheco, insisted that they should include a definition of the Immaculate Conception of Mary, explicitly stating that she was exempted from the stain of the sin which the entire human race had inherited from Adam. At one time nearly half the Fathers were inclined to go along with him, but a Dominican managed to talk them out of it. St. Thomas Aquinas, the great Dominican theologian, had opposed the doctrine three centuries earlier, and the members of his Order continued to back his position.

The Fathers at Trent decided they had more important questions to solve and define in the face of the Protestant Reformation. So they agreed on a compromise statement:

"However, this Holy Synod declares that it does not have the intention of including in its decree on original sin the Blessed and Immaculate Virgin Mary, the Mother of God."

In later times, the plea of Cardinal Pacheco was taken up by bishops, priests, and members of Religious Orders. It was pointed out that the feast of the Conception of the Virgin Mary was celebrated in the Greek Church from the 7th century, that it was popular in Sicily and Naples in the 9th century, and thence had spread to Spain, England, and Normandy. By the 12th century the feast was accepted in most of France and Germany, and soon thereafter in most of the Church. The mystery commemorated was the sanctification of Mary in the womb of her mother at the moment her soul was infused into her body.

After Trent, a number of Popes continued to clarify the Church's thinking on the Immaculate Conception. For instance, Pius V in 1567 condemned a proposition of Baius which stated: "No one except Jesus Christ is without original sin; hence the Blessed Virgin died because of the sin which she contracted from Adam."

In the middle of the 19th century, Pope Pius IX decided on a definitive study of the Immaculate Conception. In June, 1848, he established a council of theologians to study the possibility of the definition of this doctrine, and if it was opportune to do so. Six months later he established a congregation of Cardinals and other consultors, and asked them to decide whether or not they should advise the Holy See to delcare that the Blessed Virgin Mary was by special privilege conceived free of original sin.

They advised the Pope to consult the bishops of the world about it. So early in 1849 he sent out an encyclical, asking the bishops to let him know promptly the feelings of the people and clergy in each diocese on this subject, and if the doctrine should be so solemnly defined. Of 603 bishops who replied, 546 were in agreement with the proposed definition. A few, like the Archbishop of Paris, were strongly opposed. He said that in accordance with theological principles the Immaculate Conception was not definable doctrine, that it could not be made a part of Catholic faith, and that the definition of it was not opportune.

Encouraged by the favorable replies of nearly nine out of ten bishops the Pope, in 1852, set up a congregation to draft the definition. It worked more than a year and a half to complete its work, which the Pope presented to his cardinals in secret consistory on December 1, 1854, asking them whether or not he should define the dogma. Having received their approval, he set December 8, 1854, as the date for promulgation of the bull, *Ineffabilis Deus*. In it is found the following formula of definition: "By the authority of Our Lord Jesus Christ, of the Blessed Apostles Peter and Paul, and by our own authority, we declare, proclaim, and define that the doctrine which holds that the Blessed Virgin Mary, in the first instant of her conception, by a singular grace and privilege of Almighty God, and in view of the merits of Jesus Christ the Saviour of mankind, was preserved free of all stain of original sin, was revealed by God, and therefore must be firmly and constantly believed by all the faithful."

The chief Scriptural source of this doctrine, Mr. Ringler, is the greeting of the angel Gabriel: "Hail, full of grace," or "Rejoice, so highly favored" (Luke 1, 28). Mary, the most blessed of all women, had been favored by God by being chosen as the Mother of the Saviour, and the Church judges it fitting that she could benefit first and in highest measure from the graces her divine Son obtained. She who would be the mother of God's Son should never for a moment be under dominion of Satan, whom her Son came to conquer.

Mary is also the prototype of the Church. Jesus came to redeem his Church, to establish it free of original sin. Its members are free of original sin from the moment they enter it by Baptism. It is fitting that Mary, the prototype of this Church, should also be free from original sin from the moment she became a person. God united her to Himself in sanctity the moment He created her soul; even as He unites us to Himself the moment we are baptized.

49

Do You Follow Scripture in Your Divorce Doctrine?

THE LETTER:

I have never found a Church I can believe in. I have read different versions of the Catholic Bible and they don't say the same thing. In the Challoner-Rheims version in Matthew 19:9 it says: "Whoever puts away his wife, except for immorality, and marries another, commits adultery." In the King James version the word is *adultery* instead of *immorality*. The Knox version says, "He who puts away his wife, not for any unfaithfulness of hers, and so marries another, commits adultery."

I have often heard Protestants talk of "Bible grounds for a divorce." How does one really know what to believe?

Mrs. Lillian Albert

THE ANSWER:
By J.D. Conway

The passage you ask me to interpret, Mrs. Albert, is extremely difficult and has been disputed for centuries. It is of great importance because it has given rise to variant doctrines about divorce among Christians ever since Apostolic times.

But the different English translations are not important. Besides the one you mention, I find that the Revised Standard version and the New English Bible read "unchastity." Two other Protestant editions I consulted use "unfaithfulness." My copy of the King James reads "fornication." I do not find any version which uses the word *adultery*. But there is no question about the Greek word being translated: it is *porneia,* and its meaning is certain: fornication, or prostitution. It doesn't mean adultery; a different Greek word is used for that in the Gospels: *moicheia*.

However, the great majority of Scripture scholars have taken for granted that the real meaning of *porneia* in this particular verse of Matthew is adultery. They take this meaning from the context: Jesus seems to be referring to the sin of a married woman, unfaithful to her husband. And they suggest that Matthew used the generic word *porneia* rather than the technical word *moicheia* simply to avoid repetition in his sentence.

We can never properly understand a phrase of the Bible taken out of context. So I suggest, Mrs. Albert, that you open your Bible to Matthew 19:3 and read carefully from there through 19:12. You will note that the verse you cite resulted from a question which the Pharisees put to Jesus in the hope of trapping Him. They hoped to get Him involved in a controversy between two schools of Jewish scholars on the subject of divorce. All were agreed that divorce was permissible under the law of Moses, but the verse of Deuteronomy (24:1) which authorized it was difficult to interpret. It permitted a husband to divorce his wife "if he finds in her something indecent."

Those vague words "something indecent" were interpreted by Rabbi Schammai and his followers to mean adultery, and nothing else. The disciples of Rabbi Hillel took the words in a much wider sense, and held that there were many reasons for divorce, some even trivial. Some insisted that a man could divorce his wife if he found another woman more beautiful. The Pharisees hoped to get Jesus to commit Himself to one school of thought—probably that of Schammai—and thereby get Him into trouble with the other faction. The Hillel ideas were much more popular. So they asked Him if it were lawful to get a divorce for any and every cause.

Jesus evaded their trap by reminding them of God's original plan for man and woman as shown by his creation of Adam and Eve as one flesh. The ancient law did not permit divorce at all. God had joined man and woman as one flesh; they must not be separated. This answer rather confused the Pharisees. Jesus had half convinced them that the original, and therefore the more venerable, law forbade divorce. But why then did Moses tell his people that a man should give his wife a divorce notice if he intended to get rid of her? Jesus explained that Moses had permitted divorce and required the formality of a written notice because of the hardness of their hearts. In other words, it was better for a man to divorce his wife than to kill her, and better to give her a formal notice in writing than simply to throw her out of his house without any evidence of her rights. The law made no provision for a woman to divorce her husband.

Now we come to the sentence that causes you trouble, Mrs. Albert. It begins with the words, "but I say to you," regularly used by Jesus when He wished to contrast his own teachings with those of the law of Moses. Then He continues: "Whoever puts away his wife, except for immorality, and marries another, commits adultery; and he who marries a woman who has been put away commits adultery." At first glance it would seem that Jesus was giving no new law at all, but simply agreeing with the law of Moses as interpreted by the Schammai school. And yet his disciples seemed to take his words in a stricter sense, of no divorce at all, because they said: "If that's the way things are for man and his wife, it is better not to marry at all." Why should they take this attitude if He were merely quoting to them a familiar Jewish opinion?

I might mention that there are variant readings of the text quoted above in different Greek manuscripts available to us. Most modern Protestant translations omit the final phrase: "and he who marries a divorced woman commits adultery." Many authorities believe that it was not in the original, but was transferred here from Matthew 5:32, a text we should now consider. Again we find Jesus contrasting his teachings with those of the Mosaic law: "It was said, moreover, 'Whoever puts away his wife, let him give her a written notice of dismissal.' But I say to you that everyone who puts away his wife, save on account of immorality, causes her to commit adultery; and he who marries a woman who has been put away commits adultery."

An interesting interpretation of this verse is possible, presuming *porneia* to mean adultery: if a man puts away his wife for any reason other than adultery, he is responsible for the sins of adultery she may later commit; but if he puts her out of his house because she is already guilty, he is acting rightly and has no responsibility for what she later does. And here that final phrase is surely authentic: he who marries a divorced woman (any divorced woman) commits adultery. Not everyone agrees with this interpretation, but it makes sense, and is the traditional Catholic exegesis. Transferring the same interpretation to 19:9 is possible, and customary, but it forces the structure of the sentence just a bit.

Our reason for being troubled by that phrase "except for immorality" is that it seems to directly contradict similar words of our Lord as reported by Mark and Luke.

In Mark 10:2–12, the story of the encounter of Jesus with the Pharisees ends with his strong words: "What therefore God has joined together, let no man put asunder." It is only later, when He is in the house, that the disciples question Him further on the subject of divorce, and his reply leaves no room for quibbling. "Whoever puts away his wife and marries another, commits adultery against her; and if the wife puts away her husband, and marries another, she commits adultery."

Luke (16:18) omits preliminary argument with the Pharisees about the law of Moses, though he indicates that they were present and were sneering at Jesus about his teachings. Without introduction Luke simply states: "Everyone who puts away his wife and marries another commits adultery; and he who marries a woman who has been put away from her husband commits adultery."

The teaching of St. Paul on the subject of divorce seems to agree with the words of Jesus as reported by Mark and Luke: "But to those who are married, not I, but the Lord commands that a wife is not to depart from her husband, and if she departs, that she is to remain unmarried or be reconciled to her husband. And let not a husband put away his wife" (I Corinthians 7:10–11).

Despite the seeming clarity of Mark, Luke, and Paul, those two phrases of Matthew—"except for fornication" (5:32) and "not for fornication" (19:9)—have caused confusion throughout the centuries of Christianity, and consequently practices have not been uniform. In the ancient cultures of Greece and Rome, divorce was very common, and early Christianity could hardly avoid some influence from these pagan customs. And no doubt Jewish traditions of divorce exercised an influence on Christian converts from Judaism.

Consequently one scholar or another has claimed that the words "except for fornication" in Matthew 5:32 were not in the original text, but were added by early Christians to justify their practices of divorce. Some authorities of exceptional standing and of no Catholic sympathy have held the same regarding the "not for fornication" of 19:9. However, the evidence is against these claims: these phrases were most probably in the original Gospel according to Matthew.

Even after Christian influence became effective in the Roman empire, civil laws continued to recognize divorce, and these laws influenced the practice of the Greek or Byzantine Churches in cases of adultery, and they found in these two passages of Matthew justification for their practice.

The western, or Roman, Church was subject to the same laws of the empire, and later was influenced by even more lax laws of the barbarian peoples who took over the Western part of the empire. Consequently in early centuries there were many deviations in practice, but the teaching was fairly constant and increasingly clear that a consummated Christian marriage was indissoluble. After the middle of the 12th century the Roman Church was able to make and enforce its own laws regarding marriage, and they definitely excluded divorce. The great theologians of those times, men like Peter Lombard and St. Thomas Aquinas, were firm in their teachings that divorce was impossible.

It is quite interesting that despite the disagreement of the Greek and Roman Churches on the subject of divorce for cause of adultery, the subject did not come up for discussion at the Council of Florence in the mid-15th century— even though the two Churches spent a year in minute discussion of their differences and reached final agreement. It was only after the council was over and many of the Greek bishops had gone home that Pope Eugene IV discussed the divorce question with some of those Greeks who remained in Italy. They evaded the issue by stating that they could not speak for their absent brethren. A short time later, however, Pope Eugene issued a decree defining the doctrine of the Roman Church: Though it is permissible for reason of fornication to separate, it is not permitted that another marriage be contracted, since the bond of marriage once legitimately contracted is perpetual.

It is in this sense that Catholic Scripture scholars have traditionally interpreted the two texts of St. Matthew that we have been considering. Because of adultery a man is justified in separating from his wife (or the wife from her husband). They may rightly live apart the rest of their lives, but neither may marry again as long as the other lives.

The Council of Trent, in 1563, made a most interesting definition of the Church's teaching about divorce. In those days even Greek Catholics were still following the ancient customs of their Byzantine Church in permitting divorce for reason of adultery, and the council Fathers were anxious not to antagonize them. So the wording of the council decree was prepared with great care. It did not label the Greeks as heretics for believing that marriage can be dissolved because of adultery, but stated firmly that the Catholic Church is not in error in teaching the contrary doctrine as that of the Gospels and the Apostles. The exact interpretation of the canon of the council was difficult, and Greek Catholics were slow in changing their ancient beliefs and practices. It was not until about 150 years ago that all of them finally conformed.

Protestants generally agree with the Greeks in the interpretation of these texts of Matthew. Some of them have held, however, that the privilege of remarriage is restricted to the innocent spouse; while others have given a wide interpretation to the word *porneia,* which they translate as unfaithfulness, and consequently find divorce acceptable for a number of reasons.

Recently some prominent Catholic scholars have revived an exegesis of our two texts formerly held by a few great Scriptural authorities. It takes the Greek word *porneia* in its literal sense, fornication, which is a sexual sin committed between an unmarried man and an unmarried woman. The teaching of Jesus would be this: Whoever puts away his wife, except in the case in which they are not rightly married to each other and are living in fornication, commits adultery if he marries another.

So you may soon see an edition of Matthew's Gospel which will read as follows: "But now I warn you that whoever divorces his wife (except in an invalid marriage) and marries another, is committing adultery; and the man who marries a divorced woman is committing adultery."

50

Why Only One Wife at a Time?

THE LETTER:

I am a Moslem. I have many Catholic friends and I often exchange opinions with them about religion. We have just discussed marriage. According to the Catholic Church, they told me, a man and woman who are married cannot get a divorce.

But I think there are more women in this world than men. Then is it not just for a man to have more than one wife? In my religion a man is allowed to marry more than one wife when he will promise to share his love among them.

My Catholic friends would not give me more explanation about this and suggested that I ask you. I shall be very happy if you would kindly give me a clear explanation about this.

Pramono Dwidojatmoko

THE ANSWER:
By J.D. Conway

The customs of your country are quite unknown to me, Pramono, but I hope I do not give offense in addressing you directly by your first name, in the American manner. One thing I do know about your Indonesian island: it is densely populated. It is not quite as large as the state in which I live, but it must have 30 or 40 times our population. So it may be easy, when you see so many women, to judge that there are some to spare.

I am confident, however, that if you will consult population statistics you will find very nearly as many men as women on your beautiful island, and possibly even more.

Past statistics for some of your neighboring nations have shown more men than women. But for the world as a whole, year after year, the number of girl babies born just about equals the number of boy babies.

Through most of our history in the United States we have had more men than women, because there were more men than women among the immigrants. In other countries there may be more women than men because more men are killed in war, more men emigrate, and modern women live longer. The third reason has little to do with polygamy, since women past 75 seldom marry.

In England in 1921 there were 1096 women to 1000 men, making an excess of 1.7 million females; and the difference was even greater in the marriageable-age bracket of 20 to 24 years: 1176 women for each 1000 men. But this was just three years after the end of the 1st World War. In 1901, when these same men and women were children, aged one to four, there had been only 1003 girls per 1000 boys. And in 1911 that proportion was reversed to 991 girls per 1000 boys. In future years emigration will not disturb numerical balance of the sexes so much; and any major war will eliminate men and women equally. So, Pramono, polygamy is not warranted by a surplus of women in the world. If half the men in the world had two wives each, the other half of the earth's men would be wifeless.

Since you have Catholic friends you probably know about the 2nd Vatican Council. One of the leading figures in that Council was Cardinal Suenens of Belgium. During the 2nd session he urged that women be admitted to the Council as auditors. The very idea of this was shocking to some of the bishops. No woman had been admitted to a Church Council since 787, when the Empress Irene had convoked the 2nd Council of Nicea.

The cardinal's remark sounds very banal if we miss the sharp point of it: the dignity of women and their equality with men, as human persons. "Unless I am mistaken," Cardinal Suenens said, "they make up half of the human race." The Council, in its *Constitution on the Church,* said "There is in Christ and in the Church no inequality on the basis of race or nationality, social condition or sex."

The Catholic Church, Pramono, while hesitant to give women place in its Councils, has always held women in highest respect as persons. They have immortal souls created by God and redeemed by Jesus Christ with the same love shown to the souls of men. As a Moslem you are surely familiar with the exalted position held by Mary, the Mother of Jesus, in our religion.

The Universal Declaration of Human Rights, made by the United Nations in 1948, states in Article 2: "Everyone is entitled to all the rights and freedoms set forth in this Declaration, without distinction of any kind, such as race, color, sex, language, or religion."

Pope John XXIII wrote an encyclical, called *Pacem in Terris,* in which he endorsed the Declaration, and said, "Women are gaining an increasing awareness of their natural dignity. Far from being content with a purely passive role or allowing themselves to be regarded as a kind of instrument, they are demanding both in domestic and in public life the rights and duties which belong to them as human persons."

This Christian respect for the rights and dignity of women is one of the reasons the Catholic Church opposes polygamy. I do not say that the Javanese are lacking in respect for women, because I do not know your country. But I do know some Moslem countries in which the tourist gets the impression that women are inferior to men in a way Christian women would never tolerate.

Moslem law is quite strict about the obligations of a man who has more than one wife. He must love them equally and be able to support them and their children. But, of course, Moslems do not have a monopoly on polygamy. Its present practice in many countries is clearly contrary to the human equality of women. Probably every race of people has practiced polygamy in some measure in the course of its social and moral development. But it is extremely doubtful that the practice has ever been general in any group at any time. I am speaking of true polygamy, where each man would have more than one wife, on a permanent basis. I am wondering how many of your own friends have more than one wife. I know of one Moslem country in which only two percent of the men are polygamists.

In more primitive civilizations a plurality of wives was usually the special privilege of the strong man, the rich man, the chief or the king. In such societies it is usually necessary to buy a wife, and the more polygamy is practiced by wealthy men the higher the price of a wife for the poor man. The result has sometimes been that wealthy old men have collected the young, healthy, attractive women;

while a young man, strong and virile, cannot afford to marry before he is 40. I read of one old sultan who had 1200 wives, but only 147 children; and of a chief who had 400 wives and no children.

Anthropologists tell us that in the hunting and fishing stage of man's development, polygamy was little known. There may have been some promiscuity and frequent discarding of one wife for another. But hardly any man could feed and clothe more than one woman and family. Then when the herding and agriculture days arrived, some men became wealthy enough to acquire extra wives. And in those days women and children had economic value; there was work for them to do. But even in those times the average man had only one wife. The law of supply and demand permitted no more.

In higher stages of man's development there has been a general tendency for polygamy to disappear in favor of monogamy. But often there has been an intermediate stage: concubinage, which is rated higher than polygamy by sociologists, but is surely no moral improvement. The Roman and Greek civilizations, from which we "Westerners" received many of our social and legal norms, did not accept polygamy; but they had laws and customs that accepted a reasonable number of concubines in addition to the one wife.

As a Moslem you are probably familiar with our Old Testament; and you know that polygamy was a rather frequent practice among our spiritual ancestors. And some of the stories of the patriarchs illustrate the grief and unfairness resulting from the system: Abraham expelled Agar and Ismael because of the jealousy of Sara. But you may tell me, Pramono, that this was not true polygamy in which wives should be equal. But actually polygamy has often turned into a system of a main wife and a slave or servant wife, "little wives," as they were once called in China. And I wonder if Moslem law can keep a man from having a favorite wife or can prevent raging jealousies between the wives.

If man and woman have equal rights as persons, how can you permit a man to have two wives, and deny a woman the right to have two husbands? Yet both your religion and mine condemn polyandry, though we know it has existed here and there in the course of human history.

The Catholic Church has always insisted on monogamy

because it sees it as the only type of marital arrangement in which complete fidelity, generous, sanctifying love, and the mutual giving of self can be attained. It fosters sacrifice and self-control in the husband, offers most security to the wife, and provides a home in which children can receive a full, normal education, sharing the love, care, and attention of both father and mother full time.

I have no doubt that many Moslems practice polygamy from high motives, but in our Western civilization we observe that when a man with one wife seeks a second woman, it is nearly always for his own pleasure. Possibly he cannot remain continent at times when his wife's condition demands restraint; maybe he just wants variety, or the thrill of conquest. In some cases it may be that he simply wants more sexual activity than one wife can provide him. We deplore such motives and activities as selfish, unfair, and immoral. And we wonder if the male of the species isn't much the same the world over.

In our Western society we have marital customs that resemble your polygamy in many respects. I refer to divorce, successive polygamy; and I suspect that it is much more widely practiced than your simultaneous polygamy. But as your friends have told you, the Catholic Church strongly opposes it. Divorce may be free of discrimination against women, but otherwise we oppose it for much the same reasons as polygamy. It detracts from the virtue and value of marriage. The love between man and wife, if it is to be generous and sanctifying, must be exclusive and enduring. True marital love cannot say: "I love you as much as my other wife"; neither can it say, "I love you alone and faithfully, until I tire of you, or find someone I love more." And true marital love must provide security—for husband and wife, and for children. The polygamist's children are possibly better off than those of the divorcée. At least they have a mother all the time and a father half the time.

51

What Is the Unforgivable Sin?

THE LETTER:

I got a copy of the *Catholic Digest* when I attended a Roman Catholic church near us. Most of my work with people necessitates understanding their beliefs. My sons, too, are going into missionary and social work that requires a loving understanding of people of other faiths and customs. We are Lutheran, but as you no doubt know, there is much common ground of interest and benefit to both of us.

Your format and selection of articles is very good and interesting. We, too, revered Pope John XXIII and think highly of your present Pope. May God use him and you and me to his glory, to the saving of the wayward, to the bringing of peace to tormented souls, to the love of and understanding of the Christ.

In talking with people of my denomination and with other Christians there seems to be a wide difference of interpretation of the "sin against the Holy Ghost." Matthew 12:32 says that the sin will not be forgiven one in this world, neither in the world to come. What does the Catholic Church consider this sin to be?

Mrs. Elizabeth Boys

THE ANSWER:
By J.D. Conway

Only the evident sincerity of your ecumenical spirit persuades me to take up your problem, Mrs. Boys. St. Augustine wrote of the sin against the Holy Spirit: "Perhaps in all of Sacred Scripture there is no question greater or more difficult."

There are in reality three parts to the question: 1) What

is the sin against the Holy Spirit? 2) Why will it never be forgiven? 3) What is the meaning of the expression used in the King James Bible: "It shall not be forgiven him, neither in this world, neither in the world to come".

Let us first see your verse in its context. I presume you use the Revised Standard Version, so I will use it also, except when I name another.

St. Matthew, in this chapter, tells us of many miracles Jesus worked, and of his frequent clashes with the Pharisees who were plotting means of destroying him. Then a man was brought to Him who was blind and dumb and possessed by the devil. Jesus drove out the devil and healed the man so that he spoke and saw. When the Pharisees heard about this miracle they derided Jesus, saying: "It is by Beelzebub, the prince of demons, that this man casts out demons." Jesus did not hear them say this but He knew their thoughts, and He sought to confound them with arguments showing that it was not by Beelzebub but by the Spirit of God that He cast out devils. He concluded with these two verses: "Therefore I tell you, every sin and blasphemy will be forgiven men, but the blasphemy against the Spirit will not be forgiven. And whoever says a word against the Son of Man will be forgiven; but whoever speaks against the Holy Spirit will not be forgiven, either in this age or in the age to come."

This seems to say that the sin or the blasphemy against the Holy Spirit is the malicious refusal to recognize the works of the Spirit of God and the use of wanton words which credit these divine works to the devil. People can be excused or easily forgiven for not recognizing the Messiah and giving Him full credit, because his divinity is disguised by his human nature. But when God's power and goodness shine forth clearly in his works, it is blasphemy, slander, and calumny to attribute these works to an evil spirit.

Dr. K. Stendahl of Harvard proposes an interesting and slightly different interpretation: "There is the distinction between the blasphemy against the Son of Man, which can be forgiven, and the blasphemy against the Holy Spirit, which cannot; i.e., during the ministry of Jesus it was permissible and understandable not to recognize Jesus as the Messiah, but after Pentecost there was no excuse." On Pentecost the Holy Spirit came to strengthen and enlighten the faith of the disciples; refusal to believe after that would be rejection of the Spirit and his graces.

St. Mark tells us that Jesus spoke similar words in similar circumstances, but we should note a few differences. Here the Scribes accuse Jesus of being possessed by Beelzebub, and it is for this reason that He said to them: "Truly I say to you, all sins will be forgiven the sons of men, and whatever blasphemes against the Holy Spirit never has forgiveness, but is guilty of an eternal sin."

If you are using the King James Bible, you will find a different reading: The one who blasphemes against the Holy Spirit, "hath never forgiveness, but is in danger of eternal damnation." There are a few uncertainties in the Greek text at this point, which account for the variations. Traditional Catholic versions agree with the Revised Standard. Here it would seem that an attack against the Son of Man when God's Spirit is evidently working in Him is a blasphemy against the Holy Spirit. The Scribes say that the evil spirit of Beelzebub is in Jesus and is working through Him; in truth, it is the Holy Spirit that possesses Him and works through Him.

In Luke these words of Jesus are in a different setting. The disciples will be persecuted, but they need not worry about what they should say when they are brought before the rulers and judges; the Holy Spirit will teach them what to say. The martyr is possessed by the Spirit of God, but the apostate rejects the Spirit. "And everyone who speaks a word against the Son of Man will be forgiven; but he who blasphemes against the Holy Spirit will not be forgiven."

What is the sin related by the three evangelists? Rejection of the Holy Spirit and his graces. This not only answers our first question, but provides a basis for answering the second: Why is this sin never forgiven?

God has the power to forgive every sin; the mercy and love of God are unlimited: He is ready and willing to forgive every sin. And the obedience of Jesus in his death and resurrection obtained graces so that all sins may be forgiven. Why then is the blasphemy against the Holy Spirit not forgiven, either in this age or the next age?

Man's sins are forgiven only by his receiving and accepting the grace of God, which is bestowed upon him by the Holy Spirit. Man sins against the Holy Spirit when he deliberately, persistently, and maliciously rejects grace. Forgiveness is a gift of God. The man who rejects the Holy Spirit refuses forgiveness. Should he cease to oppose the

Spirit, his sin could be forgiven. But from the forcefulness of our Lord's words we judge it not very probable that the sinner who maliciously rejects the Spirit will ever reform.

And now, Mrs. Boys, let us look at the third phase of your question. The traditional Catholic translation of Matthew 12:32, is similar to that quoted above from the King James Bible. The Douay-Rheims version says of the man who speaks against the Holy Ghost, "It will not be forgiven him, neither in this world, nor in the world to come."

In past centuries many Catholic scholars thought they had found in these words a proof of the existence of purgatory. My Douay-Rheims Bible, in a footnote, names St. Augustine and St. Gregory the Great among those who held this opinion. Here is the usual argument: Jesus, when He says that this particular sin will not be forgiven in the next world, implies that other sins may be forgiven there. But in hell there is no possibility of forgiveness, and in heaven there is nothing to be forgiven; so there must be a third place, intermediary between heaven and hell, where some sins will be forgiven.

But there is probably no reference to purgatory here. We have just a translation of a Semitic idiom which is simply a forceful way of saying never. The Greek word which we translate as *age* or *world* is *aion*, which means a period of time: a lifetime, an eternity. Our word *eon*, or *aeon*, is derived from it. Both St. Matthew and St. Mark use *aion* in the verses we have quoted. Matthew says the sin will not be forgiven either in this age or the future one. Mark uses *aion* twice: "He will not be forgiven in *eternity*, but is guilty of an *eternal* sin."

Possibly you did not expect my answer to be quite as complicated as I have made it, Mrs. Boys, but really I have given you only a summary. Scripture scholars must have extensive knowledge of many languages and idioms, of theology and history, of texts and sources, of literary forms and styles of composition, of the sacred writings themselves and of centuries of commentary regarding them. I have simply picked the brains of a few of the scholars.

In summary: It is the Holy Spirit who brings us sanctifying grace, gives us a share in the divine life, and forgives our sins. As long as we reject the Person who sanctifies us, we will never be sanctified, either now or forever. As long as we blaspheme the One who comes to share his divine life with us, we can never share that life, not for all eternity. As long as we persist in sinning against the same Spirit who seeks to forgive us, we will never be forgiven, not in aeons of ages.

52

Why Do You Worship Mary?

THE LETTER:

I am a young Italian Baptist, mother of two, living in New York state. I would sincerely appreciate a reply from you on why it is that Roman Catholics worship Mary. I know Jesus loved Mary, but nowhere in the New Testament has Jesus ordered, pleaded, or even suggested that we bow at her name, kiss statues of her, light candles to her, and pray to her, as some of my friends do! Tell me where to find it in the Old or New Testament that Mary is to be revered and worshiped on the same level as Jesus.

I hope you understand and answer my letter which I felt the Holy Spirit guided and directed me to write. Thank you so much.

Josephine Arato

THE ANSWER:
By J.D. Conway

I can't show you, Josephine, where in either the Old or New Testament it says that Mary is to be revered or worshiped on the same level as Jesus, because she is not on the same level. He is a divine person, Son of the Father, equal to the Holy Spirit. She is a human person even as you and I. Because of the role she was assigned and freely accepted in God's plan for our salvation, He gave her special graces and showed her peculiar favor. But she remained entirely human in both person and nature. God, to redeem us, became man, and chose Mary, of all women, to be his mother. By that choice He gave her an essential role in the history of our salvation. Because of this role, so vital to us, we pay her special honor as the most favored member of our human race.

To understand Mary's role in the divine plan, we must see what the Scriptures have to say about her. The basic Biblical text is Luke 1, 26–38: "The angel Gabriel was sent by God to a town in Galilee called Nazareth, to a virgin betrothed to a man named Joseph, of the House of David; and the virgin's name was Mary. He went in and said to her, 'Rejoice, so highly favored! The Lord is with you. Mary, do not be afraid; you have won God's favor. Listen! You are to conceive and bear a Son, and you must name Him Jesus. He will be great and will be called Son of the Most High. The Holy Spirit will come upon you, and the power of the Most High will cover you with its shadow. And so the Child will be holy and will be called Son of God.'

" 'I am the handmaid of the Lord,' said Mary. 'Let what you have said be done to me.' "

In St. Matthew the message is given to Joseph by an angel who appeared to him in a dream: "Joseph, son of David, do not be afraid to take Mary home as your wife, because she has conceived what is in her by the Holy Spirit. She will give birth to a Son and you must name Him Jesus, because He is the one who is to save his people from their sins."

Luke tells us of Mary's visit to her kinswoman Elizabeth, who under inspiration of the Holy Spirit greeted her, "Of all women you are the most blessed, and blessed is the fruit of your womb. Why should I be honored with a visit from the Mother of my Lord?" And the Holy Spirit impelled Mary to reply, "Yes, from this day forward all generations will call me blessed, for the Almighty has done great things for me."

Luke also tells us of the birth of Jesus in Bethlehem, of the visit of the shepherds, and the presentation of Jesus in the Temple. In all these events Mary had a primary part. Matthew similarly tells us about the visit of the Magi and the flight into Egypt, events in which Mary was deeply involved.

Then Luke terminates the stories of the childhood of Jesus by telling us of his visit to Jerusalem when He was 12 years old, after which Jesus went down to Nazareth with Mary and Joseph and "lived under their authority."

St. John shows Mary in a prominent role in inaugurating the public ministry of Jesus. She persuaded Him to work a miracle at Cana in Galilee that the wedding guests might have wine.

During the public ministry of Jesus his mother appears only passingly, but we find her at the foot of his cross while He was dying. At that time Jesus spoke to her, and his words seem to indicate her role in our salvation: "Seeing his Mother and the disciple He loved standing near her, Jesus said to his Mother, 'Woman, this is your son.' Then to this disciple He said, 'This is your Mother.' And from that moment the disciple made a place for her in his home."

In verses immediately before and after this St. John quotes four times from the Old Testament; so it is probable that he has a Scriptural reference in mind also when he quotes Jesus as giving his mother the unusual title *woman,* a title used for Eve in Genesis. Mary is the new woman, the new Eve.

The original Eve was the mother of all men. She heard the word of the serpent and brought forth disobedience and death. Mary, the new Eve, is the Mother of all the faithful. She heard the voice of the angel and brought forth God's Son, source of forgiveness and life. Eve was disobedient to the command of God, and so caused her death and that of all humanity. Mary was obedient to the invitation of God, which permitted her Son to demonstrate obedience on the cross.

The final direct reference to Mary in the Scripture is in the Acts of the Apostles. She joined the Apostles in prayer, together with several other women and the brethren of Jesus.

There is a Christian tradition which sees in God's condemnation of the Serpent a preview of the role of Mary. God told the serpent, "because you have done this, I will make you enemies of each other: you and the woman, your offspring and her offspring. It will crush your head and you will strike its heel."

The original Hebrew text indicates that the offspring of Eve will eventually vanquish the devil and his seed. But the Greek version, the Septuagint, uses a masculine pronoun for offspring: "He will take care of your head and you shall watch for his heel." This credits the victory over the serpent to one of Eve's offspring, masculine; and many of the Church Fathers saw in those words the first Messianic prophecy.

For some strange reason, however, the traditional Latin text, the Vulgate, uses a feminine pronoun for offspring, and as as result we have the reading of our old Douay Bible: "She shall crush thy head, and thou shalt lie in wait for her heel." It seems that this feminine pronoun was not put into the Vulgate by St. Jerome, but by someone who copied it later; and the false reading stayed there throughout the centuries because it made sense. The enmity was between the woman and the serpent. The first woman, Eve, lost the battle; her offspring and her counterpart, the new woman, Mary, would win the battle through her Son. This became the accepted meaning of the text in Christian tradition. "She" is a mistake, but in context it is true: the woman of the garden, Eve, is in eternal contrast to the woman at the cross, Mary.

In the early centuries of the Church there is little evidence of active devotion to Mary, but she played a prominent part in the thought of the theologians. In the 5th century Nestorius denied that Jesus was really a divine Person equal to the Father. In 431 the Council of Ephesus helped clarify orthodox teaching by declaring that Mary is rightly called Theotokos (God-bearing), the Mother of God. The Fathers of Vatican II date the growth of devotion to Mary from the Council of Ephesus, and they point out that this devotion differs essentially from the adoration offered to the Incarnate Word, her Son. Indeed, true devotion to Mary increases greatly our worship and understanding of God: Father, Son and Holy Sprit. Devotion to Mary flourished greatly in the Middle Ages. It seems that during the life of St. Jerome (about 340 to 420 A.D.), there was not a single feast day of the Blessed Virgin, and possibly only one church in the world dedicated to her. Seven centuries later nearly all the great Gothic cathedrals of France were dedicated to her under the title of Notre Dame.

It may be true that devotion to Mary has at various times and places become exaggerated or distorted. It may have seemed to casual observers that she was being worshiped on the same level as Jesus. But the worshipers generally understood what they were doing: They were honoring the greatest of human persons.

The Fathers of Vatican II taught that devotion to Mary should be fostered, in liturgical cult and in pious practices which are approved. They remind us, however, to abstain from exaggerations, and to avoid everything, in word or deed, that might lead people into error regarding the true doctrine of the Church. Our devotion to Mary must be based on true faith, which sees Mary as the generous and humble handmaid of the Lord, intimately associated with Him while He was working out our redemption here on earth, and even more intimately joined with Him while He continues his work of sanctifying us through his Church.

The Scriptures do not command us to show devotion to Mary, but they do provide us, Josephine, with sound reasons why we should do so.

VI

How About This and That?
Miscellany

Sometimes questioners wanted to know how the Church regarded things that at first sight didn't have much to do with religion; but there is something religious to say about nearly everything. And a couple of questions didn't fit into the first five categories.

53

Why Do You Allow Boxing?

THE LETTER:

I have known of Catholic priests teaching boxing and of your Holy Name societies and the Knights of Columbus sponsoring boxing matches.

When one considers that boxing is the only legal sport in the United States where the objective is to injure or knock unconscious the opponent, that the brain is damaged more in boxing than in any other sport, that boxing encourages sadism among the spectators, and that many state laws regard hands as lethal weapons when used in a street fight, why does the Catholic Church condone boxing?

Laurel S. Shute

THE ANSWER:
By J.D. Conway

In your letter, Laurel, you have indicated rather precisely why Catholic moralists, in recent years, have questioned seriously the morality of professional boxing as it is conducted today, especially on TV. However, to my best knowledge there has never been an official pronouncement of the Church teaching authority on this question. One reason is the vast difference between amateur boxing at its best and the professional slugging match which thrills a bloodthirsty crowd.

Like it nor not, boxing has been widely accepted in our culture. Custom inures us to its shock. The story of pugilism and prize fighting in past centuries will put our present situation in focus.

Presumably man has fought with his fists since the days when he lived in a cave. Latin gives evidence of the popu-

lar concept of the fist as a weapon: its word for fist is
pugnus, and its word for a fight or battle is *pugna.* Our
word *pugilist* comes from the same Latin stem, and more
directly from the word *pugil,* a boxer.

Boxing was popular with the early Greeks, but it was
less a sport than a training for battle, a means of proving
strength, endurance, and courage. It was not until the
Olympic games were 200 years old that boxing became a
part of them. Those early Greeks fought in the open air,
with a ring of spectators in place of ropes. They did little
dancing or weaving; those were a coward's moves. They
did little jabbing, but gave roundhouse swings and clubbing
blows. Their only effort at cleverness was to maneuver the
opponent so that he would be facing the sun. They sought
only to prove that they could take it and dish it out.

In earliest times fists were bare, but later they were
bound with soft leather thongs, mainly as a protection for
the hands. But by the 4th century B.C. harder leather was
used, and the thongs became weapons. Later, under the
Roman empire, the Greeks adopted from Rome the brutal
cestus, a band of bull's hide, loaded with lead, iron, or
brass, and worn as a gauntlet. In Rome slaves wearing the
cestus were made to fight each other to death for the enter-
tainment of an arena crowd. With the rise of Christianity
pugilism seemed to die out. The early Christians really
loved one another, and you hardly show your love by slugging your neighbor with a cestus.

In medieval times serfs fought with their fists. (A St.
Bernadius is said to have been a boxing referee around the
year 1200 and to have invented boxing gloves.) But the
nobles fought with a lance, a horse, and a coat of armor.

Modern pugilism began as an English sport, probably in
the 17th century. Each district of London had a tough
fighter with friends and admirers eager to back his ability
with bets. They would challenge a fighter from another district; the two gangs would put up a prize for the winner,
and bets would be made all around. There were no fouls;
one could wrestle, bite, kick, or hit a man when he was
down. There were no rounds, no ring, and practically no
rules.

In the 18th century a decent sort of champion, Jack
Broughton, introduced some rules. A round ended when a
man was knocked down; it was illegal to hit him, and his
friends could come to his aid; but if he was not able to fight

in 30 seconds he lost the match. Even under these rules it was possible for "Gentleman" Jackson to win the championship from Daniel Mendoza by holding his long hair in one hand while beating him with the other. Both these men later became boxing instructors and did much to interest the gentry in the sport which had previously attracted only rowdies.

In 1839 the London prize-ring rules were introduced. They provided for a roped ring 24 feet square. Kicking, gouging, butting with the head, biting, and low blows became fouls. But even with new rules the prize fight remained too much of a brawl to attract the "better people." So in 1867 John Sholts Douglas, the 8th Marquis of Queensberry, gave his name to a newer set of rules. Now gloves were used, rounds were three minutes long, and there was a knockout if a man went down for ten seconds.

The strict morality of Queen Victoria's times, arrests, and jail sentences shifted most boxing enterprises to the United States. But prize fighting, under the London rules, was illegal here, too. When John L. Sullivan defended his title as bare-knuckle champion in 75 rounds against Jake Kilrain in 1889, he was arrested and spent a year in lawsuits which cost him thousands of dollars. It was the last fight of its kind in the United States. Sullivan fought Jim Corbett under the Queensberry rules a couple of years later, and lost to a better boxer.

In our own century amateur boxing has been made quite respectable by the Catholic Youth organization, the Golden Gloves, university teams, and the inclusion of the sport in the Olympic games. Many poor boys found it a way of escaping the degradation of the slums and attaining respectability. Even professional boxing has enjoyed some respectable days. Some very worthy men have held championship titles in the past 50 years. But a moralist must look on it with suspicion today because of growing emphasis on the knockout. The crowd demands it. Their real thrill comes when they see blood or when a man is knocked to the floor. They gasp with excitement when the stronger combatant moves in for the kill.

I am personally convinced, Laurel, that there is nothing necessarily immoral about *amateur* boxing. Rarely is a man seriously hurt; gloves are reasonably padded; and there is more emphasis on boxing skill than on the damage done by blows. Most matches are won on points rather than by a knockout. There is sharp, strong fighting, but no savagery. And it is certainly a sport which develops courage and virility, along with strength, confidence, speed, and agility.

But modern professional boxing presents a different problem. As you say, it is the only legal sport in the United States in which the objective is to injure the opponent. The immediate and direct intent of the fighter is to hurt a human person. If he opens up a cut he keeps going for it to open it wider. We should ask ourselves honestly whether it is right to intentionally inflict damage in this way. If it is not, we should not encourage it as spectators, either at ringside or on TV. Intentional injury is not unknown in other sports, notably in professional football, but by the rules it is a foul. In boxing it is fair.

We might condone a flattened nose, cauliflower ears, and scarred faces, but many professional fighters suffer brain damage. The frontal lobes may be bruised only slightly as they bang up against the skull bones, but the damage done to brain or nerve tissues is never repaired. The brain doesn't heal like a cut. And when a man has taken his beating too long and been knocked out too often, he very literally becomes punch drunk.

A moralist can hardly sanction a man's permitting himself to reach such state; nor can he approve the blows that have beaten him into that condition. And the point is that his injuries are not the result of accident, as might happen in football, but are the normal, direct result of the game, according to its rules and the intent of the men who fought him.

Father Richard A. McCormick, S.J., wrote an article on this subject for *Sports Illustrated* in 1962, and most of it was reprinted in the *Catholic Digest*. Not long before Benny Paret had died from injuries received in a fight; and even the boxing world was asking itself questions. But Father McCormick, a well-known and respected moralist, said that tragedies of this kind cause us to think with our hearts rather than our heads. He then proceeded to examine in detail the moral arguments against "professional boxing as it is today" and concluded that unless these arguments can be answered, "I believe the sport would have to be labeled immoral."

In one of his arguments Father McCormick quoted Floyd Patterson, who wrote of his desire never to be vicious again, but concluded, "At the same time I know that

I must be, because I am in a business of violence." Can we condone a sport which encourages a man to be vicious, even demands that he be vicious? Certainly not, if we accept the word *vicious* in its primary sense: addicted to vice, corrupt, immoral. But even taken in the sense that Patterson probably meant it: *aroused to malice and emotional intent to injure,* a moralist must find it wrong.

Our basic rule in relation to our brother is that we must love him. Professional fighters usually meet as friends who respect each other. They meet to win, to earn money, and to attain fame. But if the nature of their meeting is such that it leads them, by its very nature, to a fervor of malice—to a vicious intent to injure—then it is surely immoral.

You make another good point, Laurel: that boxing encourages sadism among the spectators. This may well be one of the strongest moral arguments against today's prize fight. It stirs up the primitive, brute instincts in man. There were days in man's early development when he had to use these instinct to preserve his life, maintain his rights, and protect his family. For most of us those days are gone and our violent instincts lie reasonably dormant. But they are there and their arousal gives us a basic animal thrill.

Our society should ask itself honestly whether or not it is good for modern man to be aroused to such primitive violence. Does it help us toward a peaceful and ordered society? Does it encourage us to love our neighbor? Why is there so much violence in our society today? How much of it is fostered by TV shows of horror, mayhem, and murder? And among these must we not number that professional, refereed mayhem in which one man legally injures his brother, stirring up in us a vicarious caveman satisfaction?

54

Is There Anything to Parapsychology?

THE LETTER:

I was raised an atheist (if such there be) and am married to a Catholic. For the past several years, I have been studying, in my layman way, religions—both Christian and non-Christian. I have also been interested in parapsychology. A few years ago I tried to get a priest to discuss it, but he classed it with ESP as superstitious nonsense.

What is the present position of the Church? I am not referring to such things as horoscopes, seances, and fortune-telling, but the psychic phenomena that have been well-documented.

I might add that I have not had any experiences myself, but have talked to many persons who have.

What's the answer?

Lila R. Passarelli

THE ANSWER:
By J.D. Conway

In the measure that studies and theories about extrasensory perception, or ESP, and other psychic phenomena are soundly scientific, Mrs. Passarelli, they are of no direct concern to the Church. In past centuries the Church has shown considerable concern about magic, witchcraft, sorcery, and necromancy, because they involved superstitition, and were often believed to involve cooperation with the devil. On the other hand, pseudoscientific studies in alchemy and astrology seldom met opposition from Church authorities.

Fifty years ago the Church was quite concerned about psychic research because it included alleged contacts with the spirits of the dead. Such contacts would be related to Christian faith and could be occasions of deception and superstition. Faith must not deteriorate into credulity; the sacraments must not be seen as magic. We must maintain objective standards of truth and falsehood, and avoid foolish practices which lack sound basis in either divine revelation or scientific observation.

However, superstition apart, there is certainly intriguing evidence of many phenomena in the world for which science is unable to account. The latest marvels, flying saucers, have now received a more dignified designation, Unidentified Flying Objects. The Air Force has been able to explain what nine out of ten of those reported really were. And in doing so it has incurred the wrath of the credulous, who like to believe that spacemen from other planets are visiting us. Even greater is the wrath of the fearful who are convinced that the UFO's are manned by Communists spying on us and plotting our destruction. The Air Force says it is all swamp gas. Today you can stir up a fight about UFO's comparable to the conflicts of our ancestors about witches.

Phenomena that seem to violate the normal course of nature, or that cannot be explained by accepted scientific theories, are often designated as paranormal: beside or beyond the normal. And when these paranormal manifestations are in the psychic realm, they are studied by parapsychology. The best known studies in this area have been made at Duke University in a laboratory established for this purpose in 1934. Professor J. B. Rhine is associated with it.

During the early years Dr. Rhine's experiments received little attention from the scentific community. But by exercising restraint in his conclusions, he has won an increasing measure of respect. Other investigators in Europe and America have corroborated the conclusions proposed by Duke. There does seem to be some evidence for extrasensory perception.

Scientists have difficulty fitting ESP into their accepted theories. No one can rightly say that ESP is impossible; it doesn't really violate any known physical laws, but it certainly messes up our comfortable theories about the acquisition and communication of human knowledge; and, worse yet, it disturbs a basic metaphysical concept of the average scientist: that everything can be explained by physical forces.

Clairvoyance and telepathy might be considered particularly vivid forms of ESP. Other parapsychological phenomena (technically called psi) are telekinesis, or psychokinesis; prevision; dreams which prove prophetic; apparitions and poltergeist activities; and the experience of *déjà vu* (things which happen for the first time seem to be happening again).

There is much less evidence for other psi phenomena than for ESP. Most of us have experienced that sense of *déjà vu*, and there is something mysterious, faintly disturbing, and yet rather pleasant about it. Newspapers occasionally headline alleged activities of poltergeists. There is usually a boy or girl between the ages of 12 and 20 in the picture, leading the skeptic to suspect mischief. But some psi theorists believe that the noisy disturbances may be products of mental strain in this young person, a sort of subconscious psychokinesis.

The Church has frequently shown interest in certain types of apparitions, and encouraged the faithful to accept some of the better authenticated ones as supernatural. A psychologist inclines to be particularly skeptical of apparitions to children, since they are susceptible to what are called eidetic images; visual phenomena that are subjective but are projected so that they seem to be perceived objects. These images are sometimes seen with closed eyes, sometimes while looking at a surface or area. Occasionally they indicate pathology, but are frequent in normal children. Indeed, there is a theory that most persons pass through an eidetic stage during childhood There is evidence that other senses, such as hearing, are able to experience phenomena corresponding to eidetic images. Hence the well-founded suspicion that some apparitions are eidetic rather than supernatural.

We get into more complicated metaphysical problems when we encounter previsions and prophetic dreams. If we eliminate the supernatural, we are strongly inclined to doubt the evidence, rely on coincidence, or simply say it cannot happen. But the credulous can cite some strange phenomena and swear they are true.

Psychokinesis is ESP in reverse. Instead of the physical world affecting the mind without sensory stimulus, the mind produces physical effects with only psychic contact—

or by the power of positive thinking. I believe that most scientists, if they bother to think about this matter at all, take it for granted that the positive evidence is not very conclusive.

I must admit, Mrs. Passarelli, that all this paranormal business does not interest me very deeply. I never hope to learn more than a tiny fraction of the normal and demonstrable wonders of the world; I never hope to understand the natural mysteries of physics and astronomy. I prefer to devote my limited talents to the realities of God's creation, rather than to the unknown and the inexplicable, in the fringe area of possible hallucination.

However, if I were to go in for this sort of thing, I believe I would be tempted to dive off the deep end, and join the *Planète* crowd. About 1960 a slick, smart magazine *Planète* first appeared in France. It now appears in Dutch, Italian, Spanish, and German, has built up a cohesive following, spawned a library, and sponsored symposia, attracting even reputable men of science.

It has been violently attacked and strongly defended. Its field is para-everything: over and beyond science, philosophy, and religion. Its brilliance has attracted intellectuals, artists, and students; and it challenges them to face the mysteries of the universe.

Its name indicates its point of departure: Our world is nothing but a tiny planet in an insignificant solar system; we will never understand it until we see it in global perspective. *Planète* aims for the cosmic view of everything, with emphasis on the mysteries which surround all the things we seem to know. It tries to throw light on the occult and publicize the esoteric; it loves vague hypotheses, and proclaims that henceforth even the fantastic is possible. It has made a guideline from the words of Father Teilhard de Chardin: "On the scale of the cosmic only the fantastic has chances to be true."

It revels in zoopsychology and spiritualism, in yoga and yen, in parapsychology and magic, in outer space and inner forces, in the unusual, the strange, the mysterious and invisible, in the ultra and transcendent, in mind expansion and the formation of a planetary conscience. It portrays a universe in which time and space have been conquered, where we are able to explain the past by events of the future.

As might be expected, it leaves its readers confused, but

it intrigues them. And it performs at least one acknowledged service. Into the rationalistic world of science,
drained of mystery, it has injected imagination, dreams,
and even a bit of delirium. Into the world of precise technology it has brought values which derive from love and
fantasy. It has probably fouled up the rational thinking of
its readers and scrambled their consciences, but it has given
them a thrilling view of man and his world as seen from
outer space.

Of course we have our own domestic output of books
and magazines which deal with the strange and the psychic,
with artificial astrology and case studies of reincarnation.
But the ones I have seen somehow lack the imaginative
ardor and skill to launch us beyond the realities of the rational and scientific world and give us a cosmic trip without LSD.

I have gone far beyond the range of your question, Mrs.
Passarelli, but once you begin to conquer space and time
you hardly know where or when to quit.

55

How Do You Stand on Body Transplants?

THE LETTER:

I would like to know the stand of the Catholic Church in
regard to willing the body to science. A Boston paper ran a
story recently in which it stated that only two groups objected to this idea. Since the Catholic religion was among
those in approval, I question the point as to disposal of the
remains. Is it possible to avoid any funeral whatever?

Mrs. K.

THE ANSWER:
By J.D. Conway

Human cadavers are regularly dissected in Catholic
medical schools, Mrs. K., and autopsies are performed in

Catholic hospitals; and the Church indicates no disapproval
of either practice. Without a cadaver to work on, medical
students would never learn their anatomy, physiology, or
various related sciences. Without autopsies a hospital could
not maintain its accreditation, especially for internships;
and the medical staff would be deprived of much knowledge, valuable for the treatment of future cases.

From this we may rightly conclude that the proper use
of a human corpse for scientific study is lawful. Surely then
a person may arrange for his own body to be used for this
lawful purpose after his death. With regard to an autopsy
there is no problem at all—except maybe for the em-
balmer. The funeral can be held in the usual manner.

As a hospital chaplain I frequently had the task of per-
suading relatives to permit an autopsy when a person had
died from causes that were not clearly known. I have never
known relatives to regret having given this permission.

Most medical schools use unclaimed bodies for routine
dissection, the bodies of poor unfortunates who have no
money for their burial and no relatives or friends to be
interested. Our local undertaker tells me that it is very rare
that anyone voluntarily leaves his body for scientific study;
and that he has never known a Catholic to do so. Indeed,
he expresses an opinion that is quite common among Catholics: that this is somehow contrary to Church law, which
requires that the bodies of the faithful be buried in consecrated ground; and that it involves a measure of sacrilege
against the body, which was sanctified by the sacraments
and was the privileged home of the soul.

When I argued that it is necessary for a medical school
to have cadavers for study, his reply was: Yes, but it is not
necessary for them to have Catholic bodies. This recalled to
me the practice of the Sisters in a certain hospital far away:
they were quite cooperative in helping the local medical
school obtain unclaimed bodies, except that they would
never let them have the body of a Catholic. They would
even see to its burial at their own expense, if necessary.

This is a type of prejudice to which I cannot subscribe. If
it is sacrilege to dissect a body sanctified by the sacraments,
then the bodies of Protestants may not be used, because
they received the same Baptism as Catholics, and probably
some of the other sacraments also. The natural forces of
God's creation show no more respect for the body of a
Christian than for that of a pagan. Worms devour both.

We certainly owe respect to the human body, which God fashioned with loving care, making it and the soul somehow share his own image, and which He plans to raise from the dead to share his glory forever. However, we need not be overly worried about the fate of the molecules that form it, once it is dead. Its sanctity and its immortality are somehow stored in the memory and the plans of God, who treats it the same here and now as any other organic mass.

Burial and funeral services do present a problem. Canon 1205 says that the corpses of the faithful are to be buried in a cemetery which has been consecrated or blessed. And the Roman Ritual requires that the funeral services be integral, and they are made up of three parts: 1) accompanying the body from the home to the church; 2) the ceremonies in the church; and 3) accompanying the body to the cemetery, with the burial ritual.

Canon 1203 also states that the bodies of the deceased faithful are to be buried, and their cremation is condemned. However, there are special circumstances like plagues or disasters that would excuse from this legislation and permit cremation.

Commentators I have consulted state that the use of a body for scientific study also excuses from the law. One commentator even states that it is permissible to exhume bodies for this purpose: certainly it is not the intent of the law that bodies be buried only to be dug up later.

We might note in passing that the Church is easing its former severity regarding cremation. She does not insist that the severe penalties of her law be applied unless it is evident that cremation is requested or performed as a repudiation of belief in the resurrection.

As regards the integrity of the funeral ritual, it has long since vanished from most parts of our country. In our cities there is no possibility of accompanying the body from the home to the church, and thence to the cemetery, as the ritual stipulates: by procession through the streets. We seldom meet the body at the home—or even at the funeral home. We await it at the church. Hardly ever do we have the Office for the Dead, which is a part of the ritual. So I do not believe we need be scrupulous about omitting the committal prayers. They are sometimes omitted anyway when the body is transported, after the funeral, to a distant cemetery where no priest is available.

There is certainly no need to omit the funeral entirely.

Usually a body given to a medical school is embalmed, and can be taken to the church for the requiem Mass and other ceremonies. Even if, in a particular case, the body could not be taken to the church, the funeral Mass and absolution could still take place. The ritual makes provisions for special cases.

Most people are naturally a bit squeamish about having the body of a loved one dissected; but it really isn't any worse than putting it in the ground, where the worms will eat it. Probably it is in the hope of avoiding either fate that after having made the body pretty for the funeral we seal it up in an airtight vault, safe from germs and water. Possibly our sentiment makes us feel that we are thus preserving it intact for the resurrection. Our only real accomplishment is to make the body temporarily useless to the world of the living.

Related to your question, Mrs. K., are several others which I would like to discuss. Ophthalmologists are now performing cornea transplants that restore sight to those who suffer corneal defects. A little piece is cut out from a clear cornea and inserted into a hole made in the cloudy cornea of the patient. Usually the transplanted piece will be accepted and grow fast to its new host.

In some hospitals needed operations of this kind must be long delayed because of a shortage of good eyes from which to take the little corneal piece. So people are urged in charity to will their eyes to these hospitals. Routines are worked out for the quick removal of the eyes after death, and for their transportation to the hospital without deterioration. There they can be kept until needed. False eyes fill the cavities in the donor's head; and when the eyelids are closed, no one at the wake will be able to tell the difference.

There is certainly no moral objection to your being an eye donor in this manner. On the contrary, it is an act of love and generosity by which you prolong your charity to your fellow man beyond your death. If a drop of cold water given in the name of Jesus receives its reward, how much more will you be blessed if you give the very eyes out of your head!

Quite another type of moral problem is raised by recent efforts, much publicized, to transplant entire organs from one body to another. Until recently this was popularly believed impossible, unless the transplanted organ had the same cellular genes as its host, and could hardly happen except in identical twins. So we have cases in which the life of one twin has been saved by transplanting a good kidney from the other twin. But now I believe this same operation has been performed with success, taking the kidney from a person with different genes. A liver transplant of this kind was seemingly successful, but the patient died—after 18 days, I think.

Most of us do not have identical twins; so until recently we have not been greatly concerned about the morality of donating a living organ in this manner. Oh, there was a bit of question raised at one time about donors of blood for transfusion, and of skin for graft. But the sound view quickly prevailed that you are not really mutilating yourself when you give a pint of blood, or when you permit a bit of epidermis to be shaved off. Both are quickly replaced by natural processes of body repair; but your gift can be a lifesaver to someone else.

The giving of an organ is something else; it does mutilate the body, and it will not grow back. Moralists have traditionally applied to the question of voluntary mutilation a principle of totality. Pope Pius XII spoke at length on this subject when he welcomed delegates to a Congress of Urology, in October, 1953; and he made it quite definite that the health of the entire body is the only cause which justifies the amputation, excision, or paralyzing of a limb or an organ. Usually it is done because the organ itself is diseased, as a cancerous kidney. But sometimes healthy glands may be removed to inhibit the spread of cancer in another area of the body. These procedures are morally correct, because you sacrifice a minor part for the health of the whole.

Pope Pius did not discuss our problem of mutilation for purposes of transplant, but many interpreters believe his principles general and definite enough to imply that it is not licit, since it is not done for the health of the whole body. Such interpretation represents the traditional attiude of most moralists, who would tell us that it is not licit to give your kidney to your brother even though you have two good ones, and really need only one; and he will surely die without your gift.

In disagreeing with this traditional view I am giving you much more than my personal opinion. Sound moralists, after careful study, have offered the opinion that you may do for love of your neighbor the things which are permissible for love of yourself. In other words, if it is licit to have your kidney removed to save your own life, you may have it removed to save the life of your neighbor. My preference for this opinion is not only that it better exemplifies the law of love, but that it better fits the realities of modern science. Traditional opinions were worked out in a vacuum, by making logical deductions from general principles. And the ultimate source and universal validity of these principles is not always quite clear.

The modern opinion is worked out face-to-face with real problems. Principles are not forgotten, but their application is real rather than theoretical. And the conclusions are tested by true human and spiritual values. There must be something wrong with a principle which would tell a strong, healthy man with two kidneys that he must permit his identical twin to die rather than save him by sharing with him. When a reasonable, practical sacrifice, inspired by brotherly love, is called immoral, it is time to recheck the process of deduction.

56

Why Do So Many People Dislike the Catholics?

THE LETTER:

I am a retired information officer and also have been with the news media in Canada since 1929. Married, three children, 10 grandchildren, still writing.

I have always been puzzled at the attitudes of many non-Catholics toward the Catholic Church. Many are downright hostile. I can feel their hatred for Catholics. Others not so hostile still evince enmity against Catholics. My father was devoutly Catholic, my mother a happy Baptist, so possibly I am more aware of this attitude than others might be.

For years I have wondered what such people have been told. What do they believe? There must be some reason for this anti-Catholic feeling. Is it fear? Animosity toward a faith so widespread? Or what?

                                        Paul Gormley

THE ANSWER:
By Kenneth Ryan

I think, Paul, I know what you are talking about. I remember once in a department store being treated by the saleslady with such aversion, not to say loathing, that the only likely explanation was my Roman collar. Once in my youth I went to a secular university to register for some courses without knowing too much about the procedures or exactly what courses I wanted. I was treated with such exaggerated patience and sarcastic "Father's" that I felt humiliated. Once on a golf course, after I was introduced as "Father," my physical presence was ignored by one of the players for the rest of the round.

These are the only three occasions in my whole life where I personally felt anti-Catholic prejudice, so I really should not complain. The point is that none of the persons who so instantly disliked me knew anything about me or had ever seen me before. Like you, I wondered each time where such bitterness came from. It has certainly been around a long time. In ancient Rome the pagans used to say the Christians ate children so the Christians in turn should be fed to the lions. The calumny must have derived in some way from the eating of the Body of Christ in the Eucharist.

A distorted truth can become a font of hatred. The same kind of distortions occur in all ages. In the days of Al Smith, some of the more benighted expected Al, if elected president, to invite the Pope to come over and help rule the United States. The joke that took only a little of the sting out of the distortion was that Al, upon his defeat, sent a one-word cable to the Pope: "Unpack!" The original truth was that Al Smith did look to the Pope and Catholic principles in the ordering of his own life; that he would by fraud or force impose Papal rule on Americans was the distortion.

I think, Paul, that some of the hostility Catholics experience in our otherwise peaceful, pluralistic American so-

ciety, and in your Canada, comes from Reformation times.
We Christians still suffer from 16th-century differences in
dogmatic beliefs that resulted not only in debates, recrimina-
tions, and schisms, but even open war.

Nearly all societies are subject to this kind of inborn fission. The idle crowds of ancient Byzantium split into the
rioting Blues and Greens; medieval Italy had its warring
Guelphs and Ghibellines; modern society has its ice-cold
conservatives and its red-hot liberals. On both sides the
present-day fanatics tend to feel, think, and act in syndromes. Show me a man who is passionately against the
fluoridation of drinking water and I will show you a man
who is against new taxes and for "100% Americanism."
Show me a man who screams for social reform and I will
show you a man who favors soaking the rich and amnesty
for deserters. Religion somehow gets tied in with the current syndromes.

The religious wars of Europe had politics, family feuds,
greed, and brutality as their causes, as well as differing
opinions on the best way to serve God. But after you say
all this, it is still true and baffling that religion, supposedly
obeisance to God, causes hatred as well as love of neighbor. Christ said it should not be so, that we should love our
enemies. But He also told his disciples that the day would
come when men would think they were doing a service to
God by killing them. He warned them of coming divisions
among those who followed Him.

But I think the immediate cause of prejudice here in the
United States is hate literature. There can't be much money
in it, but there must be some. When we started the *Catholic
Digest*, we began to get hate mail immediately. I remember
one charming fellow who put a spoonful of real dirt into
each piece of mail he sent us.

Not all the hate literature was so gross as to be instantly
offensive. A good deal of it had clever aspects. In those
far-off days the typical anti-Catholic society would get hold
of what we always called a "renegade priest," the partisan
recital of whose ecclesiastical and personal difficulties
would be moving enough to win sympathy. Nowadays,
priests who don't want to be priests anymore just call a
press conference and announce what their new occupations
will be, but 50 years ago the clerical refugee was hard put
to support himself. He usually lost any job he got as soon
as his background became known, and all too often he

ended up in the sheltering arms of one of the professionally anti-Catholic societies. It would exact its pound of flesh: ringing denunciations of Roman Catholic authorities for use in its hate publications.

We had an older editor on the staff who had the most straightforward, simple, and honest Catholic piety of any man I ever knew. But it was he, rather than any of us battle-ready younger troops, who would suffer vague misgivings about his own faith when a particularly effective missile dropped among us. The lesson is that if such a devout Catholic could be so affected, people of no religious preference can be easily brought to hate by the insidious stories of apostates.

The hate mail that went out to the general public always carried the aura of attack. Attack is generally better strategy than defense. Despite the truism, the sermons Catholics have listened to since the beginnings of the United States have been chiefly devoted to the defense of Catholic teaching. To the best of my recollection most of the religious instruction I got in my high-school days was defensive. Most of the twice-a-Sunday sermons I preached for so many years defended, rather than proclaimed, the Catholic position. But that defense was necessary; the defense was occasioned by an offense.

I have only limited personal experience, but I think too large a percentage of the non-Catholic preaching in the old days was offensive (in both senses). I remember a vacation trip I took through the South. Listening on my car radio to the indigenous sermons on Sunday mornings, I heard hostility preached as often as Christian love. The oldtime preachers, ignorant perhaps, seemed yet to know that people will listen to your attacks on some third party with more relish than to your reproofs or exhortations to sanctity. They provided another source of what might be called pure and unreflecting anti-Catholicism.

I suppose that this type of preaching was part of the anti-Yankee, anti-liquor, anti-Irish syndrome that became so evident at the time Al Smith dared aspired to the presidency. It says a good deal for the general climate in the United States that when John Kennedy had to face the same problem, it received rational rather than inflammatory discussion and was no longer a determining factor in the election.

Now all I have done so far, Paul, is agree with you that some people do not like us. Apart from the historical pre-

cedents, your "Why?" still stands. Well, just before and
during Vatican II, there was much talk and writing about
"triumphalism" in the Catholic Church. It was usually defined as an attitude of mind in which the Church was an
army intent on the defeat of its enemies. The victories to be
won were not only in the fields of theological disputation,
but also in politics and finance. Happiness was having a
Catholic head of state, the biggest church buildings, the
greatest membership, and the most efficient money-raising
organizations. All this was pointed out as being a far cry
from the lonely Christ who had not where to lay his head.
Triumphalism was not only wrong in itself, it was a road-
block on the highway to ecumenism and seemed rather obviously the reason why Catholics were disliked.

Here at *Catholic Digest* we commissioned an article on
the subject. For various reasons it never appeared, but I
remember disliking it because it smelled of the same ill
winds that blew in Al Smith's time. It said the Pope and his
henchmen were selfish, power-hungry and vainglorious;
they wore silken robes and piled up golden treasure in the
Vatican. If you accepted that, you would become anti-
Catholic rather readily. But despite admissible examples,
like the prelate who allowed a department store to exhibit
his new bedroom furniture in the show window before its
delivery, it has been generally realized since the Council
that the trappings and postures of the medieval kingdoms
no longer go well in our modern democracies.

The outward display of officialdom has been tardily
toned down. I think it also has been realized that any
young man whose true ambition in life is to attain riches or
power, is not likely to gain them in an ecclesiastical career.
Political machination and confidence games in finance and
real estate would bring him much quicker results. I would
admit that the gorgeous apparel worn by a Cardinal when
his portrait appears in the public press might well antagonize a person of Puritan descent, but the hierarch probably
never thought of increasing his influence or glory by wearing it.

So, Paul, while triumphalism might be the cause of some
of the enmity you mention, it has certainly been taken care
of now at every level of Catholic authority. The monsignor-
pastors no longer dress like the "cock robin" of the Fulton
Sheen anecdote. He tells how he, robed in his red, floor-
length *feriola,* was once so addressed ("There you are,

cock robin!") by an overworked waitress when served a glass of water. If triumphalism caused the anti-Catholicism, then anti-Catholicism will soon disappear.

I think it will persist, though. I have never seen the point made, but the opposite of triumphalism must be defeatism. Catholics who blame anti-Catholicism on the proud triumphalism of the Church often themselves go in for defeatism. Most of the squabble issues in the present liturgical reform such as receiving Communion standing up, Communion in the hand, Communion from the common cup, elimination of saints' days, use of the mother tongue in worship, removal of statues, were all part of the reformers' programs in the days of Luther and Cranmer. For the most part the non-Catholic customs have prevailed now within the Catholic Church so that it is fair to call their Catholic proponents defeatists. None of the customs have much to do with the truth or falsity of the religion using them, but they have been fought over as were the battle flags of old, and the reformers have won.

Of course, the reforms have not been made in the name of defeatism, but in the name of better understanding of the liturgy in general. But if it was a defeat for triumphalism to have such changes made, it is taking a long time for the beneficial effects to be noticed. The anti-Catholics who do notice our adoption of their customs are not exactly flocking to join us, despite the fine efforts of the ecumenists.

So to answer your question, Paul, I think we have to go back to what we said in the beginning: religious bigotry stems from what we called syndromes. My old moral theology professor used to tell how, in the district in which he lived, if you were 1) Catholic, you were also 2) Irish, and 3) a Democrat. A better known and acknowledged syndrome now is WASP: 1) white, 2) Anglo-Saxon, and 3) Protestant.

The latter is not the syndrome now causing anti-Catholicism. It is rather the syndrome of the intellectual, the liberal, and the reformer. If you are one of these nowadays, you are usually the other two as well. The intellectual who has given up faith, the liberal who has given up tradition, and the reformer who wants change for the sake of change, when combined in one person, is almost automatically anti-Catholic. Many persons bear the mark of this syndrome in our countries now.

If such anti-Catholicism brought about only personal hu-

miliations or the adoption of non-Catholic liturgical odd-
ments, it would be of less concern. The trouble is that bigotry has affected the Church in the public as well as the
religious sector. For instance, the clear constitutional issue
of the freedom of parents to educate their children in their
own faith with their own tax money has been twisted in the
tax-credit decisions into a discussion of the separation of
Church and State. Father Virgil Blum has pointed out that
the United States Supreme Court ruled (Nyquist case) that
certain tax benefits in New York were unconstitutional because the benefits would "flow primarily to parents of children attending sectarian schools," meaning, of course,
Catholic parents. The same day it ruled a South Carolina
law was constitutional even though it provided state assistance exclusively to non-Catholic denominational colleges.

In the abortion issue the pro-lifers found it expedient to
point out repeatedly that there were people in their movement who were not Catholic. Obviously they thought their
case in court would find a better hearing if this were understood. In cases like this it would seem that anti-Catholicism
has slopped over into antimorality. When things get that
bad, Paul, Catholics have to fight back, even when there is
no hope of quick victory.

Besides his warning to the disciples that they would be
persecuted and even killed, our Lord said, "I have come to
set a man at variance with his father and a daughter with
her mother. . . ." He mourned over Jerusalem that killed
the prophets and told the parable about the people that
killed the King's son. At no time did He interrupt his remarks to say that He would presently put a stop to all this.
From what He said the disciples could understand that the
world He was sending them into would continue to be a
hostile world. As for the Lord himself, He went on to be
crucified.

57

Let's Sing Only the Good Old Hymns!

THE QUESTION:

I am in my mid 60's, brought up with the Latin Mass and Latin hymns as well as hymns sung in my native tongue. I am now interested in church music to the extent of working with the children in our parish choir. I do not have any say in what is appointed to be sung by the organist and liturgical committee. They choose things like "Born Free" "Joy is like the Rain" "I Believe" "Be a New Man" and "The Circle Game."

I am a newcomer here to one of the oldest Catholic churches in Maine. But since I am part of the choir, some of the older parishioners ask me, "Why don't we sing some of the older hymns we all know and have known since we were children?" They say, "It would be so nice to hear some of the old hymns again!" I have no answer for them.

Can you tell me if there is a way I can bring back some of the older hymns? Very few of the older people will sing along with the choir these days.

Elisabeth B. Gregus

THE ANSWER:
By Kenneth Ryan

As they say, Mrs. Gregus, you got a problem. The young people won't sing the old songs and the old people won't sing the new. I just noticed today that a church-music magazine is conducting a composers' contest with the idea of developing music for Mass acceptable to both young and old. No way. There is no such thing.

Now that doesn't answer your request for a way to bring back the older hymns, but your problem is a tough one and

I had to say something like that first. Before mounting a campaign for the use of any particular kind of music, the promoter must realize that music is like food. People do not so much eat what they like as like what they eat. Your diet as a child usually continues to be your favorite into old age. I have a very rich friend who vastly prefers peanut-butter sandwiches to porterhouse steaks and everyone knows how former President Nixon preferred cottage cheese and catsup to what was on the White House lunch menus. The same factor operates in music: What you listened to as a child, you will love ever after.

So everyone begins with prejudice in musical taste. Original prejudices are made stronger by certain physical facts. In a picture gallery or a movie you can shut your eyes. In a church or concert hall you can't shut your ears. In church nowadays most people feel they are part of a captive audience. They have to stay there to satisfy the obligation to hear Mass, but they can't shut their ears to music they don't like. Each time this happens resentment reinforces the original prejudice.

I propose the above statements as true on the basis of personal experience. I conducted a volunteer parish choir for some 25 years. We had no liturgical committees to contend with as you have, and had fine pastors who encouraged us, whatever music we chose. But even in those halcyon days our collective choir conscience would be sometimes troubled by articles in church-music magazines which condemned Masses we were singing. We had a good organist who knew the White List by heart. This list of approved Masses was put out by a national Catholic music society and for a choir to sing anything not on the list meant losing caste whenever diocesan music meetings were held. The purpose of the list was to blackball the operatic airs and operatic style in Mass music. But our music cabinet had a few of the old favorites down on the bottom shelf under a lot of other things and occasionally I would have to give in to the pleadings of the old-timers and dust off one of the melodious, Puccini-flavored works. We, and most of the listening congregation, would thoroughly enjoy it, despite the pricking of our consciences.

But in general we followed the teachings of those who were then the reformers. Of course, those reformers have now taken their turn at being reformed. For instance, they often fastened on the old hymns which contained such flights of verbal fancy as "I know not how my transports to control!" and "Let me to Thy bosom fly!" and angrily repudiated the old-fashioned, Victorian-age piety which produced them.

Just recently in a fit of nostalgia I dug up some of the antique (circa 1915) hymnals and found myself agreeing with the critics. The words, read today, sound artificial and even insincere. Yet, right in these bright, post-Vatican II times, you can find hymns from the antique collections in the interim (1971) American version of the Prayer of Christians, possibly chosen to counterbalance the Ray Repp novelties.

A better version of the official prayer of the Church has now come out, thank goodness; for the interim version made the naive assumption that the hymns would be updated by changing the old-fashioned *thee's* and *thou's* to *you*. "Faith of Our Fathers" now has a verse reading: "Our fathers chained in prisons dark/ Were still in heart and conscience free/ And blest would be their children's fate/ If they, like them, should die for you!" Whatever charm the old battle hymn retained after so many years quickly evaporated at the lack of rhyme. *Free*, as any versifier will tell you, screams for *thee*. The lesson, need I draw it, is that tinkering with old hymns ruins them, does not update them, and does nothing to attack your problem, Mrs. Gregus, of getting the young to sing the old and the old to sing the new.

But in the words of the radio hit of the 30's, "The music goes round and round." There is always somebody demanding change. Once when I was teaching in high school, I was given the task of providing the singing for the "devotions," a word which may need explanation to the present generation as the collective name for Stations of the Cross in Lent, Benediction on Thursday and Sunday evenings, Rosary recitation in May and October, all of which were in those days held on a regular schedule.

My first reaction was to gather just a small group of boys who really enjoyed singing and make them the choir. After a month or two came the complaints from the liturgical enthusiasts, "Why not have *everybody* sing?" "Why can't we *all* join our voices in song?" And so we abandoned the choir, went for unrehearsed community singing with all the opportunity for display of individual notions of time-beat, pitch, volume, and subject matter involved in that

Soon the people with delicate ears were asking me, "Why can't you pick out some of the better voices?" "Isn't there some way to improve the singing?" I went back to having just the small choir and good music until, of course, the inevitable requests for "participation" began again. Round and round.

There was merit in both points of view, but congregational singing has always seemed to me to suffer from the same handicaps as would, say, congregational basketball: too many people in the act, too many cooks salting the broth—in general the same results you always get from a committee of the whole. As a learned aside, the Roman Ordo I, dating from about 700 A.D., has no mention at all of any singing by the people at the Papal Mass save for two "Amen's."

The point of this detour is to show that if you leave the decision on what or how to sing up to a group of nonmusicians you tend to get the cheaper, more ephemeral, lowdown-popular type of music as opposed to music that will stand the test of time. The popular vote is usually for the newest music, the musicians' vote is always for the better music, whether new or old.

There are rules to follow in making the choice between good and bad music. In my memory the best functional music I ever heard was—despite the mean things I said above about congregational singing—a unison chorus of some six or seven hundred priests singing, at a bishop's consecration dinner, the Our Father in Latin to the tune sung ordinarily in the old days at High Mass on Sunday. An analysis of the melody shows that all the notes had equal time value; it was easy to sing. The singers all knew the melody. It had none at all of those hemidemisemiquavers for which our latest hymn writers have a weakness. The old *"Pater Noster"* was diatonic, no sentimental-sounding sharps and flats. The intervals between successive notes, except when a new phrase started, were all of only one step. The words were sublime, first uttered by the Lord himself. It made good music.

Of course, it was Gregorian chant, the very best kind of religious music. Incidentally, if you don't mind another purposeful detour, Mrs. Gregus, I think that the *"Montes Gelboe"* antiphon is the finest in all Gregorian chant. After I had spent nearly a year in a European monastery studying plain chant, I somehow missed going to Vespers the

day *"Montes Gelboe"* was sung (Saturday before the 5th
Sunday after Pentecost in the old calendar). That was one
of the keenest disappointments I have had in life, a statement which will make me an oddball in the estimation of
more than 99% of the people here reading about it. A flat
99% may not know what an antiphon, or for that matter,
what Gregorian chant, is. They will be utterly unmoved by
my still haunting sense of loss. I, of course, would be simi-
larily unmoved by the very real woe of a teenager who was
taken sick and had to remain in bed the day the Beatles
came to town. I have my own ignorances, too. I can't identify any of the hymns (if that they be) which you name in
your letter, Mrs. Gregus, not even "Born Free." And the
only reason I can remember the Beatles is because of Len-
non's outrageous publicity announcement that the Beatles
were the best known persons since the days of Christ. (He
used the Holy Name, which I will not.)

But my preference for Gregorian church music and ignorance of "Born Free" does not automatically enroll me on
the list of those who prefer old to the new music. I like to
think it does put me among those who prefer good to less
good or bad music. Right now, the reformers have eliminated from the liturgy any need for a trained choir, in the
contention that everyone must be part of the action. That,
together with the virtual prohibition of Latin, pretty well
disposes of any hope that anything like universal use will
ever be accorded the chant again. But getting good music is
not a question of just jumping back one or more generations. There was just as much bad music then as now. It is
a question of finding and singing music that may be old or
new but certainly good.

Mrs Gregus, I speak with considerable hesitation in the
role of advice-columnist. Ann Landers I am not. But it
seems to me that the only realistic approach you can take
in solving your problem of old *vs.* new is to talk your liturgical committee into considering a good *vs.* bad classification of music. Some of the old music is good, some of the
new music is good.

For example, the success of the *Lilies of the Field*
"Amen" proves it is good music. It's from a subculture and
out of the Western European tradition of the Dresden
"Amen," but once a congregation learns it, they really sing
it out. I don't approve of the "One more time!" exhortation
one occasionally gets from the leader of song, but I can't

help liking and singing the music. Once you can get your committee to abstain from the veto simply because the music you suggest is "old," your battle is half won. I guess you have to let them win the other half of the battle.